G. K. CHESTERTON AND C. S. LEWIS

G. K. Chesterton
and
C. S. Lewis

THE
RIDDLE
OF JOY

Edited by

Michael H. Macdonald
Seattle Pacific University

&

Andrew A. Tadie
Seattle Pacific University

with a Foreword by

Janet Blumberg Knedlik

William B. Eerdmans Publishing Company
Grand Rapids, Michigan

Library of Congress Cataloging-in-Publication Data

    1. English literature—20th century—History and criticism.
2. Christian literature, English—History and criticism.   3. Chesterton,
G. K. (Gilbert Keith), 1874-1936.   4. Lewis, C. S. (Clive Staples),
1898-1963.   5. Christianity and literature—Great Britain—History—
20th century.   6. Authors, English—20th century—Biography.
7. Christian biography—Great Britain.
I. Macdonald, Michael H.   II. Tadie, Andrew A.
PR478.C45R5   1989   820.9'382   89-7676

ISBN 0-8028-3665-8

To:
The People of I.S.I.,
who help make joyful things happen

Contents

Contents

V. PURSUING THE RIDDLE OF JOY

Chesterton

Combustion—Lord, how it delights and fires,
Cherubic rose with papal crimson blent!
Surprises too, for I had not supposed
My own incorporation possible
In this candescent metamorphosis,
A never willed or even fancied end —
Except for heretics, with whom, Lord knows,
I broke some lances past and still will break
All future spears until the bond is forged
That rings us all, and ringing, liberates.
Crowned came I, and more crested will depart,
Keeping the splendor only, not the dross.
Now some will say it serves me right to burn,
But I instead believe it does me good.
My wits are crisping as my body roasts,
My vision sharpening. So I detect
A round of novelties, goodly to spot,
Red-hot, amid the trivial and base
Familiarities—spirits, God-lit,
Who seem to see at last and share with me
The meaning of the morning. Goodbye, shell!
It could not be forever that we clung,
Though life itself depended on our clinging,
For we are bound to journey and adjourn,
To forge acquaintance into memory
And go our ways forgetting till we wake
And in one huge remembering recall
Ourselves, our God, our promise and our prize.
Adventure was the pristine point for me:
Risking to find, and finding, to embrace.
I fought the groove and galloped from the lull,
Rejoiced in jolts and revelled in suspense.
And now I take my way from star to star
To points removed, to wrestle there as here
With demons on the march or on the sly
Who would prevent my sighting of the soul
And clasping of all sundered to my breast.
As rosiness engulfs me I confess
I am on fire with curiosity,
As eager as a petal to unfold
And taste the air of Heaven as conceived,
To feel the synthesis of opposites,
The transformation of abuse, and know
What I had heretofore imagined only:
God and Man are one but separate
Until the blazing tryst that girdles all.

C. S. Lewis

Hellfire I would not call it; if I did,
It would consume me as this fire does not.
For these are flames of light, life-giving beams
Inducing the susceptible to burn —
Burn upward, not burn up—burn on and on
Unstanchably, with purifying zeal,
Until the fond assumptions and the false
Emotions and the fierce pretensions fade
And candor takes the field in sunny stride.
If this were Hell, complacency would reign
On common ground of torpor and contempt;
Blank faces would attest indifference,
Hushed voices the futility of speech,
Glazed eyes the dearth of paramount regard.
If this were Hell, duplicity would bloom,
Vainglory flourish and betrayal thrive.
Hellish is nothing but the picayune
Upgraded to gargantuan; Heavenly,
The fury of the flame transposed to light.
But in those moot arenas interlying
Where blows are traded by disordered selves
Blindly, with no redemption in the cards,
No inkling of a victory to follow,
Dispersal is the rule. Checkered we come
And splintered we depart, unless refined
By stringent miracle. So am I now,
As through this bottleneck, belittlement,
I labor like a diver to ascend
From grief of heart and poverty of mind
Into the blithe continuum of joy.
But death is lingering, renewal slow:
I rise in glory, but I stand in need;
Wherefore I welcome your spectatorship.
Shepherds explore, attended by their flocks —
Pupils in chief—commanders of my heart.
Do you but gather round this golden pyre,
You may partake of my relinquishment:
Purge pride, shun flippancy, abhor deceit.
Browse if you will—your nourishment is mine.
Mourn if you must, but gladden in my wake!

These two poems are from *Speeches at the Stake*, valedictories in a
hypothetical setting by Rudolph Schirmer, former chairman of the board
of G. Schirmer, Inc., and a composer of numerous musical works, including *Hymn to the Americas*.

Foreword

We all feel the riddle of the earth
    without anyone to point it out.
The mystery of life is
    the plainest part of it.
The clouds and curtains of darkness,
    the confounding vapours,
      these are the daily weather
        of this world.
Whatever else we have grown accustomed to,
    we have grown accustomed
      to the unaccountable.
Every stone or flower is a hieroglyphic
    of which we have lost the key;
With every step of our lives we enter into
    the middle of some story
      which we are certain
        to misunderstand. . . .

                        G. K. Chesterton

G. K. Chesterton and C. S. Lewis: in some ways an unlikely pairing. But each of these immensely popular Christian apologists and men of letters "felt the riddle of the earth" and came to believe that its name is Joy. Amid all the certainties we are certain to misunderstand, in spite of all the keys we have lost, these two claimed to begin with honest minds and concluded there was one thing no honest mind could miss.

The Renaissance poet and moralist John Donne put the paradox this way: "Mysteries / Are like the sun, dazzling, yet plain to all eyes." Like Donne, Chesterton and Lewis possessed minds too keen to abide sloppiness, sentimentality, or sham. This integrity made them humble, in the end. They could not lament an absence of meaning, because they were too thankful for "every . . . hieroglyphic," every riddling letter that points somewhere beyond itself.

Chesterton and Lewis simply would not surrender (in any degree) the riddling charm of the unaccountable — most unaccountable of all, perhaps, "a sense of limits and connections amid the mysteries of life" (described by David Leigh, S.J., in the last paper of this collection). So they finally re-turned (turned back again) to the simplest and subtlest of human conundrums: the discovery that what is "plain" and what is "dazzling" are somehow two faces of the same enigma. The known and the unknowable, reason and rapture, duty and bliss, the lucid and the incomprehensible mysteriously inhere *in one another*; whenever they are sundered, they cease to be.

What drew their audiences to them was not only their command of so many popular (and technical) idioms, or their arts of plain talk and curious story, or their gifts of laughter and surprise, or their immense and uncompromising intellects. No, what drew their audiences was the way they saluted something in the nature of things — the way they *would not suppress* their desire for that something. They felt (as Lewis put it in "The Weight of Glory") our "inconsolable secret," and they kept trying to know what each plain and dazzling mystery finally *might* signify to the critically honest mind (even something at once *more* than any rational accounting, yet source and fountain of knowing). In some ways, they stubbornly refused to outgrow the rest of us. But perhaps they came as close to being grown-ups as anyone has.

So, in the summer of 1987, an odd lot of people met happily in Seattle to celebrate the achievements of possibly the two most effective twentieth-century apologists for Christianity. We were a quirky lot. From Europe, Canada, and the United States came academic theologians and working mothers, pastoral ministers and visual artists, financiers and poets, educators and students from various disciplines, journalists and government advisors. We represented broadly diverse political positions, religious beliefs, and literary tastes. Even the setting had its quirky aspect, as we were sponsored by Seattle's two parochial universities — a Free Methodist institution (Seattle Pacific University) in tandem with a Catholic Jesuit one (Seattle University).

The group was brought together by a desire to hear what scholars of Chesterton and Lewis had to say *to us* about the lives, thought, and faith of these two writers. (It is for a larger audience of such readers that this collection is intended.) What we agreed upon was that Chesterton and Lewis made us feel like celebrating, and that "celebrating" means ceremonial observance, proclamation, and praise. In a week of festive meals, intense conversations, and vigorous presentations, we did indeed celebrate the writings of Chesterton and Lewis with joyous observation, proclamation, and — though not with fatuous unanimity or undissenting voice — praise.

Featured speaker Christopher Derrick led off controversially (the way Chesterton or Lewis would have relished) with crisp warnings against indiscriminate (American?) adulation, interspersed with memories (from childhood) of the Chesterton milieu and (from middle years) of Lewis at Oxford. His speech appears here as the first of five papers of personal remembrance, tribute, and evaluation. (Derrick makes the opening move in a lively debate by praising John Beversluis's *C. S. Lewis and the Search for Rational Religion*, a sweeping attack on Lewis's argument from natural law. Purtill, Hooper, and Kreeft among others comment oppositely.)

Speakers also poked about in the literary achievement, the social thought, and the apologetical techniques of Chesterton and Lewis, turning up at times their prescient insights and always their delicious paradoxes. Three speakers particularly hastened after the riddle of "Joy" — from philosophical, literary, and psychological starting points. Their exploratory efforts are the final papers of this collection. Beginning the volume are two celebratory poems by Rudolph Schirmer, valedictories to Chesterton's and Lewis's purgatorial gaiety.

We offer all of these tributes to those two fellow minds who, amidst the "dark curtains" and "confounding vapours" (the "daily weather of this world"), have helped us to learn that Joy "widens out and comes where we had never thought." Reality, as Lewis wrote in *Mere Christianity*, "is usually something you could not have guessed. . . . Christianity . . . has just that queer twist about it that real things have." But all of this (unaccountable) bounty springs, *gratis*, from the "plain" and "dazzling" *choices* of One who "is all a burning joy and a strength."

*   *   *   *   *   *

For the editors and all the participants, I gladly record here our indebtedness to Seattle University and Seattle Pacific University for sponsorship, with the Intercollegiate Studies Institute, Inc. (ISI), of the "1987 Conference to Celebrate the Achievement of G. K. Chesterton and C. S. Lewis." Without the strong support and generous financial backing of the Intercollegiate Studies Institute, the conference would have lost much of its sumptuous table.

In particular, we wish to thank John Lulves, Carol Russell, and Ann Wendig of ISI for their splendid and cheerful help with this project. Sonja Nutley of Seattle Pacific University worked endlessly (or so she feared) on this manuscript; she has our gratitude. Finally, special recognition and thanks belong to Michael H. Macdonald for his inexhaustible energy in coordinating the conference (and those nine previous C. S. Lewis Institutes at Seattle Pacific University which laid the groundwork for 1987).

Seattle Pacific University   *Janet Blumberg Knedlik*
Seattle, Washington

I. RIDDLING
REMEMBRANCES FROM
THOSE WHO KNEW THEM

Some Personal Angles on Chesterton and Lewis

Christopher Derrick

We are gathered together here in the sight of God and in the face of this congregation (and I quote from the official program) "to celebrate the achievement of G. K. Chesterton and C. S. Lewis": two Brits or Limeys, I note with chauvinistic satisfaction, and—as I'm sure we can all agree—two very great men. (I trust that among the other meanings of a complex word, we shall remember the modern sense in which "celebrating" is normally done in a pub.)

That presumptively high opinion of Chesterton and Lewis on your part generates certain difficulties for me. You would hardly be here unless you already had some familiarity with their achievement and some enthusiasm for it. I cannot stand here as one who introduces a subject, still less as one who enlightens ignorance. Perhaps I should fall back on the well-known principle that an opening or keynote speaker needs only to make soothing platitudinous noises, so that the assembled company can recover from its travels and digest its dinner without needing to keep seriously awake.

But at the risk of waking you up, I do feel like offering a few

CHRISTOPHER DERRICK is a frequent lecturer on the cause of integrity in Catholic faith and morals. He is the author of many books, articles, and reviews.

Christopher Derrick

personal angles, less than totally platitudinous, I hope, and perhaps a shade challenging at certain points. Please forgive me if I start off on an autobiographical note.

Chesterton died when I was an inky schoolboy of fifteen, and I cannot exactly claim to have *known* him. But he was a conspicuous figure in my younger days, a bulky presence and a powerful influence.

My father had a Quaker background and was born in 1885, making him eleven years younger than Chesterton. He came up to London as an art student and a Fabian socialist, and as a young man he used to attend public meetings and debates in that cause. We talk a lot about "dialogue" nowadays, but in those blissful days before television, it actually happened. People would turn out on a wet night to attend a public debate, at which someone like H. G. Wells or George Bernard Shaw would discuss the first principles of life and society with someone like Hilaire Belloc or G. K. Chesterton. My father was initially in sympathy with those people like Wells and Shaw: to his extreme rage, he found himself increasingly convinced that they were wrong and that the people like Belloc and Chesterton were right. He thus became a disciple and friend of Chesterton's, and when he was received into the Catholic Church—by that marvelous saint and lunatic Father Vincent McNabb O.P.—it was (*salva gratia*) under that influence and following that example.

All this had consequences for the atmosphere and company in which I grew up, for my education as well; and here in the United States, I've gotten a lot of mileage out of that background. There are many people here for whom Chesterton and Belloc and their circle—Lewis too—are quasimythological figures, heroes of a remote Golden Age. When I mention them as fat men whom I used to meet casually, I often find myself gazed upon with a kind of awe, as though that made *me* into some kind of great man. Such reflected glory is not less enjoyable for being totally unearned, totally undeserved.

As for Lewis—well, late in 1939 and under the disturbed conditions of wartime, I secured a place at Magdalen College, Oxford, as his pupil. What with Hitler, I had only one eight-week term at Oxford before going off to the Air Force. I came back

AN INTERCESSION

O LORD Jesus,
Who knowest them that are thine,

When thou rewardest thy servants the prophets, remember, we beseech thee, for good, those who have taught us, rebuked us, counselled us, guided us;
And in that day show them mercy.

When thou rewardest the saints, remember, we beseech thee, for good, those who have surrounded us with holy influences, borne with us, forgiven us, sacrificed themselves for us, loved us;
And in that day show them mercy.

When thou rewardest the great that fear thy Name, remember, we beseech thee, for good, those who have been our patterns of any virtue or grace, of repentance, acknowledgment of offenses, begging of pardon, obedience, patience, perseverance;
And in that day show them mercy.

When thou rewardest the small that fear thy Name, remember, we beseech thee, for good, ignorant disciples, halting followers, weak cross-bearers, kneelers on feeble knees, faithful believers who faint not utterly;
And in that day show them mercy.

Nor forget any, nor forget us;
But in that day show us mercy. Amen.

Hillspeak Card No. 72-B, designed for the Episcopal Book Club and printed in the U.S.A. at Eureka Springs, Arkansas 72632 in 1945 and completed my degree course with Lewis as my tutor, thus coming to know him very well; and I kept in touch with him thereafter, by post and also by many meetings at both Oxford and Cambridge, until he died in 1963. On many an occasion, therefore, I have sat with Lewis over the beer and discussed all things and a great deal more — with Lewis alone or with others, and sometimes with that group which has now passed into literary legend as the Inklings. When so privileged, I knew that I was in excellent company. But I didn't realize how historic it would later prove to be. It's a common thing, I suspect, for us to recognize our great moments in retrospect alone.

That's the story; and it means that while I have any number of Lewis anecdotes, I have absolutely no Chesterton anecdotes of my own.

Now it may seem curious that we here bracket them together and speak of their "achievement" in the singular, as though they had been partners in some joint operation. During his lifetime, Chesterton's name was commonly (though rather arbitrarily) bracketed with Belloc's; if we bracket Lewis at all, it's mostly with Tolkien and Charles Williams and the other members of that circle. Nobody speaks of a Chesterlewis, and it would be a strange monster whose two components had never met. I see no reason to suppose that Chesterton had even heard of Lewis. There was influence between them, but all of it ran in the one direction.

It started to run during the First World War, when Lewis— being sick in hospital—chanced to read a volume of Chesterton's essays. "I had never heard of him and had no idea of what he stood for," he wrote later, "nor can I quite understand why he made such an immediate conquest of me" (*Surprised by Joy* 180). It wasn't so strange or inexplicable, since Chesterton already had a habit of making immediate conquests of highly diverse people. Even today, more than fifty years after his death, he frequently displays a power and privilege which he once attributed to Samuel Johnson: "He can walk into the heart without knocking" (Ward 193).

I don't know which of his essays made that conquest of Lewis, or how many of his countless books were to give it consolidation later on. The one which Lewis mentioned constantly, recommending it to one and all, was *The Everlasting Man*, a

5

book which appeals much more strongly and more precisely to the imagination than to the intellect. Lewis defined himself as an imaginative man above all else, and I'm not entirely convinced by his claim that Chesterton's influence upon him was primarily a matter of thought or reason. However that may be, it seems clear that *The Everlasting Man* played a crucial part in Lewis's re-conversion and the later development of his mind.

Two men of different generations, displaying various kinds of affinity and certain clear resemblances. Both were prolific and best-selling writers, in prose and in verse, equally at home in dialectic and in fantasy; each combined a powerful rationalism of the intellect with an equally powerful creative imagination, a visual imagination in particular. In Lewis, this seems to have been related to his lifelong passion for countryside and walking, and it operated realistically, even when he had invented the landscapes in question. I have much sympathy with the lady who said that she couldn't read *Perelandra* because it made her feel seasick; and look at what Lewis does in *The Great Divorce*. He has two scenes there, both English and both entirely obvious: a squalid industrial slum on a winter's evening, and a lovely countryside on a spring morning. A pair of clichés, you might say, until you see what Lewis does with them.

By sharp contrast, Chesterton's visual imagination was always symbolic, always heraldic—partly, perhaps, because it's entirely absurd to imagine him striding off across the hills and the fields and the valleys, after the style of Lewis and his friends or of Belloc.

One great bond of unity—though it isn't peculiar to these two—is that each went through a black spell of nihilism and despair when young and emerged into a robustly dogmatic Christianity, of which I shall have more to say later on. At the time when Chesterton made that conquest of him, Lewis was still deep in the religious nihilism—strongly Gnostic in flavor—which he had embraced as a schoolboy and would still retain for many years. As he tells the story, what did the trick was Chesterton's perceptible *goodness*—a quality which he had already recognized in George MacDonald and which he could value deeply in others while making no attempt to be good himself.

Everybody who knew Chesterton bears witness to his goodness, and I'm cynical enough to call it very slightly into question. Some of his characteristic behavior patterns, although most entertaining to read about, seem to me to display a gross lack of consideration for other people, and for his wife in particular. There was doubtlessly no question of positive malice. Even in the absence of that, however, the sins of omission can be serious.

Boldly but (I hope) not too offensively, I propose to say one or two other slightly negative things. I revere each of these two great men. But they were men, not gods, nor—as far as I know —even saints. I would not wish to debunk either in any general way. But I would always wish to debunk the decidedly cultic *admiratio* which they are accorded by some, and—in my experience—much more often by Americans than by Englishmen.

So let me say, in technically psychiatric language, that each of them had a private kink, a decidedly odd region of the mind, a touch of nuttiness. Do we catch a note of paranoia, for example, in Chesterton's way of talking about the front benches and the Party System, or in Lewis's way of talking about the Inner Ring, in *That Hideous Strength* as well as in the lecture so named? Perhaps; but if I wanted to develop this subject at length, I wouldn't start there. I would probably start with Chesterton's (I think) clearly pathological thing about fighting and bloodshed and the sword. The gentlest of men, he kept "a vast collection of swords and daggers and rapiers" in his house; and when dictating to a secretary, it was his practice to stride about with one of these, stabbing and spearing at the cushions. You can excuse that, no doubt, as a mere version of the fidgets. But it's less excusable that you cannot venture far into the world of Chesterton's imagination without coming across a duel in progress somewhere; and it's always given the high romantic treatment.

This is a strange thing in a Christian writer. If you tell me that Chesterton used dueling as a metaphor for the spiritual combat to which all Christians are committed, I shan't altogether believe you. He was also in love with the idea of actual swordsmanship, actual bloodshed, and killing: it excited him and he indulged freely in that excitement, even though the practice in question had been condemned repeatedly by the popes and the church generally for a thousand years if not

7

longer. How would we feel if we found a Christian writer make a comparably positive use, emotional and imaginative, of (say) abortion or rape?

There were tendencies in the young Lewis that suggest a broadly similar kink in the mind; this may possibly be responsible for his astonishing statement that "I have no sympathy with the modern view that killing or being killed is a great evil" (*Letters* 176). That baffles me: how could a thoughtful Christian ever talk as though killing and being killed were morally cognate subjects? I'm also bothered by his curious ambivalence about something which he denounced furiously on paper while enacting it eagerly in practice — male submissiveness before the aggressively dominant female. In neither man do we see much possibility of a straightforward and relaxed and happy relationship with the other sex. I can't feel that Frances Chesterton enjoyed her pedestal very much.

Yet Lewis does seem to have been relatively free from one of Chesterton's more dangerous obsessions. "Surely one of the things we learn from history is that God never allows a human conflict to become unambiguously one between simple good and simple evil" (*Letters* 183). He said that in a letter during the Second World War, and it was a lesson which Chesterton had most definitely *not* picked up from history. He habitually coerced that untidy subject into the simplicity of great myth, speaking as though the absolute struggle between good and evil, between Ormuzd and Ahriman, had become fully incarnate in some particular human confrontation and fight — as between Rome and Carthage in *The Everlasting Man*, or Alfred and the Danes in the *Ballad of the White Horse*, or Christendom and Islam in *Lepanto*. One can share his general partisanship in any such case, while still desiring to point out that the historical reality was less morally simple than Chesterton needed to suppose. As Lewis knew and caused Screwtape to complain, Satan has never become incarnate. But Chesterton, so devoted to particularity and the real, was chronically vague about its relationship to the mythopoeic turbulence of his own imagination.

This is a point at which certain people most definitely need to be warned off Chesterton, especially in the perilous world of today. The trouble is that the passionately combative mind naturally requires a dualistic world, since you can't have a good fight without first having a clear-cut and absolute enemy whom you can equate with Satan. Chesterton, so naturally and rightly hostile to dualism in its Gnostic and Manichaean and similar versions, could thus swallow it in a different version that now involves extreme moral danger, encouraging others to do the same. To those whom it may concern, I would urge a re-reading of *The Four Loves*, chapter two, with special reference to what follows —all too naturally—when we equate our country's cause with the cause of God.

I hope I have not managed to suggest that we are only concerned, in this celebration, with a couple of nuts. Perfect normality, of the mind as of the body, is presumably a rare thing; and anyone who writes as abundantly as these two must always display his inmost being for public scrutiny, any oddities included. The psychological oddities of Chesterton and Lewis, although undoubtedly real and somewhat similar, should be kept in proportion. Maisie Ward mentions a noted psychologist who, when asked to define sanity, simply said "Read Chesterton!" (5); and we have all heard of people whose tottering reason was saved by the counter-paranoid fantasy *The Man Who Was Thursday*. Such things are often said of Lewis as well. So much characteristically modern thought seems petty and crabbed, and our world can so easily appear to be inhabited—or at least managed—by lunatics: any number of people have confessed that on reading either or both of these two writers, they get a sense of having escaped into a *largior aether* of the mind, into a different and far more civilized world, suffused at every point with massive sanity.

Then why do I mention such oddities as they did display? My excuse is that I'm a shade hypersensitive to the dangers of cultic *admiratio*. I've seen such a lot of it, of Lewis-worship and of Chesterton-worship, too; and if you respect their judgment, do be guided by them and avoid such folly altogether. They would quite certainly have rivaled one another in laughing it to scorn.

It has often hit me, chiefly in respect of Lewis. A few years ago, I wrote a short book about what I take to be certain intellectual faults or weaknesses in Lewis's religious thinking, and it brought me a small torrent of hostile mail, all of it from American ladies. But they didn't challenge my findings, they didn't fault my arguments. In every single case, their tone was "How *dare* you criticize our idol!" or even "How *dare* you blaspheme our god!" More recently, I reviewed a book which cast doubt upon what some consider the flawless rationality of—once again—Lewis's religious thinking. It seemed to me that the writer, Beversluis by name, had done his chosen task rather well, and I said so. Once again, the angry letters came, and their dominant tone was "Here, Derrick—which side are you on?"

Chesterton considered that Americans were, on the average, rather more intelligent than Englishmen. I wouldn't have put it quite like that, but I see what he meant. My heart sings within me whenever my jet leaves Heathrow for Kennedy (or Seattle/Tacoma), and one of the factors that cause it to sing is the prospect of far better and livelier conversation than I can easily find in foggy old England, even when other things are equal. That's the good news. The bad news—if I may say so, and even if I may not—is that the American mind does so frequently offer the response of a mere partisan ("Which side are you on?") where the response of a philosopher might have been more interesting.

Chesterton came here, of course, not as often as myself— this is my forty-fifth visit—but most enjoyably, with deep appreciation on both sides or in both directions. He naturally thought poorly of Prohibition; and it has to be confessed that he had little sympathy with what may be called the American ideal, the American dream. "There is nothing the matter with Americans except their ideals," he once wrote in the *New York Times*. "The real American is all right: it is the ideal American who is all wrong" ("Mr. Chesterton" 1). Maybe his notion of the ideal American was a shade insufficient.

As for Lewis, he was often invited to this country but never came: he once told me that he looked upon every such possibility with horror. The fact is that he knew practically nothing about the United States. His idea of this country came partly from Hollywood and partly from stories of the American wilderness; and as he very seldom went to the movies, even Hollywood's version of America was very imperfectly familiar to him. For the rest, it's symptomatic that when declining one invitation to the United States, he said: "Oh what a pity. To think that I might as your guest have seen bears, beavers, Indians, mountains" (Lewis, *Letters* 215). Those were somewhat unrealistic expectations for a prospective visitor to cherish. The mountains are there all right. But I assure you that an English visitor can travel repeatedly all over the United States without seeing a single bear or beaver or Indian. It's hotels and airports that the lecture circuit chiefly put before him.

Lewis had all the crude chauvinism of the untraveled and often came out with anti-American remarks of the utmost fatuity. I'd repeat some of them if I weren't too polite or too frightened. It seems to me clear beyond all doubt that if he had overcome his prejudices and the various practical difficulties and actually visited the United States, he would have responded very much as to his first experience of aviation: "We found it — after our initial moment of terror—enchanting" (Green and Hooper 269). He'd have enjoyed himself quite as much as I have.

So I find it fairly easy to bracket these two men together: as visitors or potential visitors to the United States, as massively wise people with various touches of lunacy, as writers, and so forth. As writers, of course, they differ enormously. *Perelandra* and *The Man Who Was Thursday* can both be called fantasies; still, nobody could read a page of the former and suppose it was written by Chesterton or a page of the latter and suppose it was written by Lewis. And of course they had totally different habits of work. Lewis wrote meticulously, cherishing time like a jewel: Chesterton wrote chaotically, making time into a disheveled mess and somehow getting away with it. Then, one never loses sight of the difference between the scholar of stupendous erudition and the half-educated though widely read journalist. "What wonderful things Chesterton would have had to say," said Evelyn Waugh, "if only he had been an educated man!" (Hollis 191). But would he? I suspect that anything like a full academic discipline would have dried him up completely.

But he could only have profited, I feel, from a slightly more disciplined approach to the use of the mind and of the pen. Even his keenest admirers ought to admit that Chesterton wrote far too much, far too quickly, far too carelessly, and often—probably without suspecting it—in very considerable ignorance. He used to charge into battle more unthinkingly than was really prudent: he would bring the whole heavyweight barrage of his merriment to bear upon "the moderns," as he called them too sweepingly — even upon "the scientists" — without first taking the trouble to find out what they were really trying to say, or how far it really needed denunciation *in causa Christi*. He thus had a remarkable talent for being simultaneously wrong about all the detailed particulars and resoundingly right about the question centrally at issue. That doesn't bother his confirmed admirers: they make allowances for it instinctively. But in general, it's unwise for a controversial writer to give an impression that he doesn't know what he's talking about, even in small matters.

Lewis once agreed with me that Chesterton was his own worst enemy as a thinker and a writer, too. There are some people who claim to read him for the fun and fireworks of his style, taking no interest in the substance of what he was trying to say, but I find that incomprehensible. It's the other way round for me, and I can't really trust myself to speak in a temperate manner about his stylistic perversities. When reading Chesterton, I dread the words "It is as though . . .": they usually mean that some rather obvious point is going to be underlined by a whole series of needless analogies, each more farfetched and irrelevant than the last. And if some present-day writer becomes hampered by this terrible worldwide shortage of semicolons, it's because Chesterton used them all up.

In *Till We Have Faces*—though not elsewhere—Lewis seems to be indulging an uncontrollable lust for parenthesis; and at one point in *An Experiment in Criticism*, he is guilty of a sentence with ten commas in it. But you aren't overwhelmed by such blemishes, as in Chesterton: you have to search for them. Lewis's education, his professional work, and the general cast of his mind made him far more responsible as a thinker, far more lucid and precise as a writer. As much as for any other reason, I read him for the pure aesthetic delight conferred by his sentence construction.

Let me confess that for a disastrous period in my youth—

until I was laughed out of it—I modeled my own literary manner upon Chesterton's. I never purr more loudly than when some reviewer compares my more recent manner to that of Lewis, as some do.

It is only as writers, of course—and more precisely, as writers on religious subjects—that these two men can really be regarded as having a shared vocation and achievement, suitable for joint celebration, as in our present program. Chesterton had no working life except that of a writer. He did have that early vocation to graphic art, and it continued to yield its own kind of harvest for the rest of his life; but to the annoyance of some, I shall call that a pleasing accomplishment rather than a great achievement. He could write about anything or everything, of course, and he did, never confining himself to explicitly "religious" subjects. But however secular his foreground topic of the moment might be —Browning or Cobbett or G. F. Watts, for example, rather than St. Thomas or St. Francis—he always saw it *sub specie aeternitatis* and in deeply religious terms. His early attempts to be a political animal and a political writer were assiduous but carry little conviction when seen in retrospect. He was a most passionate democrat. But "democracy" was a metapolitical concept for him, even a theological concept, and the Distributist League has to be classed as a truly spectacular nonachievement [see the Jay Corrin article for more on the Distributist League—ed.].

Lewis's achievement is more complex. He was mostly an Oxford don by profession, having his greatest monument in the well-known brilliance of all those who were fortunate enough to be his pupils; and he was of course a scholar of the most colossal erudition, universally recognized as such, even in the atheistic and envious city of Oxford. That side of his reputation is secure. It's a liberal education in itself to read his study of the so-called Renaissance, "New Learning and New Ignorance," which serves as the introduction to his volume of the *Oxford History of English Literature*, *English Literature in the Sixteenth Century, Excluding Drama*—especially if one were to follow that majestic essay with *The Allegory of Love*, *A Preface to Paradise Lost*, *The Discarded Image*, and even *Studies in Words*. (The last-named book deserves particular recommendation to those Catholic philosophers who, in their inordinate fear of nominalism, avert their eyes from the fact of semantic change.)

There was nothing comparable to all that in the life and work of Chesterton. It's in religious writing alone that the two come together and begin to form a kind of semidetached team.

If we are to speak of achievements, it may be salutary to remember that when judged by the harshly objective criterion provided by sales figures, Lewis is—above all else—a writer of children's stories. I don't know how far that same criterion would require us to label Chesterton as—above all else—a writer of detective stories. In continental Europe, I have often found him remembered and valued in that capacity alone. But in each case, there was marked continuity between what the writer put into his fiction and what he said elsewhere.

So the joint achievement that we are here to celebrate is chiefly a matter of marked success in religious writing for the popular market—success by the popular standards of that market, but also by the different standards of the critical specialist. Let us not call them theologians. We debase the currency when we apply that word to people not formally qualified and professional in the field. In this land of hype, I have sometimes blushed to find it applied—absurdly—to myself. Nor let us call Lewis a moral theologian or even a moralist, though he did apply that second term to himself. In that area, his greatest skill was in the psychology of moral choice, and of temptation in particular. When it comes to the specifics of precept and counsel, we often find him writing in a decidedly amateurish manner.

It would make a kind of sense, in fact—though it might seem rather odd — to celebrate Lewis as a great if unsystematic psychologist above all else, amazingly deep and wide in his understanding of the human mind and of human behavior, and—to an astonishing degree in one who married so late and so strangely—of the female mind and female behavior in particular. Orual and Jane Studdock will serve to remind us of the brilliant realistic novelist that Lewis might have been. It's quite otherwise with Chesterton. His fictional characters, with their melodramatic names, seldom strike me as human beings: each seems more like a personification of some religious or metaphysical position.

I'm trying to feel my way towards the theme of our celebration. Any greatness of achievement is of course a mystery. It always strikes us as being random in its incidence, not to be explained in terms of either nature or nurture, of childhood influences or later education and experience or anything else that we can understand. As Lewis himself said in another connection, the Elizabethans would have explained it in terms of "constellation," of astrological factors (*OHEL* 2). I'm afraid I haven't yet cast the horoscope of either great man.

But while we can seldom know the "efficient cause" of exceptionally great achievement, its "formal cause" should be much less of a mystery. We can agree that Chesterton and Lewis were great religious writers. Wherein does their greatness consist? That's a question that we may reasonably hope to answer, and I'm sure that the next few days will cast many kinds of light upon it.

I have one or two additional personal angles. One is the crudely obvious fact that both of them are tremendous fun to read. That's a rare thing. Even devout believers should be able to admit that religious writing has a marked tendency to be boring. In the Rule of St. Benedict and the monastic tradition generally, we find it taken for granted that *lectio divina*, although necessary, is going to be a penance rather than a pleasure. It's no penance with these two.

Then and relatedly, we find in each a truly remarkable zest or gusto. They are exceptionally interesting writers because they were exceptionally interested men. Chesterton, said his old friend E. C. Bentley, "had at least a double dose of the faculty of enjoying things, from a nineteenth-century sausage-and-mash to a fifteenth-century Madonna and Child" (Ward 17), and Lewis — according to Chad Walsh — had "alert curiosity about almost anything conceivable" (Green and Hooper 159). The fact is that interest, like boredom, is highly infectious. That was Lewis's great strength as a university lecturer. Students can be apathetic, heaven knows, and pundits can be tedious. But there was no apathy or tedium when Lewis was on the rostrum; and I have often wondered what happened to those undergraduates who, driven wild with excitement by *The Allegory of Love* or by the lectures which eventually became *The Discarded Image*, hoped to find a continuation of that same excitement when they turned to the actual pages of Macrobius or Martianus Capella. Not all of them will have found it there.

Then, there may be some kind of psychological link between that remarkable zest or gusto and the visionary or imaginative power of each writer's mind; and it's there, I suspect, that the achievement of each was at its greatest. Both were controversialists, of course, and Lewis — unlike Chesterton — was highly trained in logic and dialectic. But while there was much skepticism and irreligion in their respective and overlapping lifetimes, as there is today, I can't believe that very much of it had or has even the semblance of any rational basis, such as might make it vulnerable to a strictly rational apologetic; and of all Lewis's books, I suggest, the one which the world needed least is *Miracles*. It was for the Christian and potentially Christian *imagination* that Chesterton and Lewis did their greatest deeds; and to say that is not to disparage them in the least.

I'd even go so far as to define their joint achievement as that of two very great *translators*.

Let me explain. It has long been a commonplace to say that present-day people simply can't understand the traditional language of Christianity. I've always been rather skeptical about that. The verbal or lexical difficulties aren't so great. Where people fail to understand Christianity or Catholicism—and I regard those two words as normatively synonymous — I think it's mostly because they don't want to understand it.

However that may be, there's always a strong case for restating the gospel and the faith in the language of one's own time —provided that one does exactly that. The trouble is that some people claim and appear to be doing that necessary task, when in fact they're doing something radically different. It's one thing to restate the old faith so as to make it more easily understood; it's quite another thing to modify the faith so as to make it more easily acceptable. There's a great deal of that going on, even among us Catholics. The pattern of much present-day theology —both dogmatic and moral—is not governed by what Jesus said and commanded, nor yet by the hard substance of the apostolic witness: it's shaped most crucially by *what present-day people want to hear.* As in business, the product gets modified in order to meet consumer demand. It's often modified very radically indeed. We hear of a renewed Christianity, a renewed Catholicism, made more relevant and meaningful and so attuned to the needs and preoccupations of this age. On closer inspection, it turns out to be mostly a secular humanism or a Marxism or something similar, just garnished with a top-dressing of Christian or Catholic terminology.

Now the great merit of both Chesterton and Lewis, considered as religious writers, is that neither of them fell into that trap — that dishonesty, one might say. As a Catholic, I do have my reservations about the word "orthodoxy," as applied to Lewis and the younger Chesterton. But these are almost entirely concerned with methodology. As regards substance, each — in the vast bulk of his writing — was in fact restating the ancient faith in the language of his day, in the rhetorical language of a flamboyant journalist or with the cool lucidity of a scholar, with a thousand new angles and insights but otherwise without modification. Each might thus be called a faithful translator, though a salesman or a propagandist as well, mightily successful as such.

One might sum it up by saying that while no sane person would read *Orthodoxy* or *The Everlasting Man* in order to find out whether the Christians were right or wrong, he might well read both in order to form a deeper imaginative understanding of what the Christians were talking about. So with Chesterton generally, and Lewis as well. You sometimes meet people who know that "love" is at the heart of the matter but are utterly confused thereby. They overlook the crucifying complexity of that four-letter word, its erotic and affective senses being so overwhelmingly dominant in our culture. The remedy is simple: tell them to read *Till We Have Faces.*

Mention of that book brings me to the note on which I shall conclude. As you will remember, *Till We Have Faces* starts off as a complaint or accusation against the gods: that is, as a statement in the Gnostic or Manichaean sense. I see Chesterton probably and Lewis certainly being initially drawn to some such dualistic position and then as emerging from it by a primarily existential or experiential route. Chesterton went through his period of nihilism and black despair and discovered that gratitude was necessary for sanity; and gratitude implied God, and God implied original sin. Lewis tried to reject God but could find no other possible answer to the question, "What is it that I really *want*, with such agonizing though intermittent desire?" God is of course hidden, unseen by mortal eyes; but Lewis found that alienation or estrangement from God — or, once again, original sin — is a fact of common or universal experience, even when not recognized for what it is.

Original sin, the fall of man — that's not a very fashionable doctrine nowadays, and we can see why it isn't. It undermines various kinds of temporal optimism, it arouses needless anxieties about Old Testament exegesis and related subjects, and it challenges the implied Gnosticism that pervades our present-day culture and our supposedly "renewed" Christianities. Yet it's a doctrine vital for real Christians, if not as gospel, then certainly as *praeparatio evangelica*, as diagnosis before surgery; and, as Chesterton observed, "it's the only cheerful view of human life" (*Autobiography* 176).

What I chiefly hope to see explored, during these few days at Seattle, is the centrality of this theme in the lives and thought and work of both Chesterton and Lewis. More than anything else, it's what they're all about, though with different emphases; and it's what gives their work that characteristic savor of realism, of sanity, of truth, and (as they say) of "relevance." In Adam all have sinned: that's why we needn't and mustn't level any complaint or accusation against the gods.

When we are tempted to do so, like Orual, we should remember the majesty and absoluteness of the reply they gave her.

Works Cited

Chesterton, G. K. *Autobiography*. London: Hutchinson, 1936.
Chesterton, G. K. "Mr. Chesterton Looks Us Over." *New York Times*, Feb. 1, 1931, sec. 5:1-2, 20.

Green, Roger Lancelyn and Walter Hooper. *C. S. Lewis: A Biography.* London: Collins, 1974.

Hollis, Christopher. *The Mind of Chesterton.* London: Hollis & Carter, 1970.

Lewis, C. S. *English Literature in the Sixteenth Century* (OHEL). Oxford: Clarendon Press, 1954.

_____. *Surprised by Joy.* London: Geoffrey Bles, 1955.

Letters of C. S. Lewis. ed. W. H. Lewis. London: Geoffrey Bles, 1966.

Ward, Maisie. *Return to Chesterton.* London: Sheed & Ward, 1952.

Chesterton, the Wards, the Sheeds, and the Catholic Revival

Richard L. Purtill

In the early 1950s I was coming out of Foyle's bookstore on Charing Cross in London when I saw a rather surprising sight. In a blind alley between two parts of Foyle's was a small folding platform, rather like a stepstool with a tall railing on one side. On the railing was a crucifix and a rectangular sign on which was painted in rather faded gold letters, "Catholic Evidence Guild." Standing on the platform, leaning on the railing, was a young man who was speaking with an Australian accent about the Catholic faith. He was surrounded by a small crowd whose members frequently interrupted him with questions and objections.

As I walked over to the platform the young man was arguing about free will with an older man in the crowd. In light of later knowledge, I imagine that they had gotten onto the topic by way of the problem of evil and the argument that a good deal of the evil in the world is due to human misuses of free will. The man in the crowd was defending determinism, denying that we *have* free will, and I was not entirely satisfied with the young man's reply. I don't remember if I intervened in the argument,

RICHARD L. PURTILL is professor of philosophy at Western Washington University and the author of many works of fiction, philosophy, and literary criticism, including *C. S. Lewis' Case for Christianity*.

but after the young man had finished speaking and come down from the platform, I buttonholed him and said something like this: "Why didn't you refute what he was saying by telling him that if determinism were true he was determined by causes beyond his control to believe in determinism and you were determined by causes beyond your control not to believe in it, so there would be no use arguing."

I think my thought was something along the lines of C. S. Lewis's argument against naturalism in *Miracles*: since the man did think there was some use in arguing, this in itself was an argument against determinism. The young man with the Australian accent, whose name turned out to be Tony Coburn, replied amicably that he was trying to convince the man, not just refute him, and we got into an interesting discussion.

Presently Tony said, "Some of us are planning to have some tea at a shop near here. Why don't you join us?" I then saw that some of the crowd were still waiting nearby and were evidently friends or associates of Tony's. We went to the tea shop, and over tea and cakes I discovered that my companions were all speakers or prospective speakers for the Catholic Evidence Guild, a group mostly composed of Catholic laypeople who explained and defended Catholic doctrine at street-corner meetings like the one I had just observed.

I told them in turn that I was a recent convert to Catholicism, currently serving in the U.S. Army in England, and on weekend leave in London. My own conversion had been due in great part to reading the work of G. K. Chesterton. I had encountered him first through a Father Brown story in a collection of detective stories for children which I had found in the children's room of the local library. Afterwards I had read the rest of the Father Brown stories, much of the rest of Chesterton's fiction, and then gone on to his essays. By absorbing G. K. Chesterton's intellectual progress into the church, I explained that I had become convinced to follow in his footsteps.

Somewhere in the midst of this explanation, a rather dowdy, older lady in the group said, "Oh, I see you have my book." The book in question was Maisie Ward's *Return to Chesterton*, a supplement to her major biography of Chesterton. Wondering if the

lady was a trifle dotty because she thought that my book belonged
to her for some reason, I said that I had just bought the book at
Foyle's.

Someone in the group laughed and said, "She means that
she wrote the book. This is Maisie Ward." I think I was a little
suspicious at first that my leg was being pulled, as the English say.
But my conversation with the lady soon convinced me that she
was indeed Maisie Ward, and I tried to convey some of my appreciation for her biography of Chesterton, which had helped me
to see his life and thought in perspective.

Toward the end of this conversation Maisie said, "You know,
with your interests, you should really join the CEG." Not making
the connection with the sign I had seen on the platform I said,
"Oh, is there a Chesterton society in London?" thinking vaguely that the "C" stood for Chesterton. I soon learned that the
CEG was the way most of its members referred to the Catholic
Evidence Guild, that there was a training program for speakers
on Saturday nights, and that I was more than welcome to attend
and see if it might be my cup of tea.

The last name in my title is Sheed, and although Maisie wrote
under her maiden name, she was Mrs. Frank Sheed, co-owner
with her husband of the Anglo-American publishing firm of
Sheed and Ward. St. Paul said you can have many teachers, but
only one father in the faith; Chesterton was my father in the faith
but Frank and Maisie were certainly my godparents. I owe a very
great deal of my happiness, my sanity, and such sanctity as I have
managed to Gilbert, Maisie, and Frank; my life has been im-
measurably richer because of them. The only comparable influence on me had been that of my older brother in Christianity,
C. S. Lewis.

The meeting with Maisie just described was tremendously
influential on my own life; without it and the meetings which
followed, I might not be a philosopher, a teacher, and a writer
today. But it also gave me some insights into the Catholic revival
in England, and it is these I want to share with you.

Maisie's father and grandfather had been major influences on
the nineteenth-century Catholic revival and had been friends of
Newman and Manning. Maisie first met G. K. Chesterton at one

of her father's parties for promising young writers. The publishing firm was founded around the time of their marriage by Maisie and Frank Sheed, a young Australian lawyer and Catholic activist who was to be a major intellectual influence on Catholicism in the English-speaking world. There was, in fact, in England and America a type of Catholic whom I always considered to be a "Sheed and Ward" Catholic, because their view of Catholicism was in line with and often influenced by the kind of books Sheed and Ward published. Often readers of Sheed and Ward books went on to be Sheed and Ward authors, as I might have myself if Sheed and Ward had still existed when I began writing books other than textbooks.

The chief characteristics of Sheed and Ward Catholicism were a deep love of the church, which did not preclude a keen awareness of the church's failings, a keen intellectual interest in the teachings of the church, and a great ability to *enjoy* the life of faith and the life of reason. Some of the best discussions I have had and some of the most uproariously good times were with the members of the Catholic Evidence Guild, which was in many ways an extension of the Sheed and Ward apostolate.

"Apostolate" is an important word here. As publishers, and as moving spirits in the Catholic Evidence Guild, Frank and Maisie were taking very seriously our Lord's command to "go and teach all nations." That people should understand the Catholic faith, and knowing it, learn to love it, was the aim of their lives, as in many ways it was the aim of Chesterton's later life. Maisie Ward was, as I have said, a rather dowdy, older Englishwoman who was genuinely shy and modest, but whose keen intellect, wide interests, and enthusiasm for her current projects were extremely impressive once you got to know her. Her daughter Rosemary, who was a strikingly attractive young woman, gave some idea of what Maisie might have been like as a young woman.

Maisie's grandfather, William G. Ward, had been a friend of John Henry Newman and had preceded him into the Catholic church. Indeed, Ward had a considerable influence on Newman's decision to move to the Roman church, although they later quarreled. Maisie's father, Wilfrid Ward, was to become the editor

of the *Dublin Review,* an influential journal of opinion, and later
a biographer of Newman and others.

Maisie's mother, Josephine, was a member of the old Catholic
aristocracy of England, those who had not changed their religion
at the time of the Reformation. Through her Maisie was related
to such members of the nobility as the Duke of Norfolk. More
important, Josephine Ward, a highly intelligent woman who
shared and encouraged her husband's intellectual interests, was a
writer herself and became one of the early speakers for the
Catholic Evidence Guild, bringing Maisie into the guild with her.

Wilfrid Ward cannot be said to have "discovered" Chesterton in the early days of Chesterton's career, but he certainly encouraged and admired him. Wilfrid's article "Mr. Chesterton
Among the Prophets" is still one of the most intelligent and
balanced assessments of Chesterton, though it was largely about
Chesterton's early *magnum opus, Orthodoxy.*

It is interesting to read Chesterton's appreciation of Wilfrid
Ward (as quoted by Josephine in a biographical note on her husband Wilfrid after his death):

> One admirable quality he had which is exceedingly difficult to
> describe. . . . I know not whether to call it a curiosity without rest-
> lessness, or a gigantic intellectual appetite rather amplified than
> moderated by patience. It is common to say of a man so acute that
> he had a restless activity of mind; for in the effort to evade the
> platitudes of praise a phrase like "restless" has almost become a
> compliment. But the mind of Wilfrid Ward had very notably a rest-
> ful activity. Thinking was to him like breathing. He never left off
> doing it; and he never thought himself remarkable for doing it; in-
> deed so massive was his modesty and unconsciousness that he very
> often thought (quite erroneously) that his friends and acquain-
> tances were doing it more than he was.
>
> Wilfrid Ward was a biographer in a sense as exact and more
> exalted than we apply to a biologist; he really dealt with life and
> the springs of life. Some are so senseless as to associate the func-
> tion with merely indirect services to literature like those of the
> commentator and the bibliographer. They level the great portrait-
> painter of the soul with the people who put the ticket on the frame
> or the number in the catalogue. But in truth there is nothing so
> authentically creative as the divine act of making another man out

of the very substance of oneself. Few of us have vitality enough to
live the life of another. Few of us therefore can feel satisfied with
our own competence in or for biography, however fertile we may
be in autobiography. But he was so full of this disinterested imagination of the biographer that even his short journalistic sketches
were model biographies. He made a death-mask in wax with the
firmness of a sculptor's monument in marble.

Yet I think the very positive qualities of his personality can
perhaps still be most easily handled and summarized as those which
made him so fine a critic of others. In his interpretations of Newman or of William George Ward he was without a suspicion of
self-display; but he achieved something quite other and stronger
than self-effacement. In truth, a magician needs a high power of
magic in order to disappear. But he did something very much more
than disappearing. He was anything but merely receptive, he could
be decidedly combative; but he could also, and above all, be strongly co-operative with another's mind. His intellectual qualities could
be invisible because they were active, when they were the very virile
virtues of a biographer which are those of a friend. (Ward, *Last
Lectures* xv-xvii)

Incidentally, it is those very virtues of Wilfrid Ward, inherited
by his daughter, which make her biography of Chesterton such a
major achievement. She was indeed a friend as well as a biographer, and with all respect to the achievements of Ms. Dale and
Mr. Ffinch, her biography gave us a picture of the essential
Chesterton which is corrected or enhanced only in detail by later
biographers. If one were to read only one biography of Chesterton, it should be Maisie's.

All of Wilfrid Ward's *Dublin Review* article "Mr. Chesterton
Among the Prophets" is well worth quoting, but the concluding
paragraphs give a good idea of the tone of admiration coupled
with frank criticism:

 . . . it is very many years since so much individuality has been
 brought to bear on controversies which are so largely long-stand-
 ing ones. *Orthodoxy* is a book to upset the pedant, to irritate Mr.
 Chesterton's *betes noires*, the "dreary and well-informed." Here it
 hits with wonderful precision the one weak spot — the heel of
 Achilles — in some ingenious but demoralizing system. There the
 reading of the relevant literature has been careless, and the mark

is missed—a lay figure is destroyed, a most amusing play is enacted in the destruction, and so the matter ends. . . . In our own late day, a work on these well-worn themes rarely affords half a dozen passages which come upon one with the feeling that we have found something original. In this work one's pencil marks half a hundred. J. S. Mill told us, fifty years ago, that we must master the whole existing literature of these discussions before we are fitted to say anything new. . . . In Mill's time, the few experts could fulfil his test, and originality could, perhaps, emerge after the severe training. Now specialism has so greatly developed that it hardly can. Perhaps in Mr. Chesterton it would have done so, had his training been that of an expert. But it has not. And one of the very few men who could, I believe, have now fulfilled Mill's test, and remained original after the second half of a training—of which the first half is still good for all—has set the example of going forth with little of equipment over and above his own extraordinary force and skill — little beyond the stone and the sling. The result is, however, something which must be taken very seriously indeed; and if even half of what he says needs qualification and correction, that will not prevent the book giving us a permanent legacy more of original and practically helpful suggestions than perhaps anything which has appeared in our own day on "the genius of Christianity." (Ward, *Men and Matters* 142-44)

In her biography Maisie may seem superficially to be a mere friend and admirer of Chesterton, but there is plenty of criticism of his weaknesses. However, I know from my own experience of writing about Lewis and Tolkien that if you write with approval, even tempered approval, of a controversial writer, those who dislike and disagree with that writer will dismiss your writing as mere propaganda by an admirer of the writer in question. The only kind of book about the author such critics will praise as "balanced" is a debunking or demolition of the writer.

All four Wards — W.G., Wilfrid, Josephine, and Maisie — were contributors to and encouragers of the Catholic revival in England in the nineteenth and twentieth centuries, especially insofar as this revival is an intellectual and literary phenomenon: Catholicism becoming intellectually respectable among the intelligentsia and Catholic writing becoming recognized as interesting and worthy of respect by the literary establishment. To appreciate their achievement you have to know something of the contempt with which Catholic writing was treated by non-Catholics in England before this Catholic revival.

Chesterton was certainly one of the stars of the later Catholic revival, though he was not to be received into the Catholic church until fourteen years before his death. And Chesterton always communicated with the ordinary person, through his newspaper columns, through his lectures, and toward the end of his life through radio broadcasts. But that person who did more than anyone except Chesterton himself to bring the Catholic revival to the ordinary intelligent person was not a member of any intellectual or literary elite. He was Maisie's Australian husband, Frank Sheed. Frank was a man of tremendous brilliance, vitality, and good humor. As a lecturer and streetcorner speaker Frank conveyed his excitement with and enjoyment of the truths of the Catholic faith. His books also manifested the beautiful clarity of his mind, and a lucidity rivaled only by C. S. Lewis. But to know Frank only through his books was to miss a great deal.

As a publisher, Frank had the same virtues which Maisie and her father had as biographers: after introducing readers to his authors, he then stepped into the background. In the case of his French and German and Italian authors, this meant getting them translated into English (often more lucid than the original) and presenting them as part of an intellectual context in which the virtues of one writer balanced the faults of another.

In the case of English and later American writers, it was often a matter of seeing what would speak to the audience. For many English intellectuals, Father Ronald Knox's wartime sermons to the schoolgirls at the convent school, where he was quartered to carry on his scholarly work, seemed embarrassingly childish, even "cute" in a bad sense. Frank had the wit to see that the simplicity and directness of these books was precisely what many readers needed, and *The Creed in Slow Motion*, *The Mass in Slow Motion*, etc., may have illumined and inspired more minds than Knox's more "respectable" works ever did.

Wilfrid Sheed, the son of Frank and Maisie and himself a writer of considerable range and diversity, has written a warm and illuminating picture of his parents. In this book Wilfrid Sheed shows how the lecturing done by Frank and Maisie in effect created the audience for the books they would later publish. This audience of "Sheed and Ward Catholics" in turn formed the basis for many movements in Catholicism, in effect passing on the Catholic revival to the next generation.

The characteristics of this next generation of the Catholic revival in England and the United States were largely the characteristics I listed earlier: love of the Catholic faith, intellectual excitement at the truths of the faith, and a feeling of joy in living the faith. These traits carried over in many of this "next generation" into Catholic activism, the fight against racial injustice, efforts to help the poor and homeless at home and abroad, and activism in the cause of peace. Maisie, in particular, was involved in all of these efforts. Frank was completely behind her, but his own efforts were largely directed toward the intellectual underpinnings of these movements: writing, publishing, and lecturing on those things which had to be understood in order to moderate and direct activism.

The fading—I will not say the failure, but certainly the decline — of the Catholic revival came because too many people lost sight of these intellectual foundations. The decline began, I believe, when Catholics joined the fight against racial injustice and began deferring, for the very best of motives, to the black leaders in the movement, letting them set tone and strategy. It was certainly a dilemma; to insist on their Catholic motivations and foundations for objecting to racial injustice might have seemed to others in the movement to be separatist or patronizing: "I will help you in your struggle, but on my terms, not yours." To avoid this predicament seemed to be an obvious good, but it set a dangerous precedent. When Catholics began getting involved in other movements, such as the peace movement, they fell victim to a pattern which I will call the "more revolutionary than thou" syndrome, by which in any revolutionary movement the extremists tend to take over on the pretense that anyone who is not as extreme as they are is a traitor to the movement. It is the operation of this syndrome which has led, for example, to the women's movement for sexual justice being influenced and led by lesbians and separatists out of all proportion to their numbers in the movement or to the number of women who agree with their aims. In English politics this syndrome has largely rendered ineffective the Labor Party and contributed to Margaret Thatcher's recent victory. The syndrome can be resisted; the American union movement has largely resisted it. But it has separated more than one movement for change from its base of supporters, and in a number of cases it has turned out that at least some of the extremists were in the pay of those opposed to change and had as their aim the alienation of the leaders of the movement from their rank and file supporters.

The effect of this syndrome on the Catholic revival was this: Catholics, excited by their faith, wanted to apply that faith to the needs of the world. To do so they allied themselves with groups who regarded the righting of certain injustices or the meeting of certain needs as so self-evidently right that Catholicism was only a *means* to the end, and if Catholicism came into conflict with those ends it was Catholicism which must give way. It is precisely the situation described by C. S. Lewis in Letter VII of *The Screwtape Letters*, where Screwtape, the senior devil, advises the junior devil, Wormwood, as to how to undermine the newfound Christianity of the men Wormwood is tempting:

> Any small coterie, bound together by some interest which other men dislike or ignore, tends to develop inside itself a hothouse of mutual admiration, and towards the outer world, a great deal of pride and hatred which is entertained without shame because the "Cause" is its sponsor and it is thought to be impersonal. Even when the little group exists originally for the Enemy's own purposes, this remains true. We want the Church to be small not only that fewer men may know the Enemy but also that those who do may acquire the uneasy intensity and the defensive self-righteousness of a secret society or a clique. The Church herself is, of course, heavily defended and we have never yet quite succeeded in giving her *all* the characteristics of a faction; but subordinate factions within her have often produced admirable results, from the parties of Paul and of Apollos at Corinth down to the High and Low parties in the Church of England. . . .
>
> Whichever he adopts, your main task will be the same. Let

him begin by treating the Patriotism or the Pacifism as a part of his religion. Then let him, under the influence of partisan spirit, come to regard it as the most important part. Then quietly and gradually nurse him onto the stage at which the religion becomes merely part of the "cause," in which Christianity is valued chiefly because of the excellent arguments it can produce in favour of the British war-effort or of Pacifism. The attitude which you want to guard against is that in which temporal affairs are treated primarily as material for obedience. Once you have made the World an end, and faith a means, you have almost won your man, and it makes very little difference what kind of worldly end he is pursuing. Provided that meetings, pamphlets, policies, movements, causes, and crusades, matter more to him than prayers and sacraments and charity, he is ours—and the more "religious" (on those terms) the more securely ours. I could show you a pretty cageful down here. (40-43)

It is, I believe, precisely this situation which happened to many of the enthusiastic products of the Catholic revival; for them the world became an end and faith a means. But faith used as a means ceases to be nourished and ceases to be faith. It sounds very well to say that certain human needs are so urgent that we have no time for "prayers and sacraments." But without the prayers and sacraments our faith starves and dies, and either the means are found to serve the original end or that end is abandoned. Some of those impelled to social activism by the Catholic revival and who fell into this trap substituted secular for religious motivations. But far more people simply "burned out" and abandoned the struggle.

Without the motivation of faith, doing good in the world at considerable personal sacrifice is not something most people can sustain. The Catholic Evidence Guild advised at least an hour in prayer for every hour spent on the platform. Those who kept this counsel were those who stuck with the guild; those who didn't, who relied on their own powers, eventually dropped out. Similarly, Mother Teresa and those who work with her are sustained in their tremendous sacrifices by prayer and the sacraments. There are, of course, exceptions: "secular saints" who seem sustained by some nonreligious vision or compulsion, but these are exceptions. To motivate ordinary people to self-sacrificing love they must be put in contact—by prayer and the sacraments—with Self-Sacrificing Love himself, our Lord Jesus Christ. Our priorities must be right. We must not want faith as a means, even a necessary means to doing good. First, we must know God, we must love God, and *then* we can serve God in our neighbor. "Seek *first* the kingdom of heaven and all these things will be added to you" (Matthew 6:33). Seek first the other things and you will lose the kingdom of heaven and the other things too.

The end of the Catholic revival—the Catholic revival of the Wards, the Sheeds, and Chesterton—came when people forgot this truth. The end of the reforms of Vatican II is perilously close at hand because people are forgetting the same truth again. Time after time great and hopeful movements have been shipwrecked on this rock. But Christianity tells us what to do about such failures: repent and change. Catholic Christianity's version of this formula is confess your sins, form a firm purpose of amendment, make reparation for past sins. To help and motivate us in this endeavor we have the same help we neglected before: prayer and the sacraments. What is more, we have the Wards, the Sheeds, and Chesterton. For unlike social energy, which comes from group interaction and ceases to exist when the group goes down, intellectual energy is stored in those marvelous storage batteries called books. We can pick up the book again, see the vision again, and go out to fight for the vision again. If the book was written in another age, in another social situation, we may need help in understanding it and applying it to our times. That is one vital function of scholarship about men and women such as the Sheeds, the Wards, the Chestertons.

But the scholar needs to have his or her priorities very much in order. Our work is important because the work of those we try to understand and elucidate is important. And their work is important because they are trying to understand and elucidate what God has revealed to us, in nature and society as well as in Scripture. "Therefore every scholar instructed in the kingdom of God is like a rich man who brings out of the storehouse things old and new" (Matthew 13:52). And "whoever sets aside one of the commandments, even the least, and teaches others to do

Richard L. Purtill

likewise is the least in the kingdom of heaven, but the one who keeps them and teaches others to keep them will be accounted in the kingdom of heaven as the greatest" (Matthew 5:19). Scholars and teachers should strive for that kind of greatness, the only kind worth having in the long run, remembering that "the one who would be great in the kingdom of heaven must be the least, and the servant of all" and remembering the great servants of God who have gone before us, William, Wilfrid, and Maisie Ward, Gilbert Chesterton, and Frank Sheed.

Works Cited

Lewis, C. S. *Screwtape Letters*. New York: Macmillan, 1943.
Sheed, Wilfrid. *Frank and Maisie*. New York: Simon & Schuster, 1985.
Ward, Mrs. Wilfrid (Josephine). *Last Lectures by Wilfrid Ward*. Freeport, NY: Books for Libraries Press, 1967.
Ward, Wilfrid. *Men and Matters*. Freeport, NY: Books for Libraries Press, 1967.

C. S. Lewis and C. S. Lewises*

Walter Hooper

I have called this paper "C. S. Lewis and C. S. Lewises" because I
think the attempt should be made to separate the real C. S. Lewis
from the growing number of fictional characters of the same name.
I want to clear the decks of a few of the better known counter-
feits in the hope that the real one will be easier to identify.

Lewis cared little for biographies, and I think he would be
pleased that far more people are interested in his books than in
his life. However, as Lewis's letters and recorded sayings are made
available, it becomes almost as difficult to separate Lewis from
his books as it would be to separate the personality of Dr. Johnson
from his. I don't think everyone has difficulty making such a
separation, but some do, and I am often asked, "What kind of
a man was C. S. Lewis?"

Those who have read Lewis's inaugural lecture at Cambridge
University as its first professor of medieval and renaissance English literature will recall that he described himself as one of the
few surviving "Old Western men." By this he meant one who

* © 1989 C. S. Lewis Pte Ltd

WALTER HOOPER has edited more than a dozen posthumously published volumes of Lewis's writings; with Roger Lancelyn Green he wrote
C. S. Lewis: A Biography (1974).

reads as a native books which, with all our modern responses, most of us can read only as foreigners (even if we are unaware we are doing so). Lewis ended that marvelous lecture with this advice: "Speaking not only for myself but for all the Old Western men whom you may meet, I would say, use your specimens while you can. There are not going to be many more dinosaurs" ("De Descriptione Temporum" 14).

In Lewis's essay "Hedonics," found in his book *Present Concerns*, he distinguishes between two things which make up everyone's life. There are, first, those events which it is easy for biographers to find out about and which "we commonly call good and bad fortune." Second, there is what Lewis refers to as "the actual quality of life as we live it—the weather of the consciousness from moment to moment"("Hedonics" 53). Last year William Griffin's biography of Lewis was published under the title *Clive Staples Lewis: A Dramatic Life.* By "dramatic" Mr. Griffin meant the way he presented Lewis's life in a chronological order of events "like frames in a film" (xxi). One of the reviewers of that book, pretending not to understand what the title meant, said he didn't find the events in Lewis's life, the good and bad fortune, dramatic at all. Happily for Lewis, his life was not at all dramatic in the way that, say, Lawrence of Arabia's was. You could never write a biography of Lewis that would not bore those hungry for physical adventures. When Lewis told a reporter, "I like monotony" ("Don v. Devil" 65), he meant a life relatively free of bustle and crises. If it is adventures of the mind that you are hungry for, then be grateful for the monotony Lewis enjoyed, as it made it possible for him to give us some of the best.

For those who want to know more about Lewis's life as well as the "weather" of his mind, I suggest you read what those other Old Western men who knew him best had to say of him —W. H. Lewis, Professor Tolkien, Owen Barfield, and other of his close friends. The biography of Lewis by his friend George Sayer is to be published soon. It is very, very good, and it provides further evidence that, much as Lewis liked monotony, no one ever found it monotonous to be in his company.

This was certainly my experience, and it was especially true of my first meeting with him. I have written of that meeting elsewhere, but it will perhaps bear being repeated. Before that first meeting with Lewis in 1963 I had got it into my head that he was rigorously protected by a formidable housekeeper and at least six secretaries all banging on typewriters at the same time. It was not like that at all. When I visited Lewis on June 7, 1963, I found him completely alone. Instead of being comforted by this, I found it terrifying. There was also the surprise, almost shock, of Lewis's English being so English. But all these things were driven from my mind by Lewis's friendliness and his talk. There were no cucumber sandwiches, but afternoon tea went on and on and on. After one pot had been drained he would make another. Because I, too, am very fond of tea, I thought it all quite wonderful. Eventually, after what had been at least two hours of steady tea-drinking, I asked, with that embarrassment the English find comic, to be shown the "bathroom." I didn't know that in most English homes the bathroom and the toilet are separate rooms. "Of course you may use the bathroom," said Lewis, and he took me to his. Pointing to the tub, he flung down a pile of towels and laid out not one but several tablets of soap. "Are you sure you have everything you need?" he asked before closing the door behind him. I stood a long time in that bathroom gazing at that tub, towels, and soap, wondering what to do. When I couldn't bear it any longer I returned to the Common Room and told Lewis it wasn't a bath I wanted. "Well, sir," said Lewis, bursting with laughter, "'Choose you this day.' That will break you of those silly American euphemisms. And now, where is it you want to go?"

As I think nearly everyone discovered, one of the most noticeable things about Lewis's conversation was the large part comedy played in it. It seemed to me that the comic spirit was as evident when Lewis was being serious as when he was at his most light-hearted — and he was light-hearted more often than some of his critics want us to think. I attribute this to Lewis's gift of seeing things in proportion and from a kind of heavenly perspective. Not long after I met him, Lewis had me move into his house, The Kilns, as his private secretary. It was during those months when I was privileged to be part of his household that Lewis sent me to Cambridge University to handle some business for him. When I got home Lewis asked what I thought of a gentlemen I shall call X. I said that X was the greatest bore I had ever come across. I remember listening to X and wondering if we had been talking for five minutes or five years. Even so, I discovered, as I told Lewis, that X was no ordinary bore. He even succeeded in fascinating me by the intensity of his boringness. "Yes," said Lewis, "but let us not forget that our Lord might well have said, 'As ye have done it unto one of the least of these my bores ye have done it unto me.'"

Just how serious Lewis was about this great bore was revealed to me shortly after Lewis's death. Not long before I met this terrific bore, the college he worked in (he was not a teacher) was divided over whether or not to renew X's contract. When they were unable to reach a decision they decided to be guided entirely by Lewis, and they asked him what they should do. Lewis wrote to them, saying:

> X is a very great Bore. I am not sure that I know anyone whose conversation fatigues and dejects me more. In view of the services we have already accepted from him I think it would be . . . foolish to allow any decision we make about him to be at all influenced by his boringness. . . . I feel v. strongly that to suffer bores patiently—'gladly' may be impossible—is a plain duty, and that it is even plainer when we owe them some gratitude. Anyway, it really comes under the Golden Rule. Each of us, no doubt, is a bore to some people. I should like those whom I bore to treat me kindly and justly and therefore I must be kind and just to those who bore me. He is, so far as I am concerned, the *only* Bore at our High Table. Can one expect to have less than one? We are being let off very lightly. (Letter from C. S. Lewis of 3 June 1959 to Dr. Richard Ladborough in the Bodleian Library)

There in a nutshell is enough of Lewis's wisdom and goodness to justify our looking further into his life for more wisdom and goodness. But unless we see the bores in our lives in much the same way as Lewis saw this one, we will not be giving either Lewis or our bores the attention they deserve. How do we do this?

There are, no doubt, many ways. However, if by some extraordinary miracle I could hold a pistol to the world's head and force everyone to do as I think they should, I would require that everyone connected with a university read Lewis's *An Experiment in Criticism.* It will be remembered that in *Surprised by Joy* Lewis says that the particular kind of longing which he called Joy was not an end in itself but a pointer to something else—in fact, God. Lewis is pointing to something larger than one's own self when, in *An Experiment in Criticism,* he says that in reading literary works

> we seek an enlargement of our being. We want to be more than ourselves. Each of us by nature sees the whole world from one point of view with a perspective and selectiveness peculiar to himself. And even when we build disinterested fantasies, they are saturated with, and limited by, our own psychology. . . . We want to see with other eyes, to imagine with other imaginations, to feel with other hearts, as well as our own. We are not content to be Leibnitzian monads. We demand windows. . . . One of the things we feel after reading a great work is "I have got out." Or from another point of view "I have got in"; pierced the shell of some other monad and discovered what it is like inside. (137-38)

In the early chapters of *An Experiment in Criticism,* Lewis distinguishes between two kinds of readers. There are, first, those who *receive* from books by setting aside, even if only while they read, all their preconceptions. After having read a book they may conclude that it is no good and that the author should be thrashed. But they know they must read a book before they can be in a position to judge it. The second kind are readers who use or "do things with" books, and that in such a way that they never find out whether the books they use have anything to offer or not. As Lewis says of this bad practice of using books: "We are so busy doing things with the work that we give it too little chance to work on us. Thus increasingly we meet only ourselves" (85). In this same chapter he goes on to say:

> The sort of misreading I here protest against is unfortunately encouraged by the increasing importance of "English Literature" as an academic discipline. This directs to the study of literature a great many talented, ingenious, and diligent people whose real interests are not specifically literary at all. Forced to talk incessantly about books, what can they do but try to make books into the sort of things they can talk about? Hence literature becomes for them a religion, a philosophy, a school of ethics, a psychotheraphy, a sociology—anything rather than a collection of works of art. (86)

This leads me to introduce you to the first of the false C. S. Lewises. I am uncertain of his origin, but C. S. Lewis the Misogynist appears to be mainly the construction of those American readers who make the real Lewis's books the "sort of thing they can talk about." I call the creators and perpetuators of C. S. Lewis the Misogynist "snappers," and you may be interested in knowing how they came by this title.

For several years many of those of us in the Oxford University C. S. Lewis Society have noticed how many articles have been written about C. S. Lewis the Misogynist / Sexist / Racist, to name only a few of the "ists" applied to him. Then, when it was discovered that I had to expose this false Lewis in my paper, we wondered if I would be torn to pieces at this conference. Doubtless I shall find out soon, as snappers are a peppery lot. Even so, a question discussed at many sessions of members of our society in the Bird and Baby pub was how Lewis came to be so misunderstood and vilified by the feminists. It was during one of these conversations in Lewis's old pub that Dr. Jeremy Dyson, former president of our society and the man who gave *Present Concerns* its name, provided us with the answer. He said, "It comes from being grown-up Snap players." Snap, he reminded us, is a card game much enjoyed by English children. On the backs of Snap cards are brightly colored pictures of moo-cows, dogs, cats, donkeys, and other things. When the children put down identical cards in succession, the first to see the resemblance yells "SNAP!" with a quick smack of the hand on the cards. Because of the intensity and vigilance with which some play the game it is not unusual for an overly fervent Snap player to imagine resemblances which are not there and yell "Snap!" too soon. This usually causes him to lose the game.

Dr. Dyson convinced me that really desperate snapping — that which is bound to lose you the game — is not confined to children. Those adults in the grip of a popular kind of moral posturing are so serious about imaginary moo-cows that their snappery runs away with them.

The first instance of snapology I have seen applied to Lewis's books is Stella Gibbons's article "Imaginative Writing," found in *Light on C. S. Lewis*. Mrs. Gibbons was moved to yell "Snap!"

when she discovered that Lewis "disapproved of women" (93). How did she reach such a conclusion? She believes that proof of misogyny and sexism (Snap! Snap!) are found in Lewis's treatment of Jane Studdock in *That Hideous Strength* and dear Mrs. Beaver in *The Lion, the Witch and the Wardrobe*. It will be remembered that, fleeing from the White Witch, Mr. and Mrs. Beaver and three of the Pevensie children are befriended by Father Christmas in a snowy wood. The episode ends with a very pleasant tea. However, as Mrs. Beaver prepares to cut a loaf of bread, she utters the words so offensive to Mrs. Gibbons and all conscientious snappers — "What a mercy I thought of bringing the bread knife." If you have ever tried to cut a loaf without a knife you will regard it as a very considerable mercy to have a bread knife. But who can think of *bread* when such a grievous instance of sexism is before us?

The Narnian stories have attracted more snappers than any of Lewis's other books. Sometimes one instance of snappery has been found to contradict another. One snapper has recently condemned Lewis for not being a pacifist (Snap!) in his Narnian tales and then condemned him even more strongly for his sexism (Snap!) in not allowing Lucy and Susan to take part in the battle recounted in *The Lion, the Witch and the Wardrobe*. The most absurd example of snappery I have seen applied to those books was a plea from a publisher who wanted to change the races of the four Pevensie brothers and sisters. Lewis's racism (Snap!) could, I was told, be put right by making one of the children black, one Red Indian, one Chinese, and one white. The same publishers begged to be allowed to correct misogyny, sexism, and racism (Snap! Snap! Snap!) by reversing the characters and the roles of the boys and girls and making the dark Calormenes and the white Narnians either all dark or all white.

I felt I had to include this false C. S. Lewis, who sinned against that modern blob "Peoplekind," not because I find his makers merely comic but because I find snappers sad and unhappy. Whether they will ever be able to see through the great window Lewis gave us I don't know.

There was almost certainly a time when such sunshiny books as the Chronicles of Narnia spoke directly to their hearts, and I

am anxious that this game of grown-up Snap be understood and
rejected before it blights the enjoyment and enlargement of those
of you who are still free. Following the invention of grown-up
Snap by Jeremy Dyson, we were amazed and then appalled by
the grip it has on some minds. What might begin as an attempt
to be fair-minded can end, as it already has with so many, as a
perpetual witch-hunt for the offending "isms" in every book,
every television program, every conversation. The snapper is so
busy doing things with Lewis's books that he meets in them nothing but his own furious self.

I must remind you that it was Dr. Dyson, not I, who discovered Grown-up Snap. Further, I am still learning the rudi-
ments of the game, but Dr. Dyson is the most eminent
Snapologist on earth. If you wish to pit your skills as a snapper
against those of someone more learned than yourself, go challenge Jeremy Dyson. If Snap is driving you insane and making
you a nuisance to those who used to like you, please consult Dr.
Dyson. This distinguished Snapologist has recently become at-
tached to the Department of Soil and Environmental Sciences
at the University of California, Riverside. He invites you to visit
him there. Why fight with me when you can be cured by him?

The next C. S. Lewis which cannot claim reality is one which
the real Lewis had often to say he was not. It is C. S. Lewis the
Fundamentalist/Evangelical. Lewis was neither a Fundamentalist
nor an Evangelical as those terms are normally used in the United
States. Some of you will be sorry that this is true. Nevertheless,
I believe that the real Lewis was able to do more good for
American Fundamentalists and Evangelicals, and many others as
well, when no one pretended that he was other than an Anglican.

I have some firsthand evidence of this. I had been in the
Army only a few months and stationed at Fort Bragg, North
Carolina, when in November of 1954 I received my first letter
from C. S. Lewis. It never struck me as even possible that he
would answer the letter of thanks I had written to him. But there
I was, a mere private first class, yet known to the chaplains for
whom I worked as "The Soldier Who Had Heard from C. S.
Lewis." It was because of this letter that I was chosen to look
after the physical needs of the famous man coming to preach at

Fort Bragg. It was Bob Jones, Jr., of Bob Jones University, at that time perhaps the most uncompromising Fundamentalist in this country. He had visited C. S. Lewis in Oxford, and the chaplains knew I wanted to talk to him about this. (I was surprised and impressed by his method of preaching. Instead of quoting a verse or two from the First Epistle to Timothy as his text, he recited the whole of that epistle from memory. As a result, there was not much time left for preaching on it.) Following his sermon, I went into his room to ask if there was anything he needed, and it was then that I asked what he thought of Lewis. A look of great severity came over his face. "That man," said Dr. Jones, weighing every syllable, "smokes a pipe, and that man drinks liquor—but I do believe he is a Christian."

Lewis apparently had not known that Dr. Jones was a teetotaler. He could remember little about the visit except that he thought he took Dr. Jones to the Bird and Baby for a pint and a smoke. The good thing about this was that neither man was offended, and Dr. Jones saw Lewis behaving as he would around fellow Christians. No doubt if Lewis had known of Dr. Jones's beliefs about tobacco and alcohol he would have given him tea. But as Dr. Jones went calling on Lewis, how much better to find him behaving naturally. In other words, I think Dr. Jones learned something very valuable about the behavior of not just one fellow Christian, but most of them. And it certainly had not led him to be bitter.

If such a fierce opponent of alcohol and tobacco can accept Lewis for what he was, why should Lewis be presented to more gentle opponents as he was not? Please understand that I would never urge Fundamentalists and Evangelicals to introduce Lewis to their brethren as a man whose most notable characteristic was his enjoyment of smoking and drinking. Yet I think it equally important that one does not represent Lewis in such a manner that the brethren feel deceived when they discover Lewis's enjoyment of beer and tobacco. C. S. Lewis knew this could happen, and he took steps to prevent his books from being altered in order to make them acceptable to some people. Here is an instance of that. In 1960 Lewis's publisher, Jocelyn Gibb of Geoffrey Bles Ltd, asked if he would permit a Baptist organization to remove all reference to alcohol and tobacco for a translation of *Miracles* into Japanese. In his reply of May 9, 1960, Lewis said: "I am afraid I can't agree to a Japanese version of *Miracles* with those expurgations. Small though they are, their aim clearly is that I should be disguised as a fundamentalist and a non-smoker. I should be trying to attract a particular public under false pretenses. I have hitherto been acceptable to a good many different 'Denominations' without such camouflage, and I won't resort to it now. The Baptist translator may, if he pleases, add notes of his own, warning readers that the book is at these points, in his opinion, pernicious. But he must not remove them. Perhaps you had best transmit . . . exactly what I say here" (letter to Jocelyn Gibb, Bodleian Library, Oxford).

I am grateful Lewis left such clear instructions regarding his books. Not long ago an American missionary society asked Lewis's English publishers for permission to delete what would have been about a third of *Surprised by Joy* for a translation into Spanish. When I saw precisely what they wished to excise, it was clear that a man very different from Lewis would emerge from such butchery. You would not recognize him as the Lewis you know. And how on earth can you offend the people of Spain by mentioning tobacco and alcohol? In any event, this hypocritical translation was not permitted—thanks be to God!

The real C. S. Lewis did more than anyone I have ever known or heard of for Christian unity, and the part played by Fundamentalists and Evangelicals in making Lewis's books well known is so valuable that an account of Lewis and Christian unity which left them out would be dishonest and worthless. Nevertheless, we must not be too easily satisfied when so much more is within our reach. What gives ecumenism a bad name in England are those Christianity-and-Water clergy and laity from various churches, each promising to sacrifice this or that doctrine just as long as it is possible to arrive at a kind of vegetarian "togetherness." It often amounts to a corporate agreement to deny Christ.

What I wish we could achieve would be similar to that funny but solid harmony which Lewis showed existing on Malacandra between the *hrossa*, the *sorns*, and the *pfifltriggi*. The three species of beings in *Out of the Silent Planet* complement one another because of what Lewis speaks of as "thought that floats on a different blood" (103). It will be remembered that the *pfifltriggi* enjoyed making elaborate things which were for the most part useless. I asked Lewis what he considered a piece of earthly *pfifltriggi*, and he said, "a back scratcher." I think the Fundamentalists and Evangelicals who absorb as much as they can of the "weather" of Lewis's consciousness will find it immensely more important and helpful than any *pfifltriggi*. I don't mean such things as tobacco and beer—they are on the periphery. I mean that they should look at the historic faith through Lewis's eyes and read some of those theologians such as St. Augustine which have been the staple diet of the Catholic church for many centuries. At the very least, Fundamentalists and Evangelicals would know what they reject. But I think they would be astounded at how much there is they could accept.

A notable admirer of Lewis's books is the enormously wise Pope John Paul II. While reading some of the pope's sermons the other day, I enjoyed imagining what would happen if those very sermons were published under the pseudonym "Richard Purtill" in *The Watchtower*. Liberal Anglicans and Roman Catholics would probably reject them as "Ulster Protestantism." I think all orthodox Christians would say, "This is very sound stuff!"

If I am not already thought to be the most ill-mannered speaker at this conference, I am quite certain to be after introducing C. S. Lewis the Doubter. He is the last of the false Lewises and in bringing him to your attention it is necessary to say more about the real one.

One of my reasons for going to England to meet Lewis was that I had signed a contract to write a book about him for the Twaynes English Author Series. When I mentioned this to Lewis, he said in a letter of July 2, 1962, "Far better write about the unanswering dead!" (This and other letters from Lewis to Hooper are in the Southern Historical Collection of the University of North Carolina at Chapel Hill. There are copies in the Bodleian Library.) A few months later he drew my attention to his essay "The Anthropological Approach," which opens: "It is not to be disputed that literary texts can sometimes be of great use to the

anthropologist. It does not immediately follow from this that anthropological study can make any valuable contribution to literary
criticism" (301). Nevertheless, I was fairly certain that *I* could
make some contribution to literary criticism. Then, in the company of Lewis, my interest in him somehow destroyed my interest in the book. The Lewis before me seemed to bear little
relationship that I could see to the man written about in the articles I had read. In any event, I forgot to mention the book to
Lewis. Then, sometime after I had moved into his house, Lewis
suggested that we test what I had written against "the anthropological approach." I liked the idea, and I rose instantly to the
bait. Lewis had made it clear that he would interrupt only to correct matters of fact.

As I was reading my chapter on the interplanetary novels aloud,
Lewis would break in every few minutes with, "Anthropological
approach!" Eventually, however, I came to the part I was the most
confident of. It concerned the source of the Head of Alcasan in
That Hideous Strength, and I was so certain of what I had written
that I was already tasting Lewis's congratulations. "This time," I
told him, "you won't be able to say, 'Anthropological approach.'
Just listen to this." I then informed him that I had discovered an
almost identical head with an almost identical plot in Edgar Rice
Burroughs's *Chessmen of Mars*. Lewis was silent as I beamed in triumph. Then, as I prepared to go on, Lewis burst out with "anthropological approach!" He had never read any stories by Burroughs.

Never had I so much enjoyed being found wrong. This was
partly because Lewis was so cheerful about it, and partly because
he by no means made light of my interest in his books. Not long
after the anthropological approach experiment Lewis asked me
to read the manuscript of *Letters to Malcolm*, which he had not
long finished. I don't think I was the first to assume that the book
was based on actual letters. When I asked, "Who is Malcolm?"
he said, "Oh, Walter! Not *you* too!"

I was to be fooled a second time. One evening Lewis told
me to bring down from my bedroom a book entitled *A Grief
Observed* by N. W. Clerk. All he would say was that he'd written it. He wanted to know what I thought of it, and he wished
to watch my reaction to it.

By this time I had heard Lewis talk a great deal about his late wife, Joy. While he, doubtless, loved her very much, he never to me seemed sad. For instance, after the second Inklings meeting I attended, I went with Dr. R. E. Havard and Lewis to The Trout for lunch. In the course of the conversation Lewis brought up the United States. He seemed particularly interested in the differences between the North and the South, and to his mind Joy represented the first and I the second. He said, "Joy said that men oppress women very badly in the United States and that women remain powerless under the domination of men. What do you say?" I tried not to answer very directly as I was afraid of offending him. But he persisted until, finally, I replied, "Joy was wrong." "Wrong?" asked Lewis. "What was she wrong about?" "*Everything!*" I said. "It's the opposite of what Joy told you." Later, when I was alone with Dr. Havard, I asked if he thought I'd hurt Lewis's feelings. "Of course not!" he said. "Besides the fact that he wanted to know what you think, he had never believed everything Joy said about the States."

As most of you know, *A Grief Observed* supposedly consists of a series of reflections written in four notebooks by a husband upon the death of his wife. However, it was without a word of introduction that Lewis leaned back in his chair, lit his pipe, and watched me read his book. I learned what it was about by reading it. However, when I reached the description in chapter three of God as the "Cosmic Sadist" and the "Eternal Vivisector," I said, "Good heavens, Jack! You've lost the Faith!" "Read on! Read on!" said Lewis sternly. And he sat there, smoking his pipe, until I finished the book and saw how the argument against the goodness of God had been completely resolved in the fourth and final part.

When I had finished reading, Lewis told me how he intended the book to be understood. "The structure of it," he said, "is based on Dante's *Divine Comedy*. You go down and down and down. Then, as in Dante, when you hit bottom and pass Lucifer's waist you go *up* to defense of God's goodness."

Lewis went on to say that, while he had to make it sound like straight autobiography if the book was to help the average sufferer, he took various precautions to prevent *anyone* thinking it was by him or about his grief. He took the pseudonym "Dimidius" (= Half), and Curtis Brown Ltd, his literary agents, sent the book to a firm Lewis hadn't published with. This was Faber and Faber, where it was read by T. S. Eliot and his wife. In a letter to Spencer Curtis Brown of 20 October 1960 Eliot said that he could guess who the author was, and that if he sincerely wanted anonymity a "plausible English pseudonym would hold off enquirers better than Dimidius." Lewis had used the initials "N. W." before and, as he said to me, "because I am by medieval standards a 'clerk,' they came together as N. W. Clerk." (Spencer Curtis Brown wrote to Lewis on 24 October 1960, enclosing a copy of T. S. Eliot's letter. Those letters are in the Bodleian Library.)

There were a good many copies of *A Grief Observed* in The Kilns when I first read it, and during my months there Lewis received others from people who said they thought Lewis would find it helpful in coping with the loss of his wife. He received as well quite a lot of letters from people who said they were quite certain Lewis was N. W. Clerk. I don't recall anything which seemed to irritate him so much. The response which he dictated to me usually began, "All right. So you know." As he made clear in a number of his books, he found it annoying when people found it impossible to understand an author's ability to "invent."

When I asked whether or not the fourth, and last, "MS. book" was part of the invention, Lewis drew my attention to the final chapter of *A Grief Observed*. It says there: "This is the fourth — and last — empty MS. book I can find in the house; at least nearly empty, for there are some pages of very ancient arithmetic at the end by J" (47). Lewis took that very notebook off a bookshelf and gave it to me. The "ancient arithmetic by J" — Jack — was some which he put there as a pupil at Wynyard School in 1910. The notebook had been preserved because it contained some of his stories of Boxen. It does not, however, contain any portion of *A Grief Observed*, which book never, before publication, consisted of anything except a single manuscript. It was this manuscript which Lewis read to his friend Roger Lancelyn Green, and which he later gave to me.

Lewis was in this instance, at least, a more accomplished

"inventor" than he meant to be. It should be emphasized that Lewis never said that *A Grief Observed* was autobiography, and he told me that it was not. This does not mean that he didn't grieve over the death of his wife. He may have grieved more than is recorded in *A Grief Observed*. But that is a story which may never be known, and which is perhaps none of our business anyway.

It has been only in the last few years that people have been saying that *A Grief Observed* is to be read as straight autobiography. As I thought it was autobiography when I was reading it in the company of Lewis, I certainly can't blame others for believing those who tell them that it is. That, unfortunately, is not the end of the story.

C. S. Lewis the Doubter is the product of those who, over the last few years, have been trotting out the doubting passages of *A Grief Observed* and insisting that they are autobiographical. It is an attempt to persuade readers that Joy's death destroyed Lewis's certainty about the Christian faith. The principal architect of this heresy is Dr. John Beversluis, and the most dangerous of all the false Lewises is found in Dr. Beversluis's book *C. S. Lewis and the Search for Rational Religion* and his article "Beyond the Double Bolted Door," published in the magazine *Christian History* (4.3 [1985]). When I read them I thought, "Oh, well. Boys will be boys." And let us not forget what Lewis said about readers such as Dr. Beversluis: "Forced to talk incessantly about books, what can they do but try to make books into the sort of things they can talk about?" (*An Experiment in Criticism* 86).

I didn't know that such intellectual dishonesty could lead to such unhappy consequences until the evening of January 14, 1986. I was having a pint with the committee of the Oxford University C. S. Lewis Society in the back room of the Bird and Baby and we looked up to see several Americans observing us. They were clergymen who had come to see the pub in which the Inklings met. After the manager told them who we were, one of them—a Baptist minister from West Virginia—sat for some time telling me his story. His faith in God had flourished as a result of Lewis's books. However, since reading in Dr. Beversluis's "The Double Bolted Door" that Lewis had lost the faith when his wife died, his own confidence in God was shaken. "As C. S. Lewis lost his faith in God at the end," he said, "how can I hope to hold on?" If you say that he set too high a store on Lewis's books, I agree. When, however, I went home and reread Dr. Beversluis's article I saw how my own beliefs would have suffered if, in my youth, I came across this extract from Dr. Beversluis's article:

> A *Grief Observed* reveals many things about Lewis but none more important than that he was ultimately undone by the problem of contrary evidence and left with a deity of dubious moral character. After reading it, we can no longer read Lewis's earlier books as we once read them. We now know that he came to have grave doubts about many of the views that he had so confidently and joyously defended in them—doubts out of which he could not find his way. This fact casts an eerie retrospective light over his entire career as an apologist. (31)

That is humbug. Double-bolted humbug. Even if you believed A *Grief Observed* to be an absolutely faithful account of what Lewis thought following the death of his wife, you couldn't come to the conclusion that "he was ultimately undone by the problem of contrary evidence and left with a deity of dubious moral character." I urged the Baptist pastor to do what Lewis had insisted I do: "Read on! Read on!" I advise you to do the same.

Another man who should have "read on" is William Nicholson, who wrote the script of the film *Shadowlands*. He, like Dr. Beversluis, found it convenient for Lewis to fall to pieces when Joy died. However, in fairness to Mr. Nicholson, he did not know a great deal about Lewis's life, and when that film was first shown on the BBC, he wrote a piece making it clear that not a word of the dialogue he gave his characters was historical. Even so, to avoid further misinterpretation, let me stress that such close friends of Lewis's as his brother, Austin Farrer, Owen Barfield, and his parish priest, Gather R. E. Head, did not find Lewis behaving in the manner described by Dr. Beversluis and illustrated by Mr. Nicholson. After *Shadowlands* appeared on television in England, Donald Swann addressed our C. S. Lewis Society. He told us that shortly after he and David Marsh began composing their opera of *Perelandra*, they went to The Kilns to discuss it with Lewis. This was the 14th of July, 1960, and Mr. Swann said that, following a very interesting hour during which Lewis made a number of suggestions, Lewis got up and said: "Now, if you gentlemen will excuse me — my wife died last night."

I continue to receive letters from people who, having read Dr. Beversluis's works or seen *Shadowlands*, ask if Lewis really did lose his faith when his wife died. It would help if you, too, would assure them that he did not. Dr. Beversluis's attempts to create a C. S. Lewis who "felt compelled to confess publicly that his faith had been imaginary" ("Beyond the Door" 31) must compel us to see that guesswork of this sort is terribly pernicious when it comes between a person and God. I am, on the other hand, very pleased to discover that a great many people have been helped by *Shadowlands*.

Although Mr. Nicholson has the Joy Gresham of his film write some very interesting letters to Lewis, it is a pity that none of her actual letters to him has survived. Indeed, it seems that perhaps all of the writings she left at The Kilns have vanished. Major Lewis, writing to an American friend in 1967, mentions there being some of her "papers" still in his possession. I have no idea what happened to them. However, very soon after Lewis's death, I read the diary Joy kept from about 1952 to 1955. That, too, has disappeared. But if my memory serves, it was in 1953 that Joy described in her diary a luncheon she had with Lewis in the Bird and Baby. The Snappers will probably get me for telling you what they talked about. Still, as I remember, Joy said to Lewis, "Claire Bloom is the most beautiful woman in the world." Then, while *Shadowlands* was being filmed in Oxford, I mentioned this to one of the producers of the film. He urged me to come on the set and repeat it to Miss Bloom. I liked Miss Bloom very much and after telling her what Joy had written about her, I meant to leave it at that. She, however, was not willing to drop it. "And what," she asked, watching my face, "did Lewis say in reply?" "Must you know?" I asked. "I'd like to," said Miss Bloom. "In reply," I told her, "Lewis said to Joy, 'But doesn't that woman wear lip-stick?'"

A book which Lewis liked parts of is Denis de Rougemont's

Love in the Western World (1940). In that great work de Rougemont explains much of the motivation behind the story told in *Shadowlands* and Dr. Beversluis's distortion of *A Grief Observed*. In the second paragraph of the book the author says: "Happy love has no history. Romance only comes into existence where love is fatal, frowned upon and doomed by life itself. What stirs lyrical poets to their finest flights is neither the delight of the senses nor the fruitful contentment of the settled couple; nor the satisfaction of love, but its passion" (15). It should, then, come as no surprise that those determined to use C. S. Lewis instead of receive from him must make him other than he was. What we get from these two recent works about Lewis is a famous writer whose books are marred by the fact that he did not know what life was about until the age of fifty-eight. The scales fall from his eyes as his life is transformed by a brilliant American lady fleeing from a desperately unhappy marriage. Despite the protestations of church and various friends, they achieve one of the happiest marriages of this century. Following one sip of Real Life, the cup is wrenched from their hands, they are separated by death, and Lewis, as Dr. Beversluis tells us, is "plunged into sorrow and overtaken by religious doubts of . . . paralyzing magnitude" ("Beyond the Door" 29). I think Lewis was described to Claire Bloom in terms similar to these, for at another meeting I had with her she said, "If C. S. Lewis is so naive and I am such a brilliant New York writer, why do I want to *marry* him?"

I am certain that you would like the real C. S. Lewis far more than any of the false ones I've tried to unmask. In time I believe there will be enough known about the real Lewis to make a trail of made-up heartbreaks and denials of God unnecessary. Here, for instance, is a detail from Lewis's actual marriage which Lewis found some pleasure in recalling. Since 1930 Lewis had as his gardener and factotum Fred Paxford, whose gloomy outlook led Lewis to use him as a model for Puddleglum the Marshwiggle. Paxford was as sweet as Puddleglum, but his almost continuous talk about the End of the World led him to look perhaps more even than Puddleglum upon the worrying side of things. Paxford's greatest pleasure was, it seemed to me, listening to the wireless or radio. Lewis told me that Paxford was extremely anxious on the morning of the third of April, 1960, when Lewis and Joy were preparing to fly to Greece. They were in the taxi which was to take them to the airport when Paxford came to see them off. Leaning through the window of the car, he said, "Well, Mr. Jack, there was this bloke just going on over the wireless. Says an airplane just went down. Everybody killed—burnt beyond recognition. Did you hear what I said, Mr. Jack? *Burnt beyond recognition!*"

Even if you have never met any of the Lewises I have been pillorying, I hope you will take to heart the real Lewis's plea for the enlargement of our being. To see through his eyes is, I believe, one of God's enormous mercies. It is because of this mercy that we are here. Many, perhaps all, of us would like to do something for the real C. S. Lewis as an act of appreciation. But what can we do? In *The Personal Heresy* Lewis said, "Unless you hold beliefs which enable you to obey the colophons of the old books by praying for the authors' souls, there is nothing you can do for a dead poet" (68).

I wish you would do that for Lewis. But if you hold beliefs which forbid you to pray for his soul, then perhaps of your charity you will pray for me.

Works Cited

Beversluis, John. "Beyond the Double Bolted Door." *Christian History* 4.3 (1985): 28-31.

_____. *C. S. Lewis and the Search for Rational Religion.* Grand Rapids: Eerdmans, 1985.

"Don v. Devil." *Time*, 8 Sept. 1947: 65-74.

Gibbons, Stella. "Imaginative Writing." *Light on C. S. Lewis.* Ed. Jocelyn Gibb. New York: Harcourt, 1965. 86-101.

Griffin, William. *Clive Staples Lewis: A Dramatic Life.* San Francisco: Harper & Row, 1986.

Lewis, C. S. "The Anthropological Approach." *Selected Literary Essays.* Ed. Walter Hooper. Cambridge: Cambridge University Press, 1969. 301-311.

_____. "De Descriptione Temporum." *Selected Literary Essays.* Ed.

Walter Hooper. Cambridge: Cambridge University Press, 1969. 1-14.

_____. *An Experiment in Criticism.* Cambridge: Cambridge University Press, 1961.

_____. *A Grief Observed.* 1961. Greenwich: Seabury Press, 1963.

_____. "Hedonics." *Present Concerns: Essays by C. S. Lewis.* Ed. Walter Hooper. New York: Harcourt, 1986. 50-55.

_____. *The Lion, the Witch, and the Wardrobe.* 1950. New York: Collier Books, 1970.

_____. *Out of the Silent Planet.* 1938. New York: Macmillan, 1965.

_____, with E. M. W. Tillyard. *The Personal Heresy: A Controversy.* London: Oxford University Press, 1939.

Rougemont, Denis de. *Love in the Western World.* Trans. Montgomery Belgion. 1940. Rev. ed. New York: Pantheon-Random House, 1956.

The Legendary Chesterton

Ian Boyd, C.S.B.

Bernard Shaw described Chesterton as "a colossal genius." But there are difficulties that come with being a genius, and one of these difficulties concerns the way in which legend grows up around genius. Yet the very process of legend-making is itself significant. As a recent critic has pointed out, legends must be respected because they are "the ordinary way of expressing the manifestation of genius in certain people, who cannot be described in ordinary terms" (Spark 11). Chesterton himself was conscious that he had become a legend in his own lifetime. He was aware of the existence of a legendary self who experienced none of the feelings of guilt and anxiety which were the sad burden of his private self. Writing to his friend, Ronald Knox, at the moment of crisis which preceded his reception into the Catholic church in 1922, Chesterton commented on the difference between his confident legendary self, on the one hand, and his private and real self, on the other:

> I am in a state now when I feel a monstrous charlatan, as if I wore a mask and were stuffed with cushions, whenever I see anything about the public GKC; it hurts me; for though the views I express

Rev. Ian Boyd, C.S.B., is editor of the *Chesterton Review* and the author of *The Novels of G. K. Chesterton*.

are real, the image is horribly unreal compared with the real person who needs help just now. I have as much vanity as anybody about any of these superficial successes while they are going on; but I never feel for a moment that they affect the reality of whether I am utterly rotten or not; so that any public comments on my religious position seem like wind on the other side of the world; as if they were about somebody else—as indeed they are. I am not troubled about a great fat man who appears on platforms and in caricatures, even when he enjoys controversies on what I believe to be the right side. I am concerned about what has become of a little boy whose father showed him a toy theatre, and a schoolboy whom nobody ever heard of . . . and all the morbid life of the lonely mind of a living person with whom I have lived. It is that story, that so often came near to ending badly, that I want to end well. (Waugh 207-8)

Fifty years after Chesterton's death, the continuing existence of the Chesterton legend presents a similar problem to the critic. There is still a legendary Chesterton who seems very different from the Chesterton revealed in biography and scholarship. In fact, there are a number of legendary Chestertons. Yet each of the legendary Chestertons is a repository of valuable truths. The work of criticism, therefore, is not to explode such legends but to discover their underlying meaning. Such legends tend to dominate the public imagination for a time and then to fade rather abruptly. Also, each legend, as long as it is dominant, claims to provide the only authentic truth about the writer; and each legend, as long as it does exist, blots out the memory of earlier and equally valid legendary images, which express equally valuable truths about the writer of genius. In these circumstances, there is a danger that the claims for a writer and the attempt to define his meaning will become a sort of contest between vivid yet apparently contradictory legends about him.

There were at least two important legends about Chesterton which existed during his own life. Each of them embodies valuable truths about the real writer, truths that were perhaps more manifest to the general public than they were to the diffident and humble Chesterton, who could not recognize himself in the idealized figure which his admiring readers seem to have created.

The first of the legendary Chestertons was the Chesterton who existed at the time of his death on St. Basil's day—June 14, 1936. This Chesterton was the great apologist and spokesman for Catholicism. He was the Catholic polemicist who carried on seemingly endless controversies with Dean Inge, Bishop Barnes, and Professor Coulton, as well as much more relaxed controversies with such friendly enemies as Bernard Shaw and H. G. Wells. Some of this religious controversy took place at public debates and meetings; some of it was broadcast over B.B.C. radio where Chesterton's talks became a regular and popular feature of British broadcasting in the early thirties. In these talks, Chesterton debated with Shaw and with Bertrand Russell or simply with himself, as he reviewed books in the radio talks and discussed the events of the day. But most of the debate and discussion which helped form the public legend about Chesterton as a religious controversialist was presented in his everyday journalism. Some of his greatest writing originated in such debates. *The Everlasting Man* (1925), for example, is at one level, at least, simply a religious answer to the irreligious version of history which H. G. Wells presented to a vast popular audience in the early twenties in his *Outline of History*.

Still, especially in the final decades of his life, the legend of Chesterton was that of a doctrinaire defender of the Catholic church. More and more, as his reputation declined among a Protestant and increasingly secular public in his own country, it grew in foreign countries and among Catholic readers. Chesterton's triumphant tours of Ireland, of Poland, of Canada, and of the United States in the early twenties and again in the early thirties confirmed the public impression that he was above all a Catholic polemicist. In 1930, for example, when he visited Toronto for the second time, his visit was sponsored by a Catholic college, and he met privately with the Catholic archbishop of Toronto, with the great Catholic philosopher Etienne Gilson, and with the local Catholic religious community of the Basilian Fathers who were his hosts during that visit. The books written during these later years also tended to confirm the same public stereotype. The later volumes of the Father Brown stories, for example, contain a good deal of almost sectarian argument about the distinctive religious doctrines which divided the Catholic minority from the non-Catholic majority among whom they lived.

Even the circumstances of Chesterton's death combined to strengthen the public image of him as a Catholic champion. By the spring of 1936, it was clear to everyone that he was aging, even though at sixty-two he was still not really old. The suddenness of his death was a shock. But it had become increasingly clear that he had never completely recovered from the heart and kidney ailment which had almost taken his life in the autumn of 1914. The earlier illness, with its drama of months of coma, had been a national event. The final illness was somehow a more domestic and more Catholic event. During the final years, pictures of him in newspapers were likely to be pictures of his visits to Catholic schools and hospitals. A recent biography contains a typical picture of a very sick-looking Chesterton surrounded by nuns at the opening of a Beaconsfield Catholic hospital (Barker). When the death did occur, the Catholic aspects of his death were emphasized. Maisie Ward would point out that he had just returned from a pilgrimage to Lisieux and that Pope Pius XI's telegram of sympathy to his widow describing him as "gifted defender of the Catholic Faith" conferred on him the same royal title which an earlier pope had given to Henry VIII. Then there was the report about Father Vincent McNabb's visit to his deathbed. It was said that Father Vincent first chanted the *Salve Regina*, as though Chesterton were a dying Dominican friar, and that, seeing Chesterton's pen on the table next to his bed and remembering the great book about St. Thomas that Chesterton had written a few years earlier, he then picked up the pen and kissed it.

These were the sorts of stories which helped confirm one particular legend about Chesterton. They were also the sorts of stories which provoked a fairly swift reaction to the legend. Orwell, who was always sympathetic to some of Chesterton's political ideas and who had done some of his first writing for Chesterton's magazine, *G. K.'s Weekly*, was only expressing a conventional opinion when he described Chesterton as "a writer of considerable talent who chose to suppress both his sensibilities and his intellectual honesty in the cause of Roman Catholic propaganda" (365-66). Nor did his legendary status help Chesterton for long among his fellow Catholics. As the years wore on, many Catholic readers began to regard Chesterton as an embarrassment: he was the champion of a minority who were beginning to resent the need of his patronizing help.

However, the most striking effect of the Catholic legend about Chesterton was the way in which it blotted out the memory of an earlier and equally significant legend about him. If Chesterton had died (as he almost did) in November of 1914, he would be remembered as a very different public figure than a Roman Catholic controversialist. The image of an aging and ailing Catholic apologist of the twenties and thirties obscured the memory of another public image, that of the *wunderkind* whose meteoric rise to fame in the early years of the century made him one of the best-known literary figures of the age. For it was the literary and imaginative character of his work which was most highly regarded in those Edwardian years; and it was literary and imaginative writing which he poured out in almost inexhaustible abundance for his Edwardian readers. During those years before the First World War, he wrote his Browning and Dickens biographies, and almost all his Dickens criticism; his critical study of Bernard Shaw; the best of the Father Brown stories; the best of his verse, including his greatest poem, *The Ballad of the White Horse*; and all but one of his novels; in addition to a seemingly inexhaustible flood of journalism, so vast that even today some of the best of it remains hidden in a score or so of the obscure journals on which he loved to lavish his best and wittiest writing. No wonder, then, that these were the years of Chesterton's greatest influence.

But all the while a legend about him was slowly being created. The exuberance and fun of the young Chesterton were decisive elements in the creation of this public image. He had acquired what he himself regarded as the surest sign of being a sort of classic: he was quoted by people who had never read his work. His sayings were rapidly becoming proverbs. Everyone knew a Chesterton joke or a joke about Chesterton. He was the delight of the cartoonist. He was one of the few writers who was recognized simply by his initials. It was said that the fame of his weekly article signed "GKC" in Cadbury's *Daily News* required that twice the usual number of that newspaper be printed for the Saturday edition in which his column appeared. In 1908, he published two of his most brilliantly imaginative autobiographies: the novel *The Man Who Was Thursday*, which succeeds both as a fictional autobiography and as a meditation and retelling of the Book of Job; and a personal philosophical treatise, *Orthodoxy*, which tells the story about his attempt to invent a new religion and subsequent discovery that it had already been invented and was called Christianity. "I did not make it," he writes. "God and humanity made it and it made me" (*Orthodoxy* 12). In November 1911, in Cambridge, an audience of nearly a thousand people came to hear him speak to a student club about the future of religion and heard him say that the Christian religion, which the secular world thought dead, was about to rise again from the dead: "Personally I think we shall win," he told his young audience. [The text of this talk, as it was reported in the *Cambridge Magazine* of January 20, 1912, was reprinted in the August, 1985, issue of the *Chesterton Review*, pp. 285-300. Chesterton's comment is found on page 289.] In 1913, at the insistence of his friend Bernard Shaw, he wrote his first play, *Magic*. Again, there were strong autobiographical elements to his imaginative writing, but the play was also an extension of the sort of public debate (about the reality of the supernatural) which Chesterton loved to provoke and which he had been conducting for years in the pages of newspapers and magazines with writers such as Robert Blatchford, Belfort Bax, and Bernard Shaw.

Yet this literary achievement was only one aspect of Chesterton's Edwardian reputation. The most endearing characteristic of his public image was the sense in which it expressed his deep commitment to, and positive engagement with, the ongoing life of his age. It was as though the abundance of his imaginative creation, the generous and even careless abandon with which he worked in a half-dozen literary *genres*, and the laughter and fun which irradiated his work were only outward signs of some inner quality which his public valued more than any of the hastily written literary works which expressed it. It was Chesterton whom they loved rather than any particular Chesterton book or essay

or poem. The Edwardian Chesterton was the embodiment of
what they valued most about themselves and about their own
national tradition. The young journalist had become the
repository for the hopes and ideals of his readers. He expressed
for them the spirit of one of the most exuberant ages since the
Elizabethan. He embodied Edwardian energy and optimism and
the spirit which he was later to describe as "the universal hunger
and even fury for life" (*Saint Thomas Aquinas* 113).

He also embodied Edwardian fears about the threat to their
Christian traditions. In his important book about Chesterton,
Professor John Coates writes of an Edwardian cultural crisis. He
points out that the people for whom Chesterton wrote and on
whom he relied for his enormous popularity were an inwardly
confused people. No longer guided by the sources of Christian
wisdom, they had not yet abandoned the Christian moral tradition which they had inherited but which they scarcely understood. Intellectually curious but only recently educated, they were
absorbing uncritically the alien and irreligious ideas contained in
the poisonous newspaper trash which they were reading in this,
the first age of mass journalism. Yet at the same time and in the
same newspapers and magazines, they were also reading Chesterton and savoring the intellectual food which he provided as a
sort of antidote to that poison.

Chesterton's legendary fame in the Edwardian era was ultimately based on this role as a moral teacher and as a defender
of an endangered tradition. It is appropriate that he should later
write a play about Dr. Johnson and that he should once appear
in an Edwardian pageant dressed as that great moralist whose
thinking was so closely akin to his own. Although he was fond
of argument and was a formidable debater, he understood that
the malaise of the age could not be dealt with by ordinary argumentation alone. Something else was needed to cleanse the
collective moral atmosphere of the age in which he lived. He,
and the Anglo-Catholic group with whom he worked, understood that it was useless to evangelize individuals, unless some
way were also found to evangelize the moral atmosphere which
affected individuals as decisively as the physical atmosphere in
which they lived. Chesterton saw his literary vocation as being

essentially pastoral. Like one of the Victorian sages whom he so closely resembled, he saw literature as a form of prophecy. The controversies with Robert Blatchford and Shaw, the writing of *Heretics* and *Orthodoxy*, and indeed all his writing during these pre-war years were part of a single effort to exercise influence on the moral and religious shape of the new age which he sensed was coming into existence. As he later explained in his 1927 University of London centenary lecture, "Culture and the Coming Peril," what was essential was training the minds of men to act upon the community and making the mind a source of creation and of critical action. And since the collective mind that he was attempting to influence was still in some sense Christian, his work was essentially a work of Christian education. In his *Autobiography*, he writes about the religious atmosphere of the age in prophetic language: "I have been granted, as it were, a sort of general view or vision of all that field of negation and groping and curiosity. And I saw pretty much what it all really meant. There was no Theistic Church; there was no Theosophical Brotherhood; there were no Ethical Societies; there were no New Religions. But I saw Israel scattered on the hills as sheep that have not a shepherd" (Chesterton 175).

Even Chesterton's apparent limitations were a help to him in performing this immense task of religious education. Since his marriage to Frances Blogg, a devout Anglican, he had been in contact with the Anglican theologians who were working out a strategy for the religious regeneration of England. He lectured and wrote for the Christian Social Union and wrote for their journal, the *Commonwealth*, as well as for less congenial journals, such as the *Church Socialist Quarterly*, the *Hibbert Journal*, and A. R. Orage's *New Age*; and he was friend of many of the Anglican social theologians, including Henry Scott Holland, Bishop Gore, Charles Masterman, and that radical Christian, Conrad Noel. He learned much from them, and it seems clear that they learned a great deal from him. But he was never an Anglican in the ordinary sense of the word. He seems seldom to have attended Anglican religious services; he was never confirmed as an Anglican; and in many ways his religious position still possessed some of the vagueness of the Liberal Unitarian universalism which characterized his childhood home. But if these things were weaknesses, they were weaknesses which made him a reassuring and comfortable figure to the vaguely religious Edwardian reading public for whom he wrote.

It was an additional advantage that he was not clearly identified with any religious group. He was a sacramental Christian who could speak to evangelical Protestants and other non-sacramental Christians unthreateningly, because he was not a Roman Catholic. Through his writings, he could work out a religious position which was all the more persuasive, because he seemed to include in it every good thing which he saw in contemporary life. He was one of the liberals whom Orthodox Catholics feared, but he was also one of the Catholic Christians whom the liberals persecuted. In his own person he seemed to include a genial friendliness to apparently irreconcilably hostile points of view, and yet he also vigorously opposed any attempt to tone down or to compromise strongly held views. It is somehow typical of him that his novels seldom have a single hero or a single point of view. It is as though he himself were the hero of his early novels. He is both Adam Wayne and Auberon Quin, the heroes of his first novel, *The Napoleon of Notting Hill* (1904); he is also Evan MacIan and James Turnbull, the heroes of his first religious novel, *The Bell and the Cross* (1910). He is both the fanatic and the critic of fanaticism, the Catholic extremist and the militant socialist hostile to such extremism. Somehow he is able to sympathize with both sides of most important questions. He is like the church that he describes in *Orthodoxy*, welcoming every point of view and seeking ways of reconciling opposite points of view with each other. Always, his genius is inclusive, and he remains a genial embodiment of a singularly ecumenical sort of orthodoxy: "When the word 'orthodoxy' is used here," he writes cheerfully in his book by that name, "it means the Apostles' Creed, as understood by everybody calling himself Christian until a very short while ago, and the general historical conduct of those who held such a creed" (*Orthodoxy* 18).

His way of writing also confirmed the Edwardian legend about him as a sort of amusing and good-natured Christian church, one who loved to use the cryptic language of riddle and parable. This language of the imagination was for him a means of discovering truths which were inaccessible to discursive reason. Trained as an artist at the Slade School, he seldom exercised his skill professionally. Yet, in another sense, all his best writings are examples of a professional artist's work. Moreover, the preference for picture and parable was clearly connected with his view of life. In one of his earliest essays, he writes, "All men are allegories, puzzles, earthly stories with heavenly meanings" ("The Literary Portraits of G. F. Watts" 80). His imaginative and inclusive view of life was expressed through a literary practice which was also imaginative and inclusive. The hero of *The Poet and the Lunatics* explains, "I doubt whether any of our action is really anything but an allegory. I doubt whether any truth can be told except in a parable" (92). Everything therefore was grist for Chesterton's journalistic mill. He was spinning a life-enhancing art open to everything that was happening in a rapidly changing world. As a defender of tradition and as a critic of modernity, he had nevertheless found a way of interpreting modern life in a positive light as an ongoing revelation of religious truths. All this was immensely attractive and reassuring to his troubled readers. What the Edwardian Chesterton was accomplishing was a work which is difficult to describe in ordinary language: he was a creator of parables who insisted that life itself was a parable; he was a lover of legends who, being a figure larger than life, could be described only in legendary terms. For T. S. Eliot, he was the man who kept alive the Christian minority; for Gilson, he was "one of the deepest thinkers who ever existed" (Ward 526); and for the ordinary reader he was simply "our Chesterton" (Ward 553).

Fifty years after Chesterton's death, the problem for his admirers is the reconciliation of these two apparently contradictory legends about him. The aggressive champion and apologist for Catholicism appears to be an utterly different person from the relaxed Edwardian figure who seemed to include in his person every point of view without being identified with any one of them. The parable-creating artist with an incurable curiosity about and friendliness towards the variety and comedy of human existence seems to have little in common with the religious controversialist who argues endlessly with the liberal rationalists of the twenties and thirties. Even his journalism in the last decades of his life seemed different and somehow narrower. The weekly articles in the *Illustrated London News* and a score of other journals and newspapers, which had made him so much a part of the English cultural scene, continued, but the later Chesterton seemed to devote more and more of his flagging energies to the support of the Distributist League and to his magazine, *G. K.'s Weekly*, the magazine which was the league's organ. To the puzzlement of friends and critics, he insisted on centering his career and his journalism on the maintenance of a small and seemingly unimportant magazine and an apparently doomed social movement, which seemed to many then as it seems to many today to be the most hopeless and quixotic of all the lost causes which he had ever supported. There was a sort of Chestertonian paradox here. It seemed as though the later and more Catholic Chesterton was less Catholic and more sectarian than the early and religiously uncommitted non-Catholic Chesterton.

The attempt to understand and perhaps to resolve that conflict ought to be the main work of all Chesterton criticism. Inevitably, there will be disagreements about which Chesterton legend represents the more valuable and more permanent aspects of his achievement, but it should also be possible to rescue all that is best in each of the competing legends. Chesterton is, after all, a single human being as well as a single writer. There may have been development or decline in his life, but his life also represented continuity and integration. There must be some underlying principle to explain both the sharp divisions which gave rise to such contradictory public images and the hidden unity which somehow integrated an apparently fragmented and contradictory personality.

Chesterton criticism has only touched upon this problem. L'Abbe Yves Denis, whose book *G. K. Chesterton: Catholicisme et Paradox* gives him special authority to speak on the subject, insists that Chesterton is primarily a Catholic writer. Brocard Sewell, who, in the late twenties and thirties, knew Chesterton personally and who worked on the staff of *G. K.'s Weekly*, insists that Distributism was the central preoccupation of Chesterton's life. John Coates, the author of *G. K. Chesterton and the Edwardian Cultural Crisis*, finds the key to Chesterton's work in the Edwardian years. Other critics make little attempt to connect Chesterton the controversialist with Chesterton the reconciler. Yet there is scope here for biographical criticism and especially for that sort of biographical criticism which would explain the ways in which madness was for Chesterton both an inner and deeply felt personal threat, and a metaphor for the disorders which he recognized in the world outside his own mind. There are other threads of continuity between his early and his later work. The controversialist of the final years is foreshadowed in his early and prophetic work as a social critic, including his lonely opposition to the sinister Eugenics movement and his insights into the treatment of prisoners in Edwardian times, insights that are being rediscovered today by modern sociologists.

Criticism will find other clues to the underlying unity in Chesterton's life in the ways in which all his work continues to attract the interest of widely divergent groups of readers. More ought to be said about what he means to Protestant Christians and to the Jewish community, which, offended by some of his writing, are often unaware of his noble defense of the Jewish people both at the beginning of his career during the Russian pogroms and at the end of his career when the Hitlerite persecution was just beginning, a defense which won a blessing for his memory from the American Jewish leader, Rabbi Stephen Wise. (Rabbi Wise's tribute to Chesterton, found in a letter to Cyril Clemens, dated September 8, 1937, is quoted by Ward 228.)

Perhaps the best hope for reconciling the two major Chesterton legends is to be found in criticism that pays close attention to Chesterton's sacramental religious faith. It is this sacramental viewpoint which provides the best explanation for the underlying unity of his entire career as a writer. Sacramentalism explains both his development as a thinker and his literary practice as a writer. Convinced that God was to be found in material realities, he developed a kind of natural mysticism about the way in which apparently profane realities are really sacramental signs of God. In an extremely early and very typical poem, he carries on a conversation with himself about the ultimate meaning of the created universe. He questions himself and addresses himself as a sort of poet-seer, the mystic visionary who has discovered the secret meaning of ordinary life:

> Speller of the stones and weeds,
> Skilled in Nature's crafts and creed,
> Tell me what is in the heart
> Of the smallest of the seeds.

His answer to his own question summarizes his sacramental mysticism:

> God Almighty, and with Him
> Cherubim and Seraphim,
> Filling all eternity,—
> *Adonai Elohim.* ("The Holy of Holies" lines 9-16)

It was this belief which gave unity to the many facets of his Edwardian journalism. The religious critique of life which he presents in all his writings is ultimately based on a belief that God is present in creation through sign and symbol. In the center of the most profane realities, it is possible to find God. He seldom wrote about directly religious subjects, but in the events of everyday life or in a piece of chalk or in a city street he found the central religious mystery. The title of an early Yeats play, *Where There Is Nothing, There Is God*, provokes him to comment: "The truth presented itself to me, rather in the form that where there is anything, there is God" (Chesterton, *Autobiography* 150-51).

Sacramentalism also explains the connection between Chesterton's social thought and his literary work. "The basis of Christianity as well as of Democracy," he writes, "is that man is sacred" (*Vox Populi, Vox Dei* 265). This sacredness, Chesterton believed, is derived directly from the Incarnation of the Word of God. Ever since creation, God was revealed in the material world he created. But ever since the Incarnation, God is most clearly revealed in the Holy One who became an ordinary human being and who continues to live in the world through the lives of ordinary people who are the luminous signs of God's presence:

> The Child that was ere worlds begun
> (. . . We need but walk a little way,

Ian Boyd, C.S.B.

> We need but see a latch undone . . .)
> The Child that played with moon and sun
> Is playing with a little hay. ("The Wise Men" 29-33)

In his book on St. Thomas Aquinas, Chesterton writes, "The Incarnation has become the central idea of our civilization" (*Saint Thomas Aquinas* 118-19). Ordinary everyday human life is a sacramental reenactment of the gospel story. Again, Chesterton expresses his belief in the divine Word, who was made flesh and dwelt among us, most movingly in his verse:

> If these dried hearts indeed forget
> That holy dew on dusty floor,
> The Four Saints strong about the bed,
> The God that dies above the door;
> Such mysteries as might dwell with men,
> The secret like a stooping face
> Dim but not distant; and the night
> Not of the abyss, but the embrace. ("The Pagans")

This was the "secret" about the people Chesterton called the "secret people." They were the bewildered and inarticulate ones for whom he was both guide and spokesman. But from the viewpoint of his sacramental faith they were also much more than anything they themselves realized, for Chesterton saw in them the One whom he called the Everlasting Man.

Sacramental faith in the Incarnation also explains the reason why the Edwardian Chesterton and Chesterton the Catholic apologist are ultimately the same person. The legendary Chesterton of the Catholic folk memory is the real Chesterton. The stubborn popular conviction of both friends and enemies that he was above all a spokesman for Catholicism turns out to be perfectly true. But why should anyone be surprised? Had not Chesterton himself always insisted that popular beliefs are usually right? The story of Chesterton's slow transformation from a genial Edwardian figure into the somewhat sadder and more mature Chesterton of Catholic legend is also the story of his full incorporation into the Christian community which he came to recognize as the unique Sacrament of God.

The story of the private Chesterton which he confided to

Father Knox ended happily. In spite of age and illness and growing misgivings about what was happening in the world around him, the sacraments of the church had restored to him the youthful innocence and happiness which the Edwardian legend had always attributed to him, but which, to his sorrow, he was conscious that he did not then rightfully possess. His final words on this subject were uttered in 1922 on the day on which he was received into the Catholic church in Beaconsfield, and they were words of triumph:

> The sages have a hundred maps to give
> That trace their crawling cosmos like a tree,
> They rattle reason out through many a sieve
> That stores the sand and lets the gold go free.
> And all these things are less than dust to me
> Because my name is Lazarus and I live. ("The Convert" 9-14)

Nevertheless, long after that happy harmony was achieved, the two legendary Chestertons continue to chase each other around the world, like the two versions of Father Brown which Chesterton describes in his last volume of detective stories. Perhaps neither of the legendary Chestertons represents fully the depth and complexity of this extraordinary man, but each of his legendary selves expresses truths about him that are worth pondering a half century after his death. Both the fighter for Christian truth and the gentle Edwardian imaginative artist are indeed a single person who is well worth knowing.

Works Cited

Barker, Dudley. *G. K. Chesterton*. London: Constable, 1973.

Chesterton, G. K. *Autobiography*. London: Hutchinson & Co., Ltd., 1937.

_____. *The Collected Poems of G. K. Chesterton*. London: C. Palmer, 1927.

_____. "The Convert." *Collected Poems* 84.

_____. "The Holy of Holies." *Collected Poems* 314.

_____. "The Literary Portraits of G. F. Watts." *The Bookman*. December 1900.

_____. *Orthodoxy.* London: Bodley Head, 1908.

_____. "The Pagans." *Commonweal.* November 13, 1929.

_____. *The Poet and the Lunatics: Episodes in the Life of Gabriel Gale.* London: D. Finlayson, 1962.

_____. *Saint Thomas Aquinas.* Garden City, NY: Image Books, 1956.

_____. *Vox Populi, Vox Dei.* 16 March, 1905. Reprinted in *Chesterton Review,* August 1985.

_____. "The Wise Men." *Collected Poems* 122.

Eliot, T. S. *The Tablet.* June 20, 1936.

Orwell, George. "Notes on Nationalism." *Collected Essays, Journalism, and Letters.* Eds. Sonia Orwell and Ian Angus. 4 vols. London: Secker & Warburg, 1968. Vol. 3.

Spark, Muriel, and Derek Stanford. *Emily Bronte: Her Life and Work.* New York: Coward-McCann, 1966.

Ward, Maisie. *Gilbert Keith Chesterton.* New York: Sheed & Ward, 1943.

Waugh, Evelyn. *The Life of the Right Reverend Ronald Knox.* London: Chapman & Hall, 1959.

The Prayer Life of C. S. Lewis

James M. Houston

To try to enter into an understanding of Lewis's prayer life is to attempt to penetrate his very mind and spirit in the most intimate way. Can we do so without presumption? I knew Lewis personally, enough to have a clear impression of his personal faith, in the years between 1946 and 1953. We met in a discussion group held in the home that I shared with Nicholas Zernov, then leader of the Society of St. Albans and St. Sergius, and it was through Zernov that I got to know Lewis. When I first met him in the 1940s he looked like Mr. Badger from *Wind in the Willows*: stout, in an old rumpled brown tweed jacket and brown shoes, pipe in mouth, and he looked like an Oxford farmer. However, once he began to speak, I realized that few people I had ever met, other than perhaps his friend Dyson, could articulate so well, so humorously, and so exactly to the point. Yet, while Lewis was a witty raconteur and provocative debater, he was essentially shy about his inner life. It would be an impossible task to describe his prayer life unless he had written significantly about prayer.

JAMES M. HOUSTON is founding principal of Regent College, Vancouver, British Columbia; professor of spiritual theology (Regent); and founding director of the C. S. Lewis Institute in Washington, D.C.

But C. S. Lewis has made a substantial contribution to the theology of prayer. His last work, *Letters to Malcolm* (completed in April 1963, just seven months before his death and published posthumously), deals frankly with issues he faced privately in prayer. His *Reflections on the Psalms*, published two years earlier, deals with his personal difficulties in reading the Psalms, and also his appreciation of the Christian liturgy of the Psalter. But Lewis was never enthusiastic about his own church life, which (in the setting of college chapel) was atypical of parish life. So his own focus on prayer was more personal than corporate. Several of his essays, notably "Work and Prayer" and "The Efficacy of Prayer," challenge us with specific issues of personal prayer. His autobiography, *Surprised by Joy*, and *The Screwtape Letters* also contain personal comments on prayer.

In my own encounters with Lewis, he never spoke about prayer. I did communicate once with him about the daily prayer meetings of the Oxford Inter-Collegiate Christian Union, where prayer was being offered for the conversion of Sheldon Vanauken, whose wife was active in our prayer group. Indeed, I told Lewis of Sheldon's conversion the day after it happened. But Lewis—never forthcoming about his own prayer life and, as a shy man, all the more sensitive to the Oxford atmosphere then prevailing, that you no more discussed religion too intimately than you talked about your kidneys—simply responded positively to the news of Vanauken, as a confidant who expected it anyway.

Lewis suffered from the cynical reactions of some of his colleagues when his first religious books were published, for it went without saying that an English don should not be dabbling in theology, much less getting publicity this way. To trespass into another academic discipline was questionable, to say the least. So Lewis was careful to introduce his own theological views modestly, though he did have the support of his friend Austin Farrar, and other theologians, when he did so. In his *Reflections on the Psalms* he begins, "I write as one amateur to another, talking about difficulties that I have met, or lights I have gained, reading Psalms, with the hope this might at any rate interest, and sometimes even help, other inexpert readers. I am 'comparing

notes,' not presuming to instruct" (9). It is only now that some
of us have awakened to the fact that if all of life is carved up
among the professions, so that there is likewise no room left for
being dilettantes or amateurs in the arts or culture generally, then
we shall all be cheated of humanness itself.

Lewis got away with it in his day, for when he was questioned
about his preaching as a layman at R.A.F. stations during the Battle of Britain, he could genuinely reply he was just doing his war-
work, like any other old don who did his duties as an air-raid
warden, certainly not expertly trained but doing his best in an
emergency. In such a crisis there is no need for any further apology than what he writes in the preface to his published B.B.C.
talks given during the war, when he first came to public attention:

> There is no mystery about my position. I am a very ordinary layman
> of the Church of England, not especially "high" nor especially
> "low," nor especially anything else. (6)

In this essay, then, I want to describe six traits that I think
characterize the personal prayer life of Lewis. Then I will look at
two aspects of his theological reflections on prayer, beginning
with a sketch of his unhappy childhood experiences of prayer.

1. The Realism of His Prayer Life

Lewis was no mystic. He admits this several times in his letters.
Others might climb daringly in the mountains of mysticism, but
he simply slogged around in the foothills. His spirituality is earthy,
full of realism, for he was dead scared of sentimentalism. The
way he prayed was expressive of a no-nonsense kind of faith. The
first poem of the collection edited after his death spells out his
similar poetic credo:

> I am so coarse, the things the poets see
> Are obstinately invisible to me.
> For twenty years I've stared my level best
> To see if evening—any evening—would suggest
> A patient etherized upon a table;
> In vain. I simply wasn't able.

To me each evening looked far more
Like the departure from a silent, yet crowded shore
Of a ship whose freight was everything, leaving behind
Gracefully, finally without farewells, marooned mankind.

. . . .

I'm like that odd man Wordsworth knew, to whom
A primrose was a yellow primrose, one whose doom
Keeps him for ever in the list of dunces,
Compelled to live on stock responses,
Making the poor best that I can
Of dull things. (*Poems* 1)

Lewis is admitting to us all that his spirituality, like his poetry, is prosaic, ordinary, immersed in the world around him. This down-to-earthness about him is perhaps the greatest impression he left upon me. Neoplatonism was anathema to Lewis. Thus his style is vivid, concrete, practical, empty of "gas," full of solid stuff. Instead of saying, "We must be spiritually regenerated," he confesses, "We're like eggs at present. And you can't go on indefinitely being just an ordinary, decent egg. We must be hatched or go bad" (*Mere Christianity* 155). So too his faith is all for "sound doctrine," not the woolly-mindedness of contemporaries he debated with, who wanted "religion without dogma." Growing up as a child in a "low" church milieu, he felt later that it did tend to be too cozily living at ease in Zion (*Letters to Malcolm* 13). That was not the tough, realistic faith and prayer life Lewis was to develop later.

2. The Practicality of His Prayer Life

Prayer is not something simple to talk about. It is not even something we "do," for Lewis. "Saying one's prayers" was for Lewis only a small part of his experience of prayer. "For many years after my conversion," he writes, "I never used any ready-made forms except the Lord's Prayer. In fact I tried to pray without words at all — not to verbalize the mental acts. Even in praying for others I believe I tended to avoid their names and substitute mental images of them. I still think that the prayer without words is the best—if one can really achieve it" (*Letters to Malcolm* 11).

But we have to remember that our exercise of prayer is only effective if we take ourselves as we really are and do not idealize how we would like to be. Thus Lewis had to learn himself that "to pray successfully without words one needs to be at 'the top of one's form'" (*Letters to Malcolm* II). Thinking that we can do always what we can do on occasion is an error that makes our prayers unrealistic, and this Lewis had to discover, as we all must.

The practical rhythm of Lewis was simple enough each day. He would rise at about 7 a.m., take a walk, attend matins at 8 a.m. in College Chapel, breakfast, and start tutorials at 9 a.m. Late in the afternoon he would make time for prayerful thought and contemplation, as he walked around the college grounds. Never would he recommend saying one's prayers last thing at night. "No one in his senses if he has any power of ordering his own day, would reserve his chief prayers for bed-time—obviously the worst possible hour for any action which needs concentration. . . . My own plan, when hard pressed, is to seize any time, and place, however unsuitable, in preference to the last waking moment. On a day of travelling — I'd rather pray sitting in a crowded train than put it off till midnight when one reaches a hotel bedroom with aching back and dry throat, and one's mind partly in a stupor and partly in a whirl" (*Letters to Malcolm* 17). In a letter to a friend in 1955, shortly after he had taken up his professorship at Cambridge, when he used to return home to Oxford at weekends, he said:

> Oddly enough, the week-end journeys (to and from Cambridge) are no trouble at all. I find myself perfectly content in a slow train that crawls through green fields stopping at every station. Just because the service is so slow and therefore in most people's eyes *bad*, these trains are almost empty—I get through a lot of reading and sometimes say my prayers. A solitary train journey I find quite excellent for this purpose. (*Letters* 265)

All this is consistent with Lewis's earlier observation, that much of prayer is really a disposition of heart, in tune with God's presence in one's life, so that the more this is so, the less fuss we need to make about how vocal and articulate we are in "saying our prayers." Provided, of course, that we do not succumb to merely having "warm feelings" or vaguely imaginative thoughts we mistake for real communion with God. Always, the most rigorous attentiveness and serious intent will be demanded for real prayer.

3. His Simple, Natural, Unstructured Attitude to Prayer

As we have noted, Lewis was a private person, concealing his soul in the midst of convivial friendships. He remarked on one occasion that friends are not like lovers who look at each other; friends are always looking away together at something they hold in common. So for Lewis, friendships were outward-looking, not introspective. Several times he observed the importance of "looking at" rather than "looking through" things. So he would never have analyzed his prayer life as we are attempting to do. (He would bury us in a loud guffaw of absurdity.) Still, we can learn something by looking at Lewis's personal history of prayer.

While still agnostic, in October 1929, Lewis read *The Diary of an Old Soul,* by George MacDonald. "He seems to know everything," Lewis confided to Greeves, "and I find my own experience in it constantly" (*Letters to Greeves* 313). He must have been reading passages such as this:

> My surgent thought shoots lark-like up to Thee,
> Thou like the heaven art all about the lark.
> Whatever I surmise or know in me,
> Idea, or symbol on the dark,
> Is living, working thought-creating power
> In Thee, the timeless Father of the hour.
> I am Thy book, Thy song—Thy child would be. (MacDonald 111)

By the following summer term he had also perused *The Practice of the Presence of God,* by Brother Lawrence, and then *Centuries of Meditation,* by Thomas Traherne. By the following term he was attending 8 a.m. chapel regularly. But on Christmas Eve, 1930, he wrote his friend Greeves, "I think the trouble with me is *lack of faith*. I have no *rational* ground for going back on the arguments that convince me of God's existence; but the irrational deadweight of my old skeptical habits, and the spirit of the age, and the cares of the day, steal away all my lively feelings of the truth; and often when I pray, I wonder if I am not posting letters to a non-existent address" (Griffin 76). The reason for the remoteness of Lewis's faith at that time was that he was still a deist rather than a Christian. However, after a long talk one night with Tolkien and Dyson in July 1931, Lewis wrote Greeves further: "I have just passed on from believing in God to definitely believing in Christ—in Christianity—my long talk with Dyson and Tolkien had a great deal to do with it" (Griffin 79). Later that year he also read William Law's *Serious Call to a Devout and Holy Life*. Lewis was now finding it meaningful to pray for his brother Warren in Shanghai. He wrote to him at the end of 1931:

> When you ask me to pray for you—I don't know if you are serious, but the answer is yes, I do. It may not do you any good, but it does me a lot, for I cannot ask for any change to be made in you without finding that the very same needs to be made in me; which pulls me up also by putting us all in the same boat, checks any tendency to priggishness. (Griffin 84)

All this may seem to be biography about prayer rather than theology. But to Lewis the one was impossible without the other. To look at prayer in detachment from its exercise was inconceivable. And since most of one's existence is usually pretty dull and routine stuff, one's prayers are not exceptional either. Indeed, the more honest we become with ourselves, the more "normal" our prayer life will be. As Lewis said early on in B.B.C. talks on Christian morality, at first Christianity seems to be all about rules and regulations, guilt and virtue, but in the end you are led out of all that into something beyond, a country where they do not talk of those things, but where "Every one is filled full with what we would call goodness as a mirror is filled with light. But they don't call it goodness. They don't call it anything. They are not thinking of it. They are too busy looking at the source from which it comes" (*Christian Behavior* 64). So too, in prayer, Lewis thinks that it should become so natural to the believer that no fuss need be made about it; we simply do it because that is the nature of the Christian life.

Similarly, speaking about the struggles we may have in prayer, the distractions and dryness in our lives, he comments:

> The disquieting thing is not simply that we skimp and begrudge the duty of prayer. The really disquieting thing is that it should have to be numbered among the duties at all. For we believe that we were created 'to glorify God and enjoy him forever.' And if the few, the very few, minutes we now spend on intercourse with God are a burden to us rather than a delight, what then? . . . If we were perfected, prayer would not be a duty, it would be a delight. (*Letters to Malcolm* 114)

Clearly our sins handicap us from the openness that prayer requires, while the unreality of the unseen realm of prayer only shows how distant we may be from God and his ways. Like friendship with a dear friend, however, prayer is never forced nor irksome. It grows as the relationship grows.

4. Supplicatory Prayers for Others

Praying for his brother was perhaps the first step that Lewis made in supplication for many other people throughout the rest of his life. In the correspondence to an American lady, begun in October 1950, we read Lewis promising again and again, "I will have you in my prayers," "of course we'll help each other in our prayers," "let us continue to pray for each other," "of course I have been praying for you daily, as always, but latterly have found myself doing so with much more concern." On this last occasion, he narrates some special circumstances. He wrote that he had felt strongly one night how good it would be to hear from her with good news. "Then, as if by magic (indeed it is the whitest magic in the world) the letter comes today. Not (lest I should indulge in folly) that your relief had not occurred *before* my prayer, but as if, in tenderness for my puny faith, God moved me to pray with special earnestness just before He was going to give me the thing. How true that prayers are His prayers really; He speaks to Himself through us" (21).

Lewis was not prepared to hold the truism that while petitionary prayer is expressing personal need before God, supplication is strictly praying on behalf of others. Early he had seen that to supplicate for others was to be changed by prayer, that it implied the pray-er was also willing to see changes in his life as he prayed for others. But petition and supplication are also part of a greater, more mysterious reality, since God intends to be not merely "all," as pantheism declares, but "all in all." If the Holy Spirit is the one who prompts us and gives us the gift of prayer itself, are we not in our supplications and petitions actually entering into divine soliloquy, to celebrate the sovereign good God has intended for all his creatures? Lewis quotes a poem he found in an old notebook, author unknown: "thus, while we seem / Two talkers, thou art One forever, and I / No dreamer, but thy dream" (Griffin 149-50). Lewis added that it is perhaps more accurate to call this "soliloquy" than "dream," because of the pantheistic connotations of "dream." In fact, Lewis sent Bede Griffiths this poem in 1938 to describe his growing conviction of what prayer meant in his life (*Letters to Malcolm* 67-68).

5. Prayer as Friendship

Lewis grew in prayer as he grew into friendships. Sometimes they were boon companionships, at other times they sprang from correspondence with strangers who became real friends, like "the American Lady." Perhaps, too, as Lewis leaned on confidants in his distresses, so he could reach out to others in their needs also. "Forgiveness," he once said, "is another name for being forgiven." This reciprocity explains perhaps the largess he gave to others in his enormous correspondence, indicative of what he felt he received from his trust in God.

At the outbreak of the war in 1939, he wrote his old pupil and friend Bede Griffiths, "I was terrified to find how fearful I was by the crisis. Pray for me for courage" (Griffin 162). Again he writes him in 1954, "I had prayed hard for a couple of nights before that my faith might be strengthened. The response was immediate, and your book gave the finishing touch [*The Golden*

James M. Houston

String, Griffiths's autobiography]" (Griffin 357). Again, on December 20, 1961, Lewis wrote Griffiths after his wife's death: "I prayed when I buried my wife, my whole sexual nature should be buried with her, and it seems to have happened. Thus one recurrent trial has vanished from my life—an enormous liberty. Of course, this may be old age" (Griffin 428).

Another special friend was Sister Penelope Lawson. His first letter to her he wrote in 1939, saying: "Though I'm forty years old, I'm only about twelve as a Christian . . . so it would be a maternal act if you found time sometimes to mention me in your prayers" (Griffin 162). Then on October 24, 1940, he told her: "I'm going to make my first confession next week, which will seem odd to you, but I wasn't brought up to that kind of thing. It is an odd experience. The *decision* to do so was one of the hardest I have ever made; but now that I am committed (by dint of posting the letter before I had time to change my mind) I began to be afraid of the opposite extreme — afraid that I was merely indulging in an orgy of egoism" (Griffin 181). A month later, he wrote again to say, "Well—we have come through the wall of fire, and find ourselves (somewhat to our surprise) still alive and even well. The story about an orgy of egoism turns out, like all the Enemy propaganda, to have just a grain of truth in it, but I have no doubt that the proper method of dealing with that is to continue the practice as I intend to do. For after all, everything—even virtue, even prayer—has its dangers and if one heeds the grain of truth in the Enemy propaganda, one can never do anything at all" (Griffin 181-82).

A particular thorn in the flesh for Lewis was Mrs. Moore, the mother of a friend killed in the First World War, with whom Lewis had had an unfortunate romance that turned sour, but whom he also adopted into his home and paid filial devotion. She continued to live with Lewis and his brother for many years, and her last years in the household got progressively worse. During one particular crisis over her, Lewis wrote to Sister Penelope, "It is a bad time, but I almost venture to say I felt Christ in the house as I have never done before." Signing himself "Brother Ass," he added contritely, "but alas such a house for Him to visit!" Years before his brother had wistfully compared their own troubled household with that of the Dysons, where life seemed one long series of delightful picnics.

Again Lewis wrote Sister Penelope on January 3, 1945: "Pray for me. I am suffering incessant temptations to uncharitable thoughts at present; one of those black moods in which nearly all one's friends seem to be selfish or even false. And how terrible that there should be even a kind of *pleasure* in thinking evil" (Griffin 241). As Mrs. Moore sank into senility and kept the household in constant discord, he wrote, "I have been feeling that very much lately: that *cheerful insecurity* is what our Lord asks of us" (Griffin 316). Again, on June 5, 1951, Lewis wrote her, "I especially need your prayers because I am (like the pilgrim in Bunyan) travelling across a plain called Ease! Everything without, and many things within, are marvelously well at present" (Griffin 324). It was at this time that he began to think of writing a book on prayer. Perhaps it began to dawn upon him that he could not do this without more experience of its reality in his own life, for on February 15, 1954, Lewis wrote again to Sister Penelope, "I have had to abandon the book on prayer, it was clearly not for me" (Griffin 349). He kept this postponement for the next nine years of his life, indeed to the year he died. But while he was writing it, his wife Joy Davidman commented how excited she was about his project, as perhaps one of the most important things Lewis would ever do.

6. Prayer Life Is Matured by Suffering

Perhaps in the meantime, Lewis began to think of what was involved symbolically in the change of locale from Magdalen College, Oxford, to Magdalene College, Cambridge. "My address will be Magdalene, so I remain under the same patroness," he wrote to Sister Penelope on July 30, 1954. "This is nice because it saves 'admin.' readjustments in Heaven." At the end of the year, he wrote his friend Veta Gebbert, "I think I shall like Magdalene better than Magdalen." He explained: "It is a tiny college (a perfect cameo architecturally) and they're so old-fashioned, pious, and gentle and conservative—unlike this leftist, atheist, cynical, hard-boiled huge Magdalen" that had caused Lewis so much hurt

(Griffin 356). In a letter to Bede Griffiths on November 1, he asked: "Has any theologian (perhaps dozens) allegorized St. Mary Magdalene's act in the following way, which came to me like a flash of lightning the other day! . . . the precious alabaster box which we have to *break* over the holy feet is her *heart*. It seems so obvious, once one has thought of it" (Griffin 356).

So Lewis had come to see that prayer grows in the breaking of the human heart before God. Perhaps his own heart had been broken by failing to receive a professorship from Oxford University, and then later by the far more poignant grief of losing his wife in bereavement. Like all of us, Lewis continued to struggle with God, when

> By now I should be entering on the supreme stage
> Of the whole walk, reserved for the late afternoon.
> The heat was over now; the anxious mountains,
> The airless valleys and the sunbaked rocks, behind me. (*Poems* 118)

Yet on June 18, 1962, he writes: "The plumbing often goes wrong. I need to be near a life-line" (Griffin 429). Worse was to come.

After the loss of his wife, Lewis asks the raw and naked question:

> Where is God? This is one of the most disquieting symptoms. When you are happy, so happy that you have no sense of needing Him, so happy that you are tempted to feel His claims upon you as an interruption, if you remember yourself and turn to Him with gratitude and praise, you will be — or so it feels — welcomed with open arms. But go to Him when your need is desperate, when all other help is vain, and what do you find? A door slammed in your face, and the sound of bolting and double bolting on the inside. After that silence. You may as well turn away. The longer you wait, the more emphatic the silence will become. There are no lights in the windows. It might be an empty house. Was it ever inhabited? It seemed so once. And that seeming was as strong as this. What can this mean? Why is He so present a commander in our time of prosperity and so very absent a help in time of trouble? (*A Grief Observed* 9-10).

In times of such bitter sorrow, Lewis admitted that "I am not in much danger of ceasing to believe in God. The real danger is of coming to believe such dreadful things about Him" (*A Grief Observed* 9).

> Of this we're certain; no one who dared knock
> At heaven's door for earthly comfort found
> Even a door—only smooth, endless rock,
> And save the echo of his voice no sound.
>
> It's dangerous to listen; you'll begin
> To fancy that those echoes (hope can play
> Pitiful tricks) are answers from within;
> Far better to turn, grimly sane away.
>
> Heaven cannot thus, Earth cannot ever, give
> The thing we want. We ask what isn't there
> And by our asking water and make live
> That very part of love which must despair,
> And die, and go down cold into the earth,
> Before there's talk of springtide and re-birth. (*Poems* 126)

Yet, this is perhaps the deepest experience of prayer, to be able to say, "Lord, not my will but thine be done."

Lewis's Theology of Prayer

If Lewis's personal experience of prayer has these six traits—realism, practicality, natural simplicity, strong supplicatory concern for others, warm and honest expression of friendship, and maturation by sufferings—how do these characteristics shape his theology of prayer? Perhaps the two intellectual problems he stressed most in his writings were the problem of causality in prayer and the nature of petitionary prayer. Like other human beings he had first to overcome morbid childhood experiences before he could enter into deeper understanding about the nature and exercise of prayer.

Children tend to transfer to God the patterns of their relationships with their parents. This correlation, unless corrected and healed, may persist, unconsciously, throughout life. "My real life — or what memory reports as my real life — was increasingly one of solitude," Lewis reports. He had bad dreams, "like a window opening on what was hardly less than Hell" (*Surprised by Joy* 11). As a child of seven, he admits "solitude was nearly always at my command, somewhere in the garden, or somewhere in the house. . . . What drove me to write was the extreme manual clumsiness from which I suffered," so that he hated sports. His early years he described as "living almost entirely in my imagination," or at least "the imaginative experience of those years now seems to me more important than anything else" (*Surprised by Joy* 15-18). Then at the age of ten his mother grew ill. He remembered what he had been taught, that prayer offered in faith would be answered. Then when she died he shifted his ground, thinking now that he must believe in a miracle, and seeing God merely as a magician. This loss left him with theological confusion about God for years to come. Like the solid continent of Atlantis that disappeared under the waves, "all that was tranquil and reliable, disappeared from my life. . . . It was all sea and islands now" (*Surprised by Joy* 21).

At boarding school later, Lewis says he began "seriously to pray and read my Bible and to attempt to obey my conscience" (*Surprised by Joy* 34). But his alienation from his distanced father increased, and there was emotionally no solid ground for the child. Sometimes he would awake at night afraid that his brother had slipped off with his father to America and left him behind. His prayers became acts of sheer despair. Having said them at night, his conscience would whisper he had not said them properly, so he would try and try again until he fell asleep in frustration and lack of abiding assurance. A deepening pessimism eventually led him at university to decide he was an atheist, a declaration which has given many the cold comfort of forgetting God in a conversion of relief. Perhaps the dread of frustrated prayers at nighttime never fully left him, and the need for a reasoned faith about prayer was colored as much from his early alienation as from the growth of his intellect. Perhaps Lewis's cure finally was to rest in the presence of God, rather than be always inquiring about the appropriate philosophy of prayer.

1. Lewis's Emphasis upon "Festoonings" in Prayer

Lewis's bad experiences of prayer as a child explain perhaps the emphasis he made later in life upon the importance of placing one's self in what he called "prayerful situations," or "festoonings." Perhaps he learned this from his own failures as a child to ever pray "properly" at all. In his honest humility, Lewis also learned to see that at prayer one is in a more "real" situation than ever one could be in the "real world." Prayer is the struggle for the "real I" to meet with the reality of God. Prayer is saying, "May it be the real I who speaks. May it be the real Thou that I speak to." This is the prayer that precedes all prayers. Then, as the great Iconoclast, God in mercy may shatter all our false ideas and conceptions of him, removing the hindrances of our real prayer life.

Another area where "festoonings" of prayer are needed is in the realm of causality. Several times in his writings, Lewis recites the *Pensées* of Pascal: "God instituted prayer in order to lend his creatures the dignity of causality." Lewis's comment is that God perhaps "invented both prayer and physical action for that purpose" (*God in the Dock* 104-7). God has granted us the dignity of both work and prayer together, so a proper attitude to both is to pray as we work responsibly with the gifts that God has given to us, as well as to go on praying when we can work no more. Indeed, prayer is a stronger force than causality. For if it "works" at all, then it does so unlimited by space and time. Prayer is not therefore a direct action over nature. It is action in cooperation with God; thus we are most in harmony with God's provident actions when we are in prayer before him. Perhaps the post-Einsteinian worldview, still little appreciated in Lewis's day, now frees us from being so "hung up" with causality as some of his contemporaries were.

2. Lewis and Petitionary Prayer

Wisely, then, Lewis argues that it is a wrong kind of question to ask, "Does prayer work?" It misleads us about the nature of prayer. The quiet composure of heart before God that is true prayer rests in a relationship that is deeper than words can ever express. This helps explain why Lewis thought so little need be said about prayer. It is to be experienced rather than superficially talked about. Yet Lewis did have difficulty with the apparently inconsistent character of petitions he noted in the Gospels, for he observes two types of prayer which appear inconsistent with each other. What he calls type A is the prayer taught by our Lord: "Thy will be done," seen in the light of the great submission of his Passion: "Nevertheless, not my will but thine be done." [See the essay "Petitionary Prayer: a Problem Without an Answer," *Christian Reflections* 142-51.] Type B is the petition in faith, able to "move mountains," to heal people, to remove blindness, and do much else. The apostle seems to advocate it when he urges us to "ask in faith, nothing doubting" (James 1:6-8).

Lewis asked many wise people about the contradiction, receiving no clear answer nor solution. Hesitantly, Lewis suggested himself that until God has given us the faith to move mountains, it is perhaps best to leave the mountains alone, for he created them, and that is his business. Instead, it is advisable to concentrate more attention on Type A prayers, prayers indicating that surrender of self-will and self-love is more important than getting our own way, for we can easily misinterpret our perception of things in foolish, willful ways. Perhaps what Jesus actually did, when he prayed submissively as he did on the night of his betrayal, was to identify himself with our weaknesses, so that even the certitude of the Father's will was withdrawn from him. Our struggles may be, says Lewis, not to believe that God is an Enabler, but to believe even that God is a Listener.

Thus Lewis remained modest, extremely so, about his prayer life. Perhaps nothing keeps us humbler than a healthy realism about the inadequacy of our personal relationship with God. Lewis knew times of dryness in his prayer life, what the medieval monks used to call "accidie." He warns us wisely against viewing our prayer life in relation to our emotions. "Whenever [humans] are attending to the Enemy Himself," wrote Screwtape to his assistant Wormwood, "we are defeated." The Devil's advice to his evil apprentice is to distract their attention from God to their feelings about God. "When they meant to ask Him for charity, let them, instead, start trying to manufacture charitable feelings for themselves and not notice that this is what they are doing. . . . Teach them to estimate the value of each prayer by their success in producing the desired feeling" (*Screwtape Letters* 28). At all costs, avoid the real nakedness of the soul before God in prayer. It is that, argued Screwtape, which is so deadly to the demonic cause: being in the actual living presence of God.

These then are the things Lewis teaches us from his own prayer life. The profound need of realism, of humility, of exposing our own vulnerability and unreality as we seek God in prayer. Prayer, then, is the primary language of the soul in encounter with God. This is something we cannot demythologize, as Bishop Robinson and other contemporary liberals were trying to do. For their own demythologizing was no more than a cruder, more secular mythology, far less real than the simple prayers of devout souls who did re-present, embody, and experience the reality of God.

We will give the last word to Lewis, writing about his own experiences of prayer. "Prayer in the sense of asking for things," Lewis writes, "is a small part of it; confession and penitence are its threshold, adoration its sanctuary, the presence and vision and enjoyment of God its bread and wine. In it God shows Himself to us. That He answers prayer is a corollary—not necessarily the most important one — from the revelation. What He does is learned from what He is" (*The World's Last Night* 8).

Works Cited

Griffin, William. *Clive Staples Lewis, A Dramatic Life*. San Francisco: Harper & Row, 1986.

Lewis, C. S. *B.B.C. Talks*. 1941; rpr. New York: Macmillan, 1960.

_____. *Christian Behavior*. London: Geoffrey Bles, 1943.

_____. *God in the Dock*. Ed. Walter Hooper. Grand Rapids: Eerdmans, 1970.

_____. *A Grief Observed*. London: Faber & Faber, 1964.

_____. *Letters*. Ed. W. H. Lewis. New York: Harvest Books, 1966.

James M. Houston

————. *Letters of C. S. Lewis to Arthur Greeves (1914-1963)*. Ed. Walter Hooper. New York: Macmillan, 1979.

————. *Letters to an American Lady*. Ed. Clyde Kilby. London: Hodder and Stoughton, 1967.

————. *Letters to Malcolm: Chiefly on Prayer*. New York: Harcourt, Brace, Jovanovich, 1964.

————. *Mere Christianity*. London: Geoffrey Bles, 1952.

————. *Poems*. Ed. Walter Hooper. New York: Harcourt, Brace, Jovanovich, 1964.

————. *Reflections on the Psalms*. London: Collins, Fount Paperbacks, 1984.

————. *Screwtape Letters*. London: Geoffrey Bles, 1961.

————. *Surprised by Joy*. New York: Harcourt, Brace, Jovanovich, 1955.

————. *The World's Last Night and Other Essays: The Efficacy of Prayer*. New York: Harcourt, Brace, Jovanovich, 1949.

MacDonald, George. *The Diary of an Old Soul*. Minneapolis, Minn.: Augsburg Publishing House, 1975.

II. SPELLING THE RIDDLE: LITERARY ASSESSMENTS

Looking Backward: C. S. Lewis's Literary Achievement at Forty Years' Perspective

Thomas T. Howard

My title stresses Lewis's *literary* achievement, since no conceiva-ble paper of reasonable length could cover the whole range of his works — theological, apologetic, critical, meditative, and fic-tional. My own guess is that it is the last one of these categories in which we will find the works that will endure for the longest time.

You can't very easily compare *Miracles*, say, with *The Horse and His Boy*, or *Spenser's Images of Life* with *The Abolition of Man* on any very useful literary accounting, except to say that every-thing Lewis wrote was written with vigor, clarity, perspicacity, agility, and a certain ineluctability. (I have often complained that it is no use having a discussion group on one of Lewis's books since once you have read the text, there is nothing left to be said: everyone's contributions to the discussion may be said to be gild-ing the lily.)

However, before leaving roughly forty of Lewis's fifty or so books behind with an insouciant wave of my critical hand, allow me to say at least this about his "expository" works, as opposed

---

THOMAS T. HOWARD is a speaker and for many years professor of En-glish at Gordon College. He is author of *Christ the Tiger*, *Splendor in the Ordinary*, and *The Achievement of C. S. Lewis*.

to whatever we might wish to call his "feigned" (in Philip Sidney's sense of the word) works. Theology, for example, comes and goes according to vogue, with more or less the same speed as *haute couture* varies. You have the Thomists, then the Reformers, then the Latitudinarians, then the Deists, then the Unitarians, then Schleiermacher, then Rauschenbusch, then Barth, then Brunner and Tillich, then Harvey Cox and Altizer, then Rahner, then Boff and Gutiérrez. Hence, it would be hard to locate works like *Mere Christianity* and Lewis's other theological essays on any sort of chart, if we want the chart to show us what is dominating theological discussion at the moment. On the other hand, even when we have granted that Lewis has no recognized place in the above list, nevertheless, probably most of us here suspect that indeed *Mere Christianity* (and probably *Screwtape* and *The Problem of Pain* and *Miracles*) may well be found in print on the shelves long after the Bishop of Woolwich and Sam Keen (he was the visceral theology man, if your memory fails you) have crumbled to dust on the remaindered tables. I will not argue with anyone about this, but I *think* it will be the case, for the following reason: Lewis did, in fact, achieve what he set out to attempt, namely, to speak simply, clearly, and unapologetically (no pun intended) for that faith of which it may be said, *Quod ubique, semper, et ab omnibus creditum est.* Neither your sages nor your dunderheads, your kings nor your peasants, your shopkeepers nor your ordinary clerks and householders (that is to say, none of us) can cling to, let alone adore, The Man for Others, or The Ground of Being, or Caring and Sharing. No. We mortals must come to that odd place where the poor Jewish girl heard the archangelic salutation, and to the Creche, and to the Cross and to the grave that has a *corpse missing* from it. Somehow your mumbling Sicilian peasant women find themselves kneeling next to Augustine, Thomas, St. Thomas More, Pascal, Etienne Gilson, and C. S. Lewis in these peculiar spots.

Lewis wrote unabashedly about that supernatural, miraculous story that really *did* break through the scrim that hangs thinly between time and eternity and was played out on the real stage of our real history, so that we all say, in the Creed, "*Crucifixus etiam pro nobis sub Pontio Pilato,*" to declare to all and sundry that we

Christians are not speaking of the cloud-obscured heights of Parnassus and Olympus, nor the Gardens of the Hesperides, nor the land of the Hyperboreans. If history cranks on for another ten thousand melancholy years, my own guess is that, if there are any books left at all amongst all the post-electronic tackle, a man might find *Mere Christianity* there, along with some old missals and the King James Bible.

With respect to Lewis's literary criticism, before I give you my notions as to his *literary* achievement at forty years' perspective, I may venture to say that I find myself somewhat bemused when it comes to putting forward any very helpful surmise on this front. This is not because I doubt the worth of what Lewis wrote in his *A Preface to Paradise Lost*, or his *English Literature in the Sixteenth Century Excluding Drama*, or his Spenserian studies, not to mention his *Studies in Words* and his *Experiment in Criticism*. Heaven knows, if I were running the world of graduate English studies, almost everything that is required reading nowadays would be destroyed in an immense book burning, and Lewis would be made required reading. But literary critical vogue comes and goes. Aristotle; Horace; Gascoigne, Puttenham, and Harvey; Ben Jonson; Dryden; Samuel Johnson; Coleridge; Arnold; James; Cleanth Brooks; Ezra Pound; Paul de Man, Saussure, and Harold Bloom: Lord love a duck — how can a man keep *up*? Where shall we put Lewis?

I don't know. We all know how utterly out of fashion his ontology, and hence his epistemology, and hence his way of handling a text, are now. Who of us will predict just when present trends will spend themselves? Or whether Lewisean modes of criticism will ever return? Most of us here would urge that what he says of *Paradise Lost* will always be useful, not to say indispensable: but neither you nor I am running the show. As long as *I* live, I'll be quoting various excerpts from Lewis on Milton to my students; whether anybody else will, I don't know.

But now, what about Lewis's achievement in belles lettres, at forty years' perspective? First of all, one category to which I will give short shrift, for obvious reasons, is Lewis's poetry. There are some conundrums here, and they puzzle me as much as do the voguish matters that affect the popularity and durability of his criticism. Is it good poetry? Hum. I think so. At least it is good on various accountings. He knew what he was doing with prosody, and his imagery is fresh and apt (who can forget Leavis with Lord Russell wreathed in flowers, or the scorpions and the mantichores and corpulent tarantulas of "Pan's Purge," or the bee in the handkerchief, or, best of all, the unicorn left behind the Ark? People who love Lewis's work love his poetry. But is its failure in the marketplace to be attributed to blackguards who have ignored it? We must not be a mere cheering section. Is it good poetry? I wish I knew. Will it last? I doubt it. Do I wish everyone were required to read it? Yes. Do I think it is timely, still, after forty years? Yes, yes, yes.

And now his fiction. How shall we name his achievement here, and what surmise shall we make about its timeliness and durability?

Suddenly we find ourselves up to our necks in the question of imagination. Wherein lies the success, both artistic and commercial, of a given item brought forth from the imagination? Winnie the Pooh and Piglet; Mrs. Tiggy-Winkle and Jemima Puddle Duck; Rat and Toad; Alice and the Red Queen: we can scrabble at the matter until the proverbial cows come home, but it is mightily difficult to chase down just exactly why these creatures seem almost sempiternal. Will Mr. Tumnus and Lucy and Uncle Andrew and Aslan be around as long as these others?

My own guess is that if any stories written since Lewis Carroll, Beatrix Potter, A. A. Milne, and Kenneth Grahame have a chance of achieving this sempiternal status, *The Chronicles of Narnia* are front-running candidates.

When it comes to Ransom, Weston, Mark and Jane Studdock, Tinidril, Wither, and Fairy Hardcastle, I am less sure. But I would like to put forward a hunch of my own and rest my case on that.

Here it is: I think that *The Chronicles of Narnia*, and *perhaps* the so-called "space-trilogy," will be with us for a long time still for the reason that they evoke, as do very few other works of imagination, the categories "terror" and "sublimity." You might say that these two words constitute the bottom line and the top line for human existence.

Lewis's fiction reaches, so to speak, all the way to heaven

and hell. Now I am aware that the obvious rejoinder here would be that Lewis does not write about heaven and hell in his fiction, except in *The Great Divorce*: he writes about Narnia and Perelandra and Edgestow and Glome. But surely the landscape of these places, and the things that we see going on in them, have the effect of awakening in us the capacity to imagine terror and sublimity so towering that only the words heaven and hell will suffice. We watch real, ultimate judgment being visited upon the characters. The scenes carry us beyond the borders that even Shakespeare set himself in his tragedies, for in those tragedies we see an Antony or a Lear or a Richard II running afoul of the *proximate* consequences of his follies; but Shakespeare, and most poets, do not undertake to carry us across the frontier into that region from whose bourn no traveler ever returns.

In myth and fantasy you can do this. You can't usually do it in tragedy, which is not to say that Shakespeare shortchanged us by choosing *not* to follow Lear across the frontier and tell us whether he made it to heaven or hell. We all hope it was heaven, since Lear had suffered enough, we feel. But Shakespeare would have muddied the waters of his drama if he had stirred up questions like that.

But for centuries the poets thought that you couldn't give a really true picture of human life if you left out the gods. And what you get in the landscapes of Narnia or Perelandra, and what any Jew and any Christian (and Hindu and Muslim and animist, for that matter) thinks is the truth about our human existence, is that it *is* beset with terror and sublimity, and that the origins and sources of that terror and sublimity are *outside* the perimeter of Midgard. What we find in the kind of story Lewis writes bears news of what is true, we might say.

Take, for example, such images as the figures of Edmund, Eustace, Uncle Andrew, Nikabrik, Weston, Wither, Rabadash, or Ginger the Cat. Because the kind of story we have here occurs under a firmament that reaches all the way up, or in, to Deep Heaven, we find to our discomfiture that the danger that besets these people (or cats, or dwarfs) is not just some set of psychological or legal consequences, but damnation. Franz Kafka, of course, tinkered with this sort of thing in his story *Metamorphosis*, and I do not for a moment deny the power of that story. But we are on quite a different footing in real mythology, or in Narnia: in a myth Actaeon really will turn into a stag, or Io into a white cow, or Eustace into a dragon. Here we are in the region that lies beyond the merely psychological. It is the region of judgment, and hence of final misery or beatitude. Terror or sublimity.

There is a frightening gallery of these pictures in Lewis's fiction. Edmund in *The Lion, the Witch, and the Wardrobe*, for example, in whom, though we see no visible transfiguration, we see a horrible progress from scarcely noticeable selfishness, petulance, and pusillanimity straight towards the sin of Judas Iscariot; and Eustace; and Uncle Andrew — certainly the most egregiously bumptious figure in all of Lewis, with his garrulous and utterly tiresome megalomania, ending up a complete fool, having to be put to sleep like a foetus, with the hope of starting all over again. Diggle, the dwarf — defensive, suspicious, surly, ending up incapable of joy and therefore damned; Rabadash — a pompous ass, ending up a real ass without any pomp; Ginger — calculating, cynical, perfidious, opportunistic, ending up, like the dwarfs, forever incapable of joy.

All of these images appear in the so-called children's stories. What about Lewis's "adult" fiction?

Weston, for example: what sort of progress towards damnation do we see in him? It all begins quite harmlessly. He is all for clear thinking and logical propositions (although a certain testiness in his attitudes bothers us from the start). He is also a crusader and visionary, with great designs for the betterment of the race, not to say the universe. So far so good. The difficulty here, alas, is that when you get a visionary crusader equipped with a powerfully analytic mind, you may have the recipe for either a St. Paul or a Hitler. Which way will things go? We watch in horror Weston's progress from what might appear to be neutral or even praiseworthy qualities, tainted a bit with irritability, through increasingly power-crazed stages, on to anger, megalomania, *hubris*, and diabolical cruelty, right down to the final stages, namely imbecility, inanity, brutishness, and the last whimpers of self-pity before annihilation. It is a dreadful picture of something that Lewis believed was true, namely that the state of damnation is a state next to non-being. The souls in hell are idiots (compare Dante). There is nothing left of them but the merest detritus, left from what had once been a human being. Evil has leached away and leeched away all the good solidity that God made when he made man in his image, and has left only this gibbering, imbecilic trace.

Lewis's most chilling image of damnation, however, is the figure of Wither. Belbury is full of horrible images, of course. There is Feverstone, the boisterous cad with his infectious, jeering laughter and bloodless cynicism; Filostrato, who is your archetypal Gnostic and Manichaean—there is too much *life* polluting the earth, and we must disinfect it of all these trees and bodies and eggs, and all this loam and flesh; Curry, your archetypal bore, who thinks in sociological categories and lives and moves and has his being in the world of committee politics; Straik, your archetypal apostate priest, the visionary secularizing radical; Fairy Hardcastle, the very perversion incarnate of Mother Dimble; Frost, with his glinting pince-nez, of whom we suspect that, if we could see through those spectacles and into his eyes, we would see, to our horror, nothing. But worst of all, Wither. Wither pacing and humming. Wither circumlocuting and evading. Wither never looking *at* you. Wither with his sagging mouth, drooling slightly. Wither with his demonically courtly omnipresence. Wither who never sleeps.

What is he? Is he not precisely what is left of a man when evil has run its full course? We find here what we found with Weston: almost nothing. Wither is a wraith. He is non-being. There is nothing solid about him, not even his syntax. He is like the Dark Riders in Tolkien. He was a man once upon a time, but he has opted for the murk of tergiversation rather than the clarity of truth, and he has got it. All the edges are blurred. "Hell is murky," said Lady Macbeth, and she was right. Our last glimpse of Wither might have been written by Charles Williams: there is a sort of indeterminate slipping into blur. If you sow the refusal of fact, you reap the absence of fact. The short word for this state of affairs is hell.

But it is not only the terror of damnation that looms in Lewis's fiction. There is something called "the Terrible Good."

The figure of Aslan seems to arouse in everyone that simultaneous desire and dread that attends the ineffable, or the holy. Both emotions are appropriate. Everyone without exception experiences the dread, even such blameless creatures as Mrs. Beaver, Lucy, and Peter, who have (usually) nothing to hide. But everyone except those who love evil more than good also experiences the awakening of fathomless desire in the presence of Aslan. The classic scene here, it seems to me, is the one in which Jill is trying to come at the stream for a drink and finds a lion in her path. The greatest danger to her, namely the lion, turns out, alas, to be the custodian of the very thing, and the only thing, she needs.

The most prolonged and dramatic rendering of this experience in all of Lewis would be Orual's story. Her arch-foes are the gods; but they are the custodians of felicity. We think also of Jane's encounter with Ransom at St. Anne's. Her whole quarrel with life is that she is not being permitted to be adult and independent, and then it turns out that the only liberty and felicity worth calling by those names are subdivisions of *obedience*. The Good is the most terrible thing of all (or so we suppose, left to ourselves), since it asks everything.

That the Good is in fact terrible, in the sense of being really and truly all-consuming and all-devouring, shows up repeatedly. The destruction visited upon Belbury is, precisely, the vengeance of good upon evil. The very beasts, who have been the victims of vivisection, are permitted to run wild upon their tormentors. The final apocalypse in *The Last Battle*, when the heavens and earth fold up, with the sun being squeezed out like an orange, and the great megalosaurians keeling over and dissolving to dust: it is the final folding up of the old fabric in preparation for the new one, in which omnipotence turns out to be synonymous with love.

Terror appears in another form that turns out to be synonymous with sublimity. I am referring to the appearance of eldils on stage. They do not seem to be figures appropriate to *modern* fiction, but once more we ask how a storyteller is supposed to catch the particular quality of experience that we find in myth or fantasy showing up in the encounter of mortals with the immortals? Zeus coming to Leda; Aphrodite coming to Adonis; Apollo coming to Ganymede; not to mention the angel of the Lord coming to Abraham or to the Virgin Mary: surely all that is not nothing? Is our world, or it is not, one which has been visited? I am not speaking of flying saucers, nor the specters and poltergeists who rattle the crockery in English country houses, nor even the mumbling spirits that you get at seances. Those visitations are either bogus or insignificant, it seems to me, next to the Annunciation, or to a visit from an eldil.

The very roster of characters in Narnia catches, it seems to me, the thing that you find in ancient myth with its different *kinds* of being, and also in the language of the liturgy when it acknowledges "angels and archangels and all the company of heaven." The old word "plenitude" may be the word we need here: the sheer, glorious array of creatures, some of them inauspicious and unlikely in themselves, some of them glorious beyond description; but taken all together, constituting the hilarious multitude of Joy. We observe them as though we were witnessing a celestial triumph, each one crowned with his own particular excellence and perfection, and bearing the palm of his own particular achievement. Reepicheep; Puddleglum; Mrs. Beaver (perhaps her golden banner has a sewing machine blazoned on it); Rumblebuffin (sheer size and plain good intentions — there is glory in that); Roonwit (great and sage and venerable antiquity); Jewel (what virginal purity does the unicorn bespeak?); Ramandu (a star: what is a star?); the Sea People—those tiny kings and queens that the children saw in the clear water as they neared the end of the world; the dwarfs, fauns, dryads, and talking beasts, including "the dogs, the dear dogs"; and Peter the High King: is it mere romance to speak of a schoolboy under the imagery of High King? What is courtesy and courage and older-brotherliness all about? And surely one of the most haunting and piercing images in all of Lewis: the Milk-white Stag. We never see it. We only hear rumors of it, once or perhaps twice, deep in the forest on the remote marches of Narnia; but dear heaven, it sounds the same note through our hearts as does Triton's horn, or the horns of elfland. Why is the most exquisite thing of all so fugitive? Why indeed?

Another mode under which the hint of felicity comes at us in these stories is in what we may call epiphanies, when we see revealed the glory that has been there in someone all along, but that may have been cloaked in ordinariness and hence hardly recognizable. The best-known case in point of this in Lewis's work must be that celestial procession in *The Great Divorce*, in which the dreamer sees a great and noble lady being drawn in a chariot and discovers that it was "only" Sally Smith of Golders Green. Here is the Transfiguration of the charwoman—and it is to be remembered that in transfigurations we get to see what is true, not what is false. This glory is simply the butterfly wings of which the mops and pails of Golders Green were the chrysalis. Or the Cabby, in *The Magician's Nephew*: why on earth make a Cockney cab-driver into your Adam figure, your High King? Because that is what he has been all along. You thought it was only a matter of his being simple and cheery and trustworthy, kind to his horse and loving to his wife. Well it was, and what does all that mean if it does not mean charity and sanctity, and what are they but the most glorious things there are, and how shall we deck glorious things if not in the imagery of kingship—crowns and scepters?

One other epiphany scene, if we may call it that, occurs in *That Hideous Strength*, at St. Anne's, when the women are choosing their gowns. As each one tries hers on, we see her suddenly transfigured and revealed gloriously for what she really is—and has been all along: it is just that the colors are clearer now. Mother Dimble, a priestess or sibyl; Ivy Maggs, a pert fairy, a dapper elf; Camilla Denniston, the Valkyrie; Jane, "submitting" to blue: who can avoid the iconography of the Blessed Virgin here, always in blue, who said, "Be it unto me . . ."? Wild fancies? No doubt. But no wilder than things Christians believe to be sober reality.

And now I must reach for the language of the writer of Hebrews, when he was trying to hail his readers with the heroes of faith in chapter 11: "And what more shall I say? for the time would fail me to tell of . . ."—of the heart-breaking clarity and stillness in the final pages of *Perelandra*, or the same heart-breaking clarity and stillness that suffuses everything as the "Dawn Treader" reaches the lilies at the end of the world; or of the same clarity and hush and then crescendo as Aslan sings Narnia into being, or as he breathes on the beasts to make them talking beasts; or of the descent of Mercury, Venus, Mars, Saturn, and Jove, on St. Anne's; or of the great leaping chase farther up and farther in to Narnia at the end of *The Last Battle*.

So. What shall we say of C. S. Lewis's literary achievement, at this distance of forty years? None of us can say what will last, of anyone's work, until a very long time has passed. Henry James himself is not safe yet. So of course I cannot predict whether Lewis's work will be in print 200 years from now. But I am perfectly happy to be on record as saying that virtually every line he wrote, fiction or argument, is as timely now as the day it was written. It is timely because it is all true.

G. K. Chesterton and Max Beerbohm

William Blissett

It was the young Max Beerbohm—dapper, choosy Max, essayist, caricaturist, theatrical reviewer, and social success—who made the first move. He was thirty and the recipient of his letter, twenty-eight. The year, 1902:

> Dear Mr. Chesterton,
>   I have seldom wished to meet anyone in particular: but you I should very much like to meet.
>   I need not explain who I am, for the name at the end of this note is one which you have more than once admitted, rather sternly, into your writings.
>   By way of personal and private introduction, I may say that my mother was a friend of your grandmother, Mrs. Grosjean, and also of your mother.
>   As I have said, I should like to meet you. On the other hand, it is quite possible that you have no reciprocal anxiety to meet me. In this case, nothing could be easier than for you to say that you are very busy, or unwell, or going out of town, and so are not able—much as you would have

WILLIAM BLISSETT is professor of English at the University of Toronto and author of *The Long Conversation, A Memoir of David Jones*.

liked—to lunch with me here either next Wednesday or next Saturday at 1:30.

I am, whether you come or not, yours admiringly,

Max Beerbohm.

P.S. I am quite different from my writings (and so, I daresay, are you from yours). So that we should not necessarily fail to hit it off.

I, in the flesh, am modest, full of common sense, very genial, and rather dull.

What you are remains to be seen—or not to be seen by me, according to your decision.[1]

The meeting took place and went well, and the two London journalists became friends. Years later, in his *Autobiography*, Chesterton recalls the occasion:

About this time I discovered the secret of amiability in another person with a rather misleading reputation for acidity. Mr. Max Beerbohm asked me to lunch; and I have ever since known that he is himself the most subtle of his paradoxes. . . . Max played in the masquerade of his time, which he has described so brilliantly; and he dressed or overdressed the part. His name was supposed to be a synonym for Impudence; for the undergraduate who exhibited the cheek of the guttersnipe in the garb of the dandy. He was supposed to blow his own trumpet with every flourish of self-praise; countless stories were told about the brazen placidity of his egoism.

But, Chesterton continues, Max's voice, the expression of his eyes, refute such stories:

Most men spread themselves a little in conversation, and have their unreal victories and vanities; but he seems to me more moderate and realistic about himself than about anything else. He is more sceptical about everything than I am, by temper; but certainly he does not indulge in the base idolatry of believing in himself.[2]

1. David Cecil, *Max Beerbohm: A Biography* (London: Constable, 1964), pp. 199-200.
2. G. K. Chesterton, *Autobiography* (London: Hutchinson, 1936, 1969), pp. 97-99.

Max and G. K. C.—to use the names that were becoming famous, like brand names for superior new products—found each other congenial opposites: concave and convex, slight and gigantic, slim and encompassing, reserved and exuberant, appraising and enthusiastic, tidy and untidy. It was, we note, the aloof, composed, dandiacal Max who made the overture to the lunging, jolly, sloppy G. K. C. Gregarious Chesterton was easy enough to meet but seems not to have sought people out, rather to have welcomed whoever came with a Whitmanian embrace, as in his invitation to "Humanity Esq., The Earth, Cosmos E — Mr. Gilbert Chesterton / requests the pleasure / of humanity's company / to tea on Dec. 25th 1896."[3] He omitted the RSVP. Max recognized this quality from the beginning: "A fashion paper for critics (why is there no such publication?) would tell us that the very latest mode is Optimism—Optimism in the very brightest colours and of the very amplest 'make'. This fashion for the coming Spring and Summer was set by (or, at least, finds its most ardent follower in) Mr. G. K. Chesterton, that excited and exciting novice, *quem honoris causa nomino*. At the cradle-side of that infant Hercules, current Life and Literature appear not as a pair of horrid snakes to be grappled with and strangled, but as two dear, kind, good snakes to be kissed and romped with, and to have a lusty admiration lisped and crowed over them from the tips of their tails to the tips of their tongues."[4] His earliest caricature of his new friend was intended to catch this aspect — "Mr. G. K. Chesterton giving the world a kiss" (1904).[5]

Let us get to know our pair as they were in 1902; first Max. By then, certainly, his special combination of talents was well defined. Already at school he had been known and admired and liked and a little feared for his caricatures; already at Oxford he had achieved some distinction for the style of his pen and pencil in essay and drawing, for the style too of his clothes and con-

3. Maisie Ward, *G. K. Chesterton* (New York: Sheed & Ward, 1943), p. 61.

4. M. Beerbohm review dated May 3, 1902, in *More Theatres* (London: Hart-Davis, 1969), p. 456.

5. Caricature listed (no. 309) and described in Rupert Hart Davids, *A Catalogue of the Caricatures of Max Beerbohm* (London: Macmillan, 1972).

versation. The essays of his first collection were written mainly in his years at Oxford. Indeed, he remained an undergraduate, leaving the university without a degree, though under no cloud. This was the small but attractive book called with "impudence" — G. K. C.'s word — *The Works of Max Beerbohm.* The last of these essays, "Diminuendo," ends thus:

> And I, who crave no knighthood, shall write no more. I shall write no more. Already I feel myself to be a trifle outmoded. I belong to the Beardsley period. Younger men, with months of activity before them, with fresher schemes and notions, with newer enthusiasms, have pressed forward since then. *Cedo junioribus.* Indeed, I stand aside with no regret. For to be outmoded is to be a classic, if one has written well. I have acceded to the hierarchy of good scribes and rather like my niche.[6]

In spite of saying, twice, "I shall write no more," Max three years later brought out a new collection of twenty essays and called it, impudently, *More,* and in the same year published *Caricatures of 25 Gentlemen.* He had clearly made his mark in two arts, but that was not the same as making his fortune. He lived at home with his mother and sisters in Upper Berkeley Street and was much in demand socially. In 1898 he had succeeded Bernard Shaw as theatrical critic for the *Saturday Review.* Shaw recommended his successor with a sentence that was an echo, witty and incongruous, both of Max's own "Diminuendo" and of Ibsen's *Master Builder,* a Max-like sentence ending in a carefully chosen and, as it proved, deathless epithet: "The younger generation is knocking at the door, and as I open it there steps sprightly in the incomparable Max."[7] Yet, while Max supported himself by his weekly column, he found the task irksome always, and it should not have been such a surprise to his friends when in 1910 he married, gave up theatrical journalism, and left England to live the rest of his long life (except for the war years) in Rapallo.

Chesterton in contrast was a "sudden newcomer." The phrase is Max's, who will write: "In the year 1900 I had been considered a rather clever and amusing young man, but I felt no

6. M. Beerbohm, *Works and More* (London: John Love, 1952), pp. 123-24.
7. *Saturday Review,* May 2, 1898.

pang whatsoever at finding myself cut out at my own game by a
sudden newcomer, named G. K. Chesterton, who was obviously far more amusing than I."[8] The "game" referred to seems to
be the invention and projection of a distinctive and winning
image, so necessary if one is to thrive in the literary marketplace.
In playing this game, they (and some other vivid literary personalities) are following in the wake of the first lord of language
and publicity, Oscar Wilde. Ironically, the two contribute equally to an exaggerated picture of Wilde's Nineties that still persists,
Max making the decade seem more sparkling and deft and stylish
than any lump of temporal phenomena can ever have been,
G. K. C. making it more decadent, pessimistic, or *(absit omen!)*
"impressionistic." They conspire to solidify it into something too
recognizable and intelligible.

In fact, before meeting him, Chesterton might well have
thought of Max too as somehow unwholesome, as resembling
that caricature of him as a menacing fetus drawn by Aubrey
Beardsley. Finding him to be, as man and artist, untainted may
perhaps more than anything else have forced Chesterton to abandon the note of melodrama in his later references to the period.
At the point of their meeting, however, the Nineties are over,
and G. K. C. is basking, Max chafing in Edwardian Fleet Street.
G. K. C., who became a journalist in 1900 in order to marry,
was never to leave journalism even after he and Frances moved
from their Battersea flat to Beaconsfield in 1909, the year before
Max and his bride turned their backs on Fleet Street and England and settled in Rapallo.

Chesterton had been trained at an art school and retained a
notable talent with pen, brush, and crayon — though to my
knowledge Max never commented on this. Chesterton had
entered literary publishing with his book of nonsense verse,
Greybeards at Play (1900), like Max amusing himself by the
pretense that he was much older than his years.[9] G. K. C. brought

8. Max Beerbohm, "Lytton Strachey" (1943), in *Mainly on the Air* (New
York: Knopf, 1958), p. 194.
9. "The gods bestowed on Max the gift of perpetual old age," Oscar Wilde
said of the young Oxonian, and kept up the joke in writing to Robert Ross
(May 31, 1898): "I see that Max has become Dramatic Critic, and has begun

out a vigorous book of serious verse in the same year, *The Wild Knight*. So thoroughly did he throw himself into journalism and so successful was the swoop that within a year his first collection of essays, *The Defendant*, appeared, to be praised thus in the *Whitehall Review*: "No one save Max Beerbohm has ever approached these Defences in whimsicality of idea and treatment."[10] If Max can write in "Defence of Cosmetics," Chesterton can write "Defences" of Penny Dreadfuls, Rash Vows, Skeletons, Publicity, Nonsense, and eleven other oddly assorted things, including a "Defence of Humility" that begins in the true Chesterton vein:

> The act of defending any of the cardinal virtues has today all the exhilaration of a vice. Moral truisms have been so much disputed that they have begun to sparkle like so many brilliant paradoxes.[11]

This sort of thing measures itself against Wilde, of course, but also against Max's first book, when he was at his most Wildean, as when, in comparing the late Victorian age with the Regency, he remarks, "We are not strong enough to be wicked, and the Nonconformist Conscience makes cowards of us all,"[12] or when in the essay on cosmetics he hails the end of "the reign of terror of nature" and rejoices now that "Artifice, that fair exile, has returned."[13] However, it must be noted that at its most brilliant and characteristic, Max's writing achieves surprise without paradox: he is the master of the turn of phrase, not the inverted truism. Knowing, as he did, both Wilde and Chesterton (did anyone else delight in, and delight, both?), he was inoculated to immunity to their excesses of style. What he shared with both was a ready channel to the wellsprings of fun, and what he shared especially with Chesterton was a sense of style as an intuition of

by his valedictory address. He is clearly entitled to his retiring pension by this time." Rupert Hart-Davis, ed. *The Letters of Oscar Wilde* (London: Hart-Davis, 1962), p. 749.

10. See D. J. Conlon, ed. *GKC The Critical Judgments, Part I*, Antwerp Studies in English Literature (1976), p. 38 for *Whitehall Review*, Feb. 27, 1902.

11. G. K. C., *The Defendant* (London: Dent, 1901), p. 131.

12. Max Beerbohm, "King George the Fourth," in *Works and More* (London: Lane, 1930), p. 50.

13. Max Beerbohm, "The Pervasion of Rouge," in *Works and More*, p. 83.

Being—not a boast of cleverness but a way of saying Glory be to God for making such dexterity possible to a creature. As stylists, they are like playing animals, or as little children saying "now watch."

Chesterton was quick to notice his new friend in print. The book of essays that anticipated his later literary biographies, *Twelve Types* (1902), makes no mention of him, but the expanded *Varied Types* (1903) includes an essay that praises the Victorian sage Ruskin for his humor: "One tenth of his paradoxes would have made the fortune of a modern young man with gloves of art yellow. He was as fond of nonsense as Mr. Max Beerbohm. Only . . . he was fond of other things too. He did not ask humanity to dine on pickles."[14] This may have been written after or before their meeting: perhaps Max sought an opportunity to dissociate himself from pickles and to protest about the association of his name with "art yellow" gloves, since as a freshman he had shuddered at the sight of Walter Pater wearing gloves of bright yellow pigskin.[15] We know for a fact that he and Chesterton talked of Browning at their first lunch and that Max, on learning that G. K. C. had just been commissioned to write the study of Browning for the English Men of Letters Series, said pensively, "A man ought to write on Browning while he is young."[16]

If *Robert Browning* (1903) is in part the fruit of that conversation, *G. F. Watts*, later that same year, opens with thoughts of the ups and downs of critical fashion: "The thing always happens sharply: a whisper runs through the salons, Mr. Max Beerbohm waves a wand and a whole generation of great men and great achievement suddenly looks mildewed and unmeaning."[17] One surmises from this that Max's championing of Rossetti and his circle could not be stretched to cover Watts.

Indeed, their rapport, though genuine, could never have been complete. Max's favorite sister became an Anglican nun, but his

---

14. G. K. C., *Varied Types* (New York: Dodd, Mead, 1903), p. 218.
15. Max Beerbohm, "Diminuendo," in *Works and More*, p. 115.
16. G. K. C., *Autobiography*, p. 99.
17. G. K. C., *G. F. Watts* (London: Duckworth, 1904, 1920), p. 3.

own concern with religion remained slight: the *fin-de-siècle* Catholicism of Oscar and Bosie and Aubrey was not for him, still less Chesterton's breezy, undecadent, religious stance. Again, G. K. C. remained a small-l liberal all his days, and Max a small-t, small-a "tory anarchist." Compare their reactions to the death of Gladstone in 1898, G. K. C. in a poem alas published, Max in a set of drawings understandably long delayed in publication.[18] The first three of the eleven drawings show Gladstone wearing down St. Peter, who has orders to exclude him, by threat of a prolonged peroration; in the second, the Grand Old Man addresses a mass meeting in heaven and pays a graceful and eloquent tribute to God; and in the third, on leaving the meeting Mr. Gladstone picks up a fallen angel. (Gladstone used to bring streetwalkers home to tea with Mrs. Gladstone, a virtuous, even heroically virtuous practice that lent itself to misconstruction.) Here, in sharp contrast, rebuking the sort of young person Max wrote and drew for, are the concluding stanzas of "To Them That Mourn":

> O young ones of a darker day,
>   In art's wan colour clad,
> Whose very love and hate are grey—
>   Whose very sin is sad,
>
> Pass on: one agony long-drawn
>   Was merrier than your mirth,
> When hand-in-hand came death and dawn,
>   And spring was on the earth.[19]

This brings us to 1904 and *The Napoleon of Notting Hill*, Chesterton's first work of extended fiction. Highly successful, it was still remembered in 1948, when George Orwell wrote *Nineteen Eighty-Four*, and in 1984, when the action of their very different visions of the future takes place. It brings G. K. C. and Max together very markedly, since Auberon Quin, who at the beginning of the tale is elected King of England, is the image of

18. *Max's Nineties* (Philadelphia: Lippincott, 1958), for "Mr. Gladstone Goes To Heaven," eleven drawings (1899).

19. G. K. C., *Collected Poems* (London: Methuen, 1927), p. 341.

Max. The illustrator, W. Graham Robertson, recalls his commission in paragraphs that deserve extended quotation:

> Once, when I was particularly busy, arrived a bulky parcel containing a novel by G. K. Chesterton, which I regarded dubiously, wondering how I should find time to read it. But, as I glanced at it, my eye fell upon the first phrase—"The Human Race, to which so many of my readers belong"—and at once dispatched to Lane an enthusiastic recommendation. A book which began like that must be all right; no one could afford to throw away such a gem in the opening sentence who had not plenty more to follow.
>
> I was enlisted to illustrate the work which turned out to be a witty and fantastic picture of a future England, reigned over by an elected King who appeared to be none other than Max Beerbohm, or at least a recognizable caricature of him. But Max, himself a caricaturist, was fair game; besides, he was in the secret and made no objections, and John Lane used to ask him and me to meet Mr. Chesterton, so that the collaboration between novelist, model and illustrator might become the more harmonious.
>
> Poor Max and I, in the freshness and innocence of our budding middle age, gambolled dutifully round the big man, all unconscious that—as he afterwards set down—he bracketed us together as interesting survivals of a bygone and evil period.
>
> He found us, it seems, "most charming people" — always an ominous opening—and then went on to describe the type which, to him, we represented. It wasn't a very nice type. It had—"an artificial reticence of speech which waited till it could plant the perfect epigram." Now that couldn't have been I or I should have gone through life dumb. It was—"a cold sarcastic dandy"— (a dandy! I, whose clothes always look like somebody else's misfits after I have worn them twice!)—"who went about with his one epigram, patient and poisonous, like a bee with its one sting." Now, I'll take my oath that this wasn't Max: of all the witty men I have met he has the kindliest and most strictly disciplined tongue. Sometimes a hint of sly malice creeps into his caricatures, but there it is surely in its right place.
>
> I consider Max Beerbohm the perfect companion, because I always part from him with the impression that I, myself, have been brilliantly amusing. He is the most generous of wits; he not only casts his pearls before swine, but actually gives the swine the credit for their production.

I regret that Mr. Chesterton did not appreciate us all the more because we both thoroughly appreciated him.[20]

It will appear that Robertson did not arbitrarily use Max's features but recognized Max in the character, and that G. K. C. and Max both assented to this. No fewer than five of the reviewers comment on the likeness to Max in Robertson's illustrations, which is unmistakable, and on the identification of the character with Max, which is much more debatable.[21] Frances Chesterton in her diary gives an account that does not quite mesh with Robertson's:

A delightful dinner party at the Lanes. . . . The talk was mostly about *Napoleon*. Max took me in to dinner and was really nice. He is a good fellow. His costume was extraordinary. Why should an evening waistcoat have four large white pearl buttons and why should he look that peculiar shape? He seems only pleased at the way he has been identified with King Auberon. "All right, my dear chap," he said to G., who was trying to apologize. "Mr. Lane and I settled it all at lunch." I think he was a little put out at finding no red carpet put down for his royal feet and we had quite a discussion as to whether he ought to precede me into the dining room. Graham Robertson was on my left. He was jolly too. . . .[22]

Years later, in 1930, Chesterton wrote "A Note on Notting Hill," recalling Max's essay on "The Naming of Streets" (1902) and how it influenced the venue of the novel:

No person is, in the most serious sense, so wise and understanding as Mr. Max Beerbohm. And I grieve to say that, in describing the effects of streets in altering his moods, he wrote: 'In Notting Hill High Street I become frankly common,' which is absurd; and impossible; and therefore quite uncommon. The fairies punished him by putting parts of him in Mr. Graham Robertson's illustrations. But I confess that the original idea, in the conscious intellectual sense, was concerned with places like that in general; and my book might have been 'The Washington of Walham Green', or 'The

20. W. Graham Robertson, *Time Was* (London: Hamish Hamilton, 1931), pp. 309-10.
21. Reviewers cited in London, pp. 84-93.
22. Ward, p. 175, for Frances Chesterton's diary.

William Blissett

Kosciuszko of Kensington Oval', or 'The Garibaldi of Gun-
nersbury', or 'The Charlemagne of Chiswick', instead of 'The
Napoleon of Notting Hill.' For I have never been able to conceal
entirely from a derisive world the fact that I was driving at something; though I had then got no further than asking in rather a wild
way 'Is there nothing that will save Notting Hill from being frankly common?'[23]

It is, nevertheless, a good joke that the original of King Auberon
should have confessed himself to feel "common," of all things,
there, of all places.

Max really did like the book and was not just going along
with the joke. Writing to Reggie Turner, he said, "I think it aw-
fully good. I wonder if you will relent about the author. You told
me he lacked 'heart.' I think there is plenty of that organ mixed
up in the book." Max was always candid with Reggie, his friend
from Oxford days; on a later occasion (1910) he said: "I thought
G. K. C.'s *What's Wrong with the World?* very cheap and *sloppy*,
though with gleams — gleams of gas-lamps in Fleet Street mud
and slush," and in the following year, "Chesterton doesn't wear
well at all, though I'm not sure whether it is that he has lost his
quality or merely that he hasn't acquired a new quality to keep
me interested." But in 1935 he was rejoicing in G. K. C.'s visit
to Rapallo — "enormous as compared with what he was; but
delightful" and thought him "*very* good" on radio.[24] But to return
to *The Napoleon of Notting Hill.*

23. G. K. C., "A Note on Notting Hill," in *The Weekend Review* (December 20, 1930), p. 915, as cited by Ian Boyd, *The Novels of G. K. Chesterton*
(London: Paul Elek, 1975), p. 202, n. 24. Max's essay of 1902 appears in *Yet
Again* (London: Heinemann, 1909), ref. to Notting Hill p. 204. It may be noted
that G. K. C.'s very first essay for the *Illustrated London News* (October 14,
1905) found him "deeply grieved to see that Mr. Max Beerbohm has been
saying that he does not find London beautiful or romantic."

24. *Letters to Reggie Turner*, Rupert Hart-Davis, ed. (New York: Lippincott, 1965), pp. 160, 193, 194-95, 275, 277. The other major collection of Max
Beerbohm letter, *Max and Will* (Rothenstein), Mary M. Lago and Karl Beckson,
ed. (London: John Murray, 1975), makes no mention of G. K. C., but David
Cecil cites a letter, apparently to Rothenstein in 1924, in which Max says: "No,
I am not nearly so witty as Chesterton for one. But certainly I have not pros-
tituted and cheapened my wit as he has" (370).

110

Of all Chesterton's fictions, it alone is unconcerned with religion.[25] Its pageantry and medievalism are in no way ecclesiastical, its issues not theological, its intense evocation of a small territory open to heaven not parochial. The foundation of Adam Wayne's fervent belief is in the Borough; all Auberon Quin's piety is a sense of humor and a style. Quin is, to use that phrase Max applied to himself, a "Tory anarchist," and Wayne is, to use a phrase G. K. C. will adopt, a "Distributist": both are opposed to bureaucracy and to Whiggery—Whiggery, that sincere belief that the nation is best governed by a governing class, that those who have all the money and position and education should also have all the power.

Max enters the book before Quin is named. Of the two young men walking the streets of London one wintry and dim morning it is said, "The lines of their frock-coats and silken hats had that luxuriant severity which makes the modern fop, hideous as he is, a favorite exercise of the modern draughtsman; that element which Mr. Max Beerbohm has admirably expressed in speaking of 'certain congruities of dark cloth and the rigid perfection of linen.'" The short young man who overtakes his taller friend with "imbecile cheerfulness" is introduced as Auberon Quin. He had "an appearance compounded of a baby and an owl. His round head, round eyes, seemed to have been designed by nature playfully with a pair of compasses. His flat dark hair and preposterously long frock-coat gave him something of the look of a child's 'Noah.' When he entered a room of strangers, they mistook him for a small boy, and wanted to take him on their knees, until he spoke. . . ." So far, a Max caricature of Max, but the sentence continues, snipping the bond of likeness: "until he spoke, when they perceived that a boy would have been more intelligent."

25. An observation of Christopher Hollis, *The Mind of Chesterton* (London: Hollis & Charter, 1970), p. 111. Most critical studies of the book are unconcerned with the Max Beerbohm connection: Lawrence J. Clipper, *G. K. Chesterton* (New York: Twayne, 1974), pp. 126-29; Lynette Hunter, "A Reading of *The Napoleon of Notting Hill*," *Chesterton Review* 3, 1976, pp. 118-28; Joseph A. Quinn, "Eden and the New Jerusalem: A Reading of *The Napoleon of Notting Hill*," *Chesterton Review* 3, 1976, pp. 230-39; Garry Wills, *Chesterton: Man and Mask* (New York: Sheed & Ward, 1961), pp. 104-7.

William Blissett

Now, it is true, these friends prove to be unreliable judges of intelligence, and Auberon will hold his own with them in his distinctive brand of nonsense; nevertheless, not even the heartiest and least aesthetic of Max's acquaintances could ever have thought his conversation childish or have compared his room to an amethyst and himself to a turnip inside it.[26] This must be a signal by Chesterton not to make too much of the Beerbohm likeness —just as he is later to insist that Father Brown is English, clumsy, nondescript, to distance him from that deft and distinguished Irishman, Father O'Connor, with his "vocalic pulchritude."[27]

Max's gravitational field, however, though tiny, was powerful, and Quin soon takes on his elegance and aloofness, all turnips forgotten. Auberon's speech from the throne is pure Max from its opening acceptance of advancing years: His Majesty explained that "now old age was creeping upon him, he proposed to devote his remaining strength to bringing about a keener sense of local patriotism in the various municipalities of London. How few of them knew the legends of their own boroughs! How many there were who had never heard of the true origin of the Wink of Wandsworth! What a large proportion of the younger generation in Chelsea neglected to perform the old Chelsea Chuff! Pimlico no longer pumped the Pimlies. Battersea had forgotten the name of Blick." And his uniform to end uniforms! "He wore an extravagantly long frock-coat, a pale-green waistcoat, a very full and *dégagé* black tie, and curious yellow gloves. This was his uniform as Colonel of a regiment of his own creation, the 1st Decadents Green."[28]

The deep resemblance between Auberon and Max, however, is that caught a few years later in the essay "Cockneys and their Jokes":

26. *The Napoleon of Notting Hill With Seven Full-Page Illustrations by W. Graham Robertson and a Map of the Seat of War* (London: John Lane, 1904), pp. 26, 30, 75-76.
27. The phrase "vocalic pulchritude" is applied by the poet and artist David Jones to Fr. O'Connor, who received him into the Roman Catholic Church as he had received G. K. C.--see *The Kensington Mass* (London: Agenda Editions, 1975), p. 7.
28. *Napoleon of Notting Hill*, p. 209.

I remember that Mr. Max Beerbohm (who has every merit except democracy) attempted to analyse the jokes at which the mob laughs. He divided them into three sections: jokes about bodily humiliations, jokes about things alien, such as foreigners, and jokes about bad cheese. Mr. Max Beerbohm thought he understood the first two forms; but I am not so sure that he did. In order to understand vulgar humour it is not enough to be humorous. One must also be vulgar, as I am.[29]

A sympathetic character who is not democratic, a humorous character whose humor is not Chestertonian—even Chesterton had to stretch, to expand, to imagine such a being; and the happy meeting with Max made it possible. And yet at the end of the story, when Adam Wayne and Auberon Quin, the pure fanatic and the pure satirist, depart together, it is not really G. K. C. and Max but the two personalities in Chesterton's own ample frame who go forth.

There is such profusion and plenty in Chesterton that his readers feel free to pocket windfalls, but his critics are obliged to pick up after him. That is what I propose to do now with the remainder of his more interesting mentions of Max, along with some places in his writing where Max may have been on his mind. The result may be a bit miscellaneous, but, hang it, Chesterton is miscellaneous or he is nothing. No chronological unfolding of interest is discernible: instead, I offer a fourfold consideration: (1) G. K. C. as it were looking back with Max at earlier periods —the Regency, the Victorian Age, the Nineties; (2) G. K. C. looking at Max's caricatures; (3) G. K. C. casually reading or remembering passages in Max's writings; and (4) G. K. C. reading Max with critical attention.

29. G. K. Chesterton, *All Things Considered* (London: Methuen, 1908), pp. 12-13. Max shot off an amusing and prompt reply, in *Last Theatres*, Rupert Hart-Davis, ed. (London: Hart-Davis, 1970), p. 355, and, after a year, returned to the subject (conceding G. K. C.'s main point): "Mr. Chesterton once chid me, in a brilliant essay, for not cherishing in my heart the ideal of democracy. It is quite true that I don't believe at all firmly in (what has always been to Mr. Chesterton a dark and mystical reality) the wisdom of the people. I would not stake sixpence on the people's capacity for governing itself, and not a penny on its capacity for governing me" (496).

William Blissett

In the mid-1920s Chesterton looked at the period that Max (and Thackeray before him) had made his own—the Regency. The essay "On Bath" (1925) is appreciative enough though not particularly high spirited: it praises Beau Nashe for his order that no swords be worn in Bath, which is more in keeping with Max's pacific nature than with Chesterton's own comically bellicose love of swords and sword-sticks. His essay for the Royal Society of Literature (1926) had for subject George the Fourth, who had been the first to encourage the society—"a man who had the makings of a very fine, because very free, patron of letters; for in his youth he loved not only literature, but liberty," but was broken and died as a man when he became king. Though he says nothing about clothes and little about style, Chesterton in assessing the moral worth of the man is closer to Max than to Thackeray. Once, by the way, he takes issue with Max by recalling that Thackeray's father, a man of the Regency, had with a chuckle recommended that the boy read Smollett's *Peregrine Pickle,* that rowdy and unimproving novel: "Even a modern so steeped in the eighteenth century as Mr. Max Beerbohm has described the typical papa of a generation who might well have been that of this papa, as a gloomy and ponderous person who talked to his children about nothing but Hell."[30]

Within the Victorian Age it was the 1880s that occasioned one of Max's most Maximilian sentences, the mild disclaimer that "to give an accurate and exhaustive account of that period would need a far less brilliant pen than mine."[31] True, he could never have allowed himself the ample scope of Chesterton's Dickens essays or his *Victorian Age in Literature* (where G. K. C.'s pen is quite brilliant enough to give his publisher the shivers), though by implication the deft drawings and their amusing captions in Max's *Rossetti and his Circle* comprise an excellent and indispensable critical and historical comment on the later Victorian

30. "On Bath," in *Generally Speaking* (London: Methuen, 1928), pp. 118-23; "The Romance of a Rascal," in *The Common Man* (New York: Sheed & Ward, 1950), p. 43. [The R. S. L. essay, which is not quoted, is sufficiently identified in the text].
31. *Works and More,* p. 46.

decades. Chesterton likewise could never have created Enoch Soames, the quintessential decadent poet of Max's *Seven Men*. I am afraid he would have come down hard on poor Enoch and missed some of the absurdity and most of the pathos, for he observed that Robert Louis Stevenson escaped the world of Enoch Soames as from a city of the dead — this being perhaps the last, and least, example of Chesterton's melodramatization of the Nineties.[32]

One of the funniest sentences in his high-spirited romance, *The Flying Inn* (1914), is this: "Lady Enid Wimpole still overwhelmed her earnest and timid face with a tremendous costume, that was more a procession than a dress. It looked rather like the funeral procession of Aubrey Beardsley." Max, who was an exact contemporary of Aubrey, knew him, and felt the anguish of his early death, could never have written so; Chesterton seems a whole generation removed, not just two years younger.[33]

Like Max, Chesterton met Swinburne "only once, upon a sort of privileged embassy; and such impressions may easily be illusions." When, severally, they met him, late in the poet's life, he was (to quote Chesterton) "a sort of god in a temple, who could only be approached through a high priest. I had a long conversation with Watts-Dunton and then a short conversation with Swinburne. Swinburne was quite gay and skittish, though in a manner that affected me strangely as spinsterish; but he had charming manners and especially the courtesy of consistent cheerfulness. But Watts-Dunton, it must be admitted, was very serious indeed. It is said that he made the poet his religion; but what struck me as odd, even at the time, was that his religion seemed to consist largely of preserving and protecting the poet's irreligion. He thought it essential that no great man should be contaminated with Christianity." The brief account concludes with a vigorous restatement of the argument that Swinburne's pantheism is incompatible with his revolutionary fervor. The contrast with Max's

32. *Robert Louis Stevenson* (London: Hodder and Stoughton, 1927), p. 110.

33. *The Flying Inn* (New York: Garden City, 1914), p. 123. Max's tribute to Beardsley on the occasion of his death was published in 1898 and reprinted in *A Variety of Things* (London: Heinemann, 1928), pp. 151-62.

celebrated account of his visit to "Number 2, The Pines" is in-
structive: Max's whole desire is to catch Swinburne at home,
Chesterton's to catch him out.

No subject of a caricature by Max could long remain unaware of it. Friends would flock to say, at the same time, that no
likeness existed and that the caricaturist was merciless. We know
from casual references that G. K. C. looked at examples of Max's
art. Chaucer, he says, "like Matthew Arnold in Max's caricature,
was not at all times wholly serious" (slightly misquoting the caption, from memory).[34] Again, in an essay "The False Photog-
rapher," he contrasts the blandness of a photograph of a certain
unnamed poet (surely John Davidson) with the strangeness of
his appearance in the flesh, and continues:

> I happen to possess a book of Mr. Max Beerbohm's caricatures,
> one of which depicts the unfortunate poet in question. To say it
> represents an utterly incredible hobglobin is to express in faint and
> inadequate language the license of its sprawling lines. The
> authorities thought it strictly safe and scientific to circulate the
> poet's photograph. They would have clapped me in an asylum if I
> had asked them to circulate Max's caricature. But the caricature
> would have been far more likely to find the man.[35]

Chesterton accepts by implication the extreme stylization and distortion seen in Max's caricatures of Le Gallienne or Pinero when,
in "The Man in the Passage," he writes: "His face was somewhat
square, his jaw was square, his shoulders were square, even his
jacket was square. Indeed, in the wild school of caricature then
current, Mr. Max Beerbohm had represented him as a proposition in the fourth book of Euclid."[36]

Of particular interest are evidences of concurrence in judgment between the two. Max's remark that "Whistler really

34. G. K. C., *Chaucer* (London: Faber, 1932), p. 110.
35. *A Miscellany of Man* (London: Methuen, 1912), p. 199. Max's caricature of Davidson appeared in *A Book of Caricatures* (1907) and is reproduced
in J. G. Riewald, ed. *Beerbohm's Literary Caricatures* (Hamden, Connecticut:
Archon Books, 1977), p. 165.
36. G. K. C., *The Wisdom of Father Brown* (New York: Macaulay, 1914),
p. 92.

regarded Whistler as his greatest work of art" strikes G. K. C. as an "extraordinarily sensible and sincere critique." He can pay serious tribute to Max as one "whose fine and classic criticism is full of those shining depths that many mistake for shallowness." As late as the *Irish Impressions* he admits to learning from him:

> But I think it is true, as Mr. Max Beerbohm once suggested to me in connection with Mr. Shaw himself, that there is a residual perversity in the Irishman, which comes after and not before the analysis of a question. There is at the last moment a cold impatience with the intellect, an irony which returns on itself and rends itself; the subtlety of the suicide.[37]

Here they share—Max first, then G. K. C.—an insight not only into Shaw but into such Irish intellectuals as J. M. Synge and Stephen Dedalus, Flann O'Brien and Samuel Beckett.

As well thinking *with* Max, Chesterton also thought *about* him. The contrast, in *Heretics* (1905), between the "humane aestheticism" of Max and the "cruel aestheticism" of W. E. Henley.[38] In the same year Chesterton wrote this:

> Mr. Max Beerbohm in one of his most delightful and absurd essays has denounced the fire brigade as a band of vandals who destroy a "fair thing." He has threatened to start an opposition fire brigade whose pipes shall be filled not with water but with oil. Nero was only Max made serious; Nero was only Max without his good nature; Nero was only Max in action.[39]

In the following year he observed about wits like Whistler and humorists like Max—"whose humour was so dainty and delicate as to become a kind of topsy-turvy transcendentalism" —that "these great wits and great humorists had one genuine defect— they could not laugh."[40] (I am very much afraid that by laugh he meant belly-laugh.)

37. *Heretics* (London: Lane, 1960), p. 245; *Stevenson*, p. 140; *Irish Impressions* (London: Collins, 1920), pp. 106-7.

38. *Heretics*, p. 293.

39. "The Voice of Shelley" (1905), in *The Apostle and the Wild Ducks* (London: Paul Elek, 1975), p. 138.

40. "W. W. Jacobs" (1906), in *A Handful of Authors* (New York: Sheed & Ward, 1953), p. 28.

The slight acerbity toward Max that was part of Chesterton's profound distrust and fear of the Nineties ethos wanes in his later writings, as in this high-spirited ironic defense of the somewhat conventionally Bohemian unconventionality of Robert Louis Stevenson's manner and dress:

> Everybody talks as if Stevenson had been not only conspicuous but quite unique in this sort of vanity. Everybody seems to assume that among the artists of his time he was entirely alone in his affectation. Contrasting in this respect with the humdrum respectability of Oscar Wilde, notable as the very reverse of the evangelical meekness of Jimmy Whistler, standing out as he does against the stodgy chapel-going piety of Max Beerbohm, having none of the cheery commonplaces of Aubrey Beardsley or the prosaic self-effacement of Richard Le Gallienne, he naturally aroused attention by the slightest deviation into oddity of dandyism; things notoriously so unpopular among the decadents of the "nineties."[41]

And yet, much as Chesterton enjoyed engaging, even sparring with Max, they cannot be regarded as rival essayists. Though he wrote hundreds, Chesterton often refers to the familiar essay in a tone of estrangement, most clearly in "An Apology for Buffoons" (1928), where he distinguishes writers who say "I believe" from writers who say "one does feel"—the latter being the more egotistical because they assume that their readers will be interested not in the subject but in the essayist. "All my articles and . . . none of my articles are essays," he asserts and goes on to parody a vacuous, though "light and delicate" essay, belonging in the world (though not the neighborhood) of Max. Chesterton's sort of writer, and Shaw's too, and yes, the raucous Mencken's, "deals with big things noisily and the other with small things quietly. But there is more of the note of superiority in the man who always treats of things smaller than himself than the man who always treats of things greater than himself."[42]

Having owned to the charge of being something of a

41. G. K. C., *Robert Louis Stevenson* (London: Hodder and Stoughton, 1927), pp. 88-89.
42. *The Well and the Shadows* (London: Sheed & Ward, 1938), pp. 16-19.

demagogue and something of a buffoon, Chesterton concludes thus:

> I do not really mean, of course, that the essayist is an egoist in any selfish sense. Nobody in the world, I imagine, gets more good than I do out of good essays like those of Mr. Max Beerbohm or Mr. E. V. Lucas or Mr. Robert Lynd. I only ask, in all serious-ness, that they should understand the necessities of our sort of self-assertion as well as recognizing the existence of their own. And I do ask them to believe that when we try to make our ser-mons and speeches more or less amusing, it is for the very simple and even modest reason that we do not see why the audience should listen unless it is more or less amused. Our mode of speech is conditioned by the fact that it really is what some have fanci-fully supposed the function of speech to be; something addressed by somebody to somebody else. It has of necessity all the vices and vulgarities attaching to a speech that really is a speech and not a soliloquy.[43]

So Chesterton holds his own; and if Max's satire is, in Oscar Wilde's phrase, a silver dagger, G. K. C.'s swinging sword-stick has its own effectiveness. There is something playful about both weapons, and both of these gentle, playful men refrained, most of the time, from using them to stab or bludgeon their adver-saries.

Max wields his silver dagger even when most he appears a mild essayist. He had that first requisite of a theatrical reviewer, unkindness, so that his quite frequent words of praise and en-couragement are not dulled by a tone of too easy approbation. Poor Pinero can never have quite recovered from the examina-tion, the dissection, the vivisection of his style,[44] and Max's scorn-ful dismissal of the sentimental religiosity of Jerome K. Jerome's play *The Passing of the Third Floor Back* (where a nameless, Christlike figure, challenged to identify himself, simply holds out his arms) is quite final—so corrosive indeed that it seeps through to, and devours, a little soft spot at the end of *The Man Who*

43. "On Essays," in *Come to Think of It* (London: Macmillan, 1932), pp. 1-5.
44. "Mr. Pinero's Literary Style" (Oct. 24, 1903), in *Around Theatres* (New York: Taplinger, 1969), pp. 286-90.

William Blissett

Was Thursday.[45] His lifelong rejection of Kipling amounted almost to a vendetta, and he once deplored the insipidity of Alice
Meynell's essays in an article understandably not reprinted. He
was, however, like Oscar Wilde and unlike Whistler, the sort of
wit who would rather keep his friend and lose his jest than keep
his jest and lose his friend. He certainly kept his friends, and
while some, like Chesterton, were easy to hold on to, others, like
Belloc, could be combative to the point of orneriness. He exclaimed to S. N. Behrman about Chesterton and Belloc, "They
had blind spots, but they were delightful men. Such enormous
gusto, you know, such gaiety, and feeling for life." And the liking
was reciprocal. The Chestertons enjoyed a happy visit with the
Beerbohms at Rapallo; and Evelyn Waugh, recalling his own first
meeting with Max, recalls also "how joyously Belloc and Baring
acclaimed him!"[46] Max went along cheerfully enough with *The
Napoleon of Notting Hill*, but on another occasion he and G. K. C.
engaged in something more like a collaboration. In 1909 the
caricaturist Francis Carruthers Gould (some thirty years senior
to his two young friends) drew himself playing the flute. Max
"(after F. C. G.)" drew his dapper self in the same album, also
tootling a flute, and G. K. C. on the back of the Gould drawing
completed what he called "the Great Flute Series," showing himself as wildly undapper and blowing his flute to kingdom come.
It must have been quite a lark.[47]

A somewhat puzzling parallel, or cross purpose, occurs in
1907, when Chesterton takes issue with Henry James's story "The
Turn of the Screw"—"one of the most powerful things ever writ-

45. "A Deplorable Affair" (Sept. 5, 1908), in *Around Theatres*, pp. 516-
19. *Thursday* had appeared in February of that year; at the end, Sunday answers
a similar question similarly.
46. S. N. Behrman, *Portrait of Max* (New York: Random House, 1960),
p. 280; Evelyn Waugh, "Max Beerbohm--A Lesson in Manners" (1956), in J.
G. Riewald, ed. *The Surprise of Excellence* (Hamden, Connecticut: Archon,
1974), p. 93.
47. Anton C. Masin, "The Great Flute Series--Chesterton, Beerbohm and
Gould," *Chesterton Review* 5, 1978, pp. 42-47. In 1919, they contributed
prefatory notes, G. K. C. "About the Poems" and Max Beerbohm "About the
Drawings," to Captain Lance Sieveking's *Dressing Gowns and Glue*, with illustrations by John Nash (London: Cecil Palmer & Hayward, 1918).

ten, and . . . one of the things about which it is most permissible to doubt whether it ought ever to have been written at all." He concludes, "I will approve the thing as well as admire it if he will write another tale just as powerful about two children and Santa Claus."[48] This, I say, is puzzling, since Max as long ago as 1896 had thought of writing a parody of James on a Christmas theme in which all mention of Christmas would be avoided, and in 1906 had published the set of parodies that were to become *A Christmas Garland*—and these included "The Mote in the Middle Distance," which already took up G. K. C.'s challenge to the master, and "Christmas Day," an exceptionally deft parody of Chesterton himself.[49] To complicate matters further, sometime later (remembering Max but forgetting his own challenge to James, which must have been partly serious) Chesterton appreciatively remarked that "only Max could imagine Henry James writing about Christmas."[50]

This should bring us to *The Christmas Garland*, but something more should first be said about Max's caricatures. There are eight of Chesterton alone and a further eight in which he figures along with others, few or many. The earliest of these (1904) shows "Mr. G. K. Chesterton giving the world a kiss." G. K. C. and Frances went to see it in the Carfax Gallery, and she wrote in her diary, "It's more like Thackeray, very funny though."[51] Max returned to G. K. C. in 1907 and 1911; and in 1912 he drew the famous caricature of Chesterton giving an after-dinner speech, his shirt showing under his waistcoat, his girth a whole terrestrial globe.[52] This was followed in 1913 by a similarly conceived portrait featuring a watchchain stretched across a vast arc of body, and in 1925 (as one of a set) the encounter of

48. G. K. C., "The Red Angels," first published in *The Daily News*, Dec. 21, 1907, collected in *Tremendous Trifles* (London: Methuen, 1909), pp. 106-7.

49. For the history of Max's parodies of Henry James, see John Felstiner, *The Lies of Art—Max Beerbohm's Parody and Caricature* (London: Gollancz, 1973), pp. 142-56.

50. *The Victorian Age in Literature* (London: Butterworth, 1931), p. 231.

51. Ward, p. 169.

52. Reproduced in Felsteiner, p. 170.

the Old and the Young Self.[53] The Young Self (astonishingly like the photograph of Chesterton at the age of sixteen, but how could Max have seen it?) says (and here again Max's caption is as careful and as satiric as his drawing):

> Oh yes, I drank some beer only the other day, and rather liked it, and of course the Crusades were glorious. But all this about English public life being honeycombed with corruption, and about the infallibility of the Pope, and the sacramental qualities of beer and the soul-cleansing powers of Burgundy, and the immaculate conception of France, and the determination of the Jews to enslave us, and the instant need that we should get straight back into the Middle Ages, and—

To which the Old Self replies, "Well, you haven't met Belloc."

There is another sketch and a drawing, undated, showing him full-length, gesticulating, in evening dress, but in the remaining caricatures G. K. C. shares his space with others. Some of these are large assemblies or delegations, such as the one where Max's subjects, or victims, formally beg him to lay off: G. K. C. here is placed at the back, being so large and so tall. In two, both 1909, he shares the page with Bernard Shaw. "Leaders of Thought" is an encounter of sphere and tangent.[54] "Mr. Shaw's Sortie" shows a globular, belted G. K. C. behind a wall (reminiscent in shape of Humpty Dumpty though in no danger of falling) speaking the concluding words of his book on Shaw. In the foreground, George Bernard Shaw twice over, in two operatic costumes—Shaw in a dancer's tutu, knock-kneed, carrying a spear and tooting a megaphone, and Shaw as Mephisto, looking the less bizarre and more reliable of the two. What are the vibrant words of peroration that accompany this dégringolade? "But this shall be written of our time: that when the Spirit who Denies besieged the last citadel, blaspheming life itself, there were some —there was one especially—whose voice was heard, and whose spear was not broken."

53. Reproduced in Riewald, *Literary Caricatures*, pp. 118-19.

54. Hart-Davis, *Catalogue*, reproduces "Deputation," p. 183, and "Mr. Shaw's Sortie," p. 201; "Landers of Thought" is reproduced in Dudley Bartor, *G. K. Chesterton* (London: Constable, 1979), p. 168. In "Sortie," what Sir Rupert Hart-Davis describes as "dressed as Pantaloon" I would call a ballerina's costume.

Appearing in *The Book of Caricature* (1907) is "Mr. Hilaire Belloc, striving to win Mr. Gilbert Chesterton over from the errors of Geneva." Short, burly Belloc stands on a chair to harangue the seated, grotesquely obese Chesterton; Belloc's tankard, full, is in his left hand; Chesterton is emptying his, the features of his face drawn into it.[55] Not a well-aimed caricature, for Chesterton at no time assented to the "errors of Geneva," not a kind one either, and the unkindest details are the feet. Belloc's are neat enough, but Chesterton's! In a quick poll let us recall Max's literary caricatures voting with their feet, beginning with the famous one of Oscar Wilde speaking the name of Rossetti to an audience of earnest Americans: his feet are admirable, theirs deplorable. The neatly shod include Byron, Browning, Hardy, Whistler, Lytton Strachey, Conrad, George Moore, and of course, preeminently, Max himself. The clumsy-footed include Burns, Whitman, Ibsen, Shaw, Hauptmann, Maeterlinck, the hated Kipling, the likable Chesterton. Oddly enough, Anthony Asquith recalls the smallness in proportion of Chesterton's hands and feet, and photographs confirm this. It is as if Max judged G. K. C. as the sort of person who should have big feet.

To return, finally, from caricature to parody. Max, in an essay, "A Morris for May Day,"[56] refers to the style of Chesterton as a "prance," as "dancing the Chesterton." Max's own great parody, published the year before as "Christmas Day" and included in *A Christmas Garland* as "Some Damnable Errors about Christmas" catches the cadence of this jolly Chestertonian girandole:

I look for the time when we shall wish one another a Merry Christmas every morning; when roast turkey and plum-pudding shall be the staple of our daily dinner, and the holly shall never be taken down from the walls, and every one will always be kissing every one else under the mistletoe.

55. Reproduced in Riewald, pp. 112-13. Father John O'Connor, *Father Brown on Chesterton* (London: Frederick Muller, 1937), p. 45, recalls a Max cartoon of Belloc and Chesterton, with Max's accompanying words ". . . that scoffing was true worship, and the Yah! of the rude boy in the street is but an act of reverence, being but the first syllable of the Unutterable Name!"
56. "A Morris for May Day" is included in *Yet Again* (London: Heinemann, 1925), p. 153.

William Blissett

But Max does not simply hit the brightly painted barn door of Chesterton's style and thought, but catches too his sudden modulations into gravity. The idea of Christmas as merely a time of jubilation "never entered the heads of the saints and scholars, the poets and painters, of the Middle Ages. Looking back across the years, they saw in that dark and ungarnished manger only a shrinking woman, a brooding man, and a child born to sorrow."[57] It is Max's greatness as a parodist that he catches the inward elusive virtues of a writer as well as his foibles and tricks and vices of style.

Chesterton's life of ceaseless activity and Max's of almost unbroken leisure impinged on each other from time to time, quite significantly on a few occasions, though one must resist the temptation to exaggerate. Let us put it, and leave it, in a phrase that either friend might casually and without embarrassment say to the other: "You do me good."

57. *A Christmas Garland* (London: Heinemann, 1950), pp. 54, 52.

The Centrality of *Perelandra* to Lewis's Theology

Evan K. Gibson

Although Lewis says he wrote *Perelandra* for his "co-religionists" and seems to have regarded it as his favorite story, it is not always realized how much of Christian theology he put into it. The book reveals, on a close reading, many of the concepts which Lewis believed to be central to Christian belief. To the common reader, perhaps, it is a counter-analogue of the Fall — a "what might have been" if Adam and Eve had risen to heroic heights and resisted the power of the Tempter. The Edenic islands, the innocent, newly created woman, the satanically subtle Un-man seem to be a reenactment of the Genesis story with a happy ending — a paradise regained without being lost.

But, of course, Lewis says specifically in the story that this is not his intent. In spite of the similarities, *Perelandra* is not Genesis revisited (164). It was written, however, during the same period as his *Preface to Paradise Lost*, and, inevitably, the stories overlap. As I have written elsewhere, Eve's temptation is threefold, and so is Tinidril's, and the three chapters of the Perelandrian Queen's ordeal cover the same ground as does that in the third chapter of Genesis (Gibson 58-62).

EVAN K. GIBSON is professor emeritus of English at Seattle Pacific University and the author of C. S. Lewis: Spinner of Tales.

Evan K. Gibson

But what I would like to consider here is not the story's similarities with the biblical account, or, for that matter, with the Miltonic account, but rather its relationship to the body of doctrine which we associate with Lewis as a writer of apologetics.

I have divided the discussion into four concepts to be found in *Perelandra:* the nature of the occult, the nature of sin, the nature of grace, and the nature of the universe. I am using the word occult in a specialized sense which the dictionary does not entirely support — the world of supernatural evil.

Perhaps my best defense of the word is that Lewis uses it in this unfavorable sense in *Surprised by Joy.* He speaks of the lust of the occult in discussing the period after he had given up his childhood faith. His first exposure to the black light of occultism was when he came under the influence of the matron at the school in Malvern which he calls Chartres. He describes her as "floundering in the mazes of Theosophy, Rosicrucianism, Spiritualism; the whole Anglo-American Occultist tradition" (62). The influence on the young schoolboy was, he says, something like the lust of the body, a fatal power which focused all desires upon the preternatural. Here was the first strike of the cobra which was to inject its poison into his imagination and trouble his spirit from time to time in the years of his apostasy.

The serpent raises its swaying head again at Bookham when the granite face of his materialistic philosophy was cracked by the devastating shock created by reading the prose of William Butler Yeats. To his astonishment he discovered that here was a responsible non-Christian writer who believed in magic, who believed that a supernatural world actually existed — a world something like that which his poetry and drama had reported. Then reading Maeterlinck he discovered another respected modern writer, and not a Christian, who took spiritualism, theosophy, and pantheism seriously — who, as Lewis says, "believed in a world behind, or around, the material world" (*Surprised by Joy* 165).

The lust of the occult was again aroused in him, and he tells us that he became a willing candidate to enter the dark doors of magic. "If there had been in the neighborhood," he says, "some elder person who dabbled in dirt of the Magical kind (such have

126

a good nose for potential disciples) I might now be a Satanist or a maniac" (*Surprised by Joy* 165-66). But no such teacher appeared, and incapacity plus other influences such as the discovery of George MacDonald's *Phantastes* led him away from the black pit.

Later, during his days at the University, he twice attended gatherings in the apartments of William Butler Yeats, who was then living at Oxford. But his letters seem to indicate that he was not impressed. At least, other influences soon turned the lure of the occult to fear and nausea. Probably most important was the horrifying experience of watching a friend go violently mad—a friend who had muddled his mind with theosophy, yoga, and spiritualism.

The friend was Dr. John Askins, the brother of Lewis's surrogate mother, Mrs. Janie Moore. Lewis tells, in *Surprised by Joy*, of holding him "while he kicked and wallowed on the floor, screaming out that devils were tearing him and that he was that moment falling down into Hell" (192). The experience had a tremendous effect upon Lewis. Almost in terror he wrote to Arthur Greeves, "Keep clear of introspection, of brooding, of spiritualism, of everything eccentric. Keep to work and sanity and open air — to the cheerful & the matter of fact side of things. We hold our mental health by a thread & nothing is worth risking it for. Above all beware of excessive day dreaming, of seeing yourself in the center of a drama, of self pity, and as far as possible, of fears" (*They Stand Together* 292).

As he says in *Surprised by Joy*, this "almost panic-stricken flight, from all that sort of romanticism which had hither-to been the chief concern of my life" caused him to determine to stay on the beaten track, the center of the road (191). What he calls "the squalid nightmare of magic" seems never again to have cast its hypnotic spell upon him.

His aversion to the introspective is further illustrated in his remarks to Arthur in 1930 after starting to read Jacob Boehme's *The Signature of All Things.* He found, at first, the writings of this Christian mystic helpful and urged Arthur to get and read *The Supersensual Life.* But when he got to the *Signatura Rerum*, which deals with the mystery of creation, he found it not only difficult but also frightening. He was a very immature theist at the time

—in between his capitulation to God in 1929 and his acceptance of Christ's claims in 1931. Of the second chapter of the *Signatura* he says, "There is something really dreadful" in it. And he makes an affirmation which, I think, is significant in understanding Lewis's contribution to apologetics rather than to devotional literature.

> In the meantime, I wish to record that it has been about the biggest shaking up I've got from a book since I first read *Phantastes*. It is not such a pleasant experience as *Phantastes*, and if it continues to give me the same feeling when I understand more, I shall give it up. No fooling about for me: and I keep one hand firmly gripped round the homely & simple things. But it is a real book: i.e. it's not like a book at all, but like a thunderclap. Heaven defend us—what things there are knocking about the world! (*They Stand Together* 328)

Such was his reaction to a Christian mystic. I am not suggesting, of course, that Lewis regarded Boehme's writings as belonging in the occultist tradition but that he seems to shy away from anything introspective or metaphysical.

As the Green and Hooper biography points out, Lewis much preferred the solid theological work to the purely devotional book. He did not like Brother Lawrence's *The Practice of the Presence of God*. He called it "a little too unctuous." And later he wrote, "I tend to find the doctrinal books often more helpful in devotion than the devotional books" (Green and Hooper 114-15).

Lewis's advice to Arthur, "Keep clear of introspection, of brooding"—as a reaction to John Askins's insanity—probably has a bearing upon his dislike of books which turn one's attention to the inner life. The theological works allowed one to "keep to work and sanity and open air." If we are right in making the harrowing experience of observing his friend's madness a traumatic and attitude-changing point in his life, we can, perhaps, give roots to Owen Barfield's observation that at about this time Lewis "deliberately ceased to take any interest in himself except as a kind of spiritual alumnus taking his moral finals." He concludes that "what began as a deliberate choice became at length . . . an ingrained and effortless habit of soul. Self-knowledge, for him, had come to mean recognition of his own weaknesses and shortcomings and nothing more. Anything beyond that he sharply suspected, both in himself and others, as a symptom of spiritual megalomania" (xvi). Barfield says that from then onward he had the impression of two Lewises—a friend and the memory of a friend—that is, that Lewis deliberately turned away from his inner self—that his literary personality was "willed"—not insincere, but a determination to turn his attention to something more interesting than his own inner life.

Such a shift in interest does not mean, of course, a denial of the reality of the supernatural world of evil. Although a world to be avoided, it was a world to be taken into account. He makes it clear in *The Problem of Pain* that his view of Satan is an orthodox one and lays the basis for his introduction of "the Bent One" in the space trilogy by referring to "several Dominical, Pauline, and Johannine utterances—I mean the story that man was not the first creature to rebel against the Creator, but that some older and mightier being long since became apostate and is now the emperor of darkness and (significantly) the Lord of this world." That such a power exists, he says specifically, "I myself believe" (122-23).

And so, although the refrigerium of *The Great Divorce* is fantasy and the folklore humor of *The Screwtape Letters* is not meant to be taken seriously, Lewis's general treatment of the world of supernatural evil should not be regarded as simply employed for literary purposes. The possible influence of the preternatural world upon the human spirit he illustrates in *That Hideous Strength* with Wither and Frost, the one a shapeless and distended ruin and the other an absolute zero of concentrated denial of reality.

In *Perelandra* the damage to Weston's spirit which communion with the demonic world has done is apparent almost immediately upon his arrival in Venus. The subtle change in his personality which Ransom is aware of, the defective logic, the senile, cackling laugh all are precursors of the devastating possession which destroys him. The mighty spirit which takes charge of Weston's body, thereafter called the Un-man, may not be a referent of anything which Lewis believed could actually happen.

Certainly all New Testament accounts of demon possession suggest a lack of control rather than the cold calculation with which the Un-man attacks the innocence of the Lady of the Planet of Love. We are always on shaky ground when we attempt to find what an author really believed by studying his imaginative material.

But behind the temptation of Tinidril and behind the barrage of evil spirits through which the narrator goes at the beginning of the book is the principle that we live in a hostile environment. And the Macrobes who control and finally destroy Wither and Frost, the machinations of Screwtape and Wormwood which fail to destroy their intended victim, illustrate Lewis's conviction that of vital import to the human soul is the Pauline affirmation that "we wrestle not against flesh and blood but against principalities, against powers, against the rulers of the darkness of this world, against spiritual wickedness in high places" (Eph. 6:12).

As we would expect, there is nothing original in Lewis's definition of sin. He places it succinctly in the mouth of George MacDonald in *The Great Divorce*: "There are only two kinds of people in the end: those who say to God, 'Thy will be done,' and those to whom God says, in the end, 'Thy will be done'" (66-67). The heart of the matter is in the will. Whether it is the big ghost who wants his rights, the possessive wife who wants her husband, or the apostate bishop who has lost the desire for truth, each ghost from the Grey City demonstrates that he or she had willed the condition that held them in bondage. Most of them had shaped their own character by their choices long before we meet them in *The Great Divorce*. We also see the end result of the belligerent will in Dick Devine, whom the Oyarsa of Malacandra calls only a talking animal. Long before he had become Lord Feverstone in *That Hideous Strength*, choice had poured his character into concrete.

In *Perelandra* Tinidril illustrates the unfolding blossom of her awareness of free choice by describing the momentary reluctance to receive the fruit Maleldil provided when her imagination had already pictured another fruit as the one she desired. Ransom uses this observation to explain the sin in the Bent One — the eldil who clung to the good desired and refused the good given until good became evil. And so Satan is also one to whom God must say in the end, "Thy will be done."

Weston illustrates the centripetal force of a self-seeking will that is so inward turning that its egoism is blind to all outward conditions. Ransom felt that he was in the presence of a monomaniac. Weston showed no interest, upon arrival in Venus, in the fate of his spaceship or his return to earth. He seemed to have traveled thirty million miles in search of conversation: ". . . tense, tedious and inescapable, the scientist pursued his fixed idea" (100).

In *Mere Christianity* Lewis describes pride as the great sin, "the complete anti-God state of mind" (96). And he says that it is essentially competitive. It is the desire to be better than anyone else which often drives a man to make more money than he can use or a woman to collect more admirers than she has time for. The proud man regards anyone who is more powerful or richer or more clever than he as his rival and enemy. Weston displays his megalomania by telling Ransom that he himself is a man set apart. He has been guided and chosen. "I know now," he says, "that I am the greatest scientist the world has yet produced" (*Perelandra* 105).

But even more significant are the religious implications. Lewis points out that to the proud man God is the final enemy. The Creator is always infinitely superior to the creature. But a god who can be reduced from the Creator of the universe to its soul —to a pantheistic concept of life as inherent in matter—is much more manageable to the proud man. And this seems to be Weston's position, calling the divine spirit at one time "the stuff of mind, the unconsciously purposive dynamism," and at another "a great inscrutable Force . . . that can choose its instruments." But if it can choose, it has chosen him. He claims to be the conductor of the central forward pressure of this force—and so there is no distinction between him and the universe. As he says, "I am the Universe. I, Weston, am your God and your Devil" (104, 109). It is at this point, of course, that the disaster overtakes him.

But this leads us to examine Lewis's view of some of the results of sin. We have already noted the deterioration of character in Weston and in that of Wither and Frost. The deterioration of the ghosts of the Grey City is too obvious to need elaboration. But in the Un-man Lewis carries it further. He describes this mighty spirit (apparently Satan himself), with a foot in two worlds, at work to pervert a planet, to turn the course of racial history, as a vast ruin, deteriorated until he now indulges in petty obscenities, rips open frogs, and rings the bark of trees, whose intellect, although still masterful, is only used as a tool to destroy and is not an integral part of the personality.

But no discussion of Lewis's concept of sin would be complete without noting the Un-man's attempt to change to sin the innocence of Tinidril. His initial attempt to get her to fondle in her imagination a forbidden situation—a picture of living on the fixed land—simply as a bit of fiction, would hold out to her the advantages of disobedience. He also suggests that her new knowledge will make her superior to the King, picturing to her the women of earth, who, he claims, are far superior to the men in grasping imaginative possibilities. In each aspect of the temptation the Un-man tries to tarnish her imagination by separating it from reality and stimulating her individual will to act independently. Of course, he fails because there are no holding places in her imagination for a life contrary to Maleldil's will and no ambition for a place superior to her husband or even to her offspring. She thinks with delight that perhaps her daughters will be greater than herself.

The second temptation attempts to lead her will into a deification of her own reason. The attack is very subtle in that the Un-man pretends that the breaking of the command must be the will of Maleldil. It is an unreasonable law; therefore it was meant to be broken. But, of course, his intent is to bring about a willful decision by Tinidril based upon reliance on her own reason. He makes a great deal of the importance of independence —that to be a complete woman she must depend upon herself. Depending upon her reason, he says, is "a great wave you have to go over, that you may become really old [that is, mature] really separate from Him" (*Perelandra* 133). Living on the Fixed Land will establish that independence. It is here, of course, that Ransom makes his first contribution to the contest, effectively answering the Un-man when he points out that a command without apparent reason allows love to respond in naked obedience. In a love relationship one delights in obeying simply because it is commanded. And to this Tinidril immediately responds.

In *Surprised by Joy* Lewis speaks rather disparagingly of wish-fulfillment stories in which the reader enjoys vicariously the successes of the hero. The third temptation of the Un-man is an attempt to arouse in the Queen and Lady Mother of the planet a vicarious experience which will cause her to picture herself as a self-sacrificing heroine, of her own will taking upon herself great deeds for the good of her husband and progeny. Tinidril knew that she was to be the mother of the planet, and the unknown in her future made her vulnerable to any suggestion that life might pass her by — that she might miss some unique opportunity. So it was here that the Un-man made his most potent attack. The stories he tells play upon her fear of lost moments. His aim, of course, is to turn her eyes inward and to build a self-image which she admires so much that she will be willing to shape her own destiny in accordance with that heroic image. The temptation fails because of the selfless character of Tinidril and also because Ransom concludes that the attack is no longer a temptation but a third degree and removes the tempter from the scene. But these central episodes of the story illustrate that Lewis believed that whether temptation enters through the imagination, the reason, or self-centered contemplation, the essence of sin is not so much in the doing as in the decision prior to the act.

Divine grace is frequently defined as the unmerited favor of God — a definition Lewis would not quarrel with. As a characteristic of God's nature, Lewis describes grace in *The Four Loves* by saying that "God, who needs nothing, loves into existence wholly superfluous creatures in order that He may love and protect them" (144). We usually associate divine grace with the atonement, but, although Lewis would agree that that is the greatest illustration we know of this characteristic, he would make grace a much wider web than that which rescued fallen humanity from the results of its own perversity. In fact, he sees it as a golden cord which binds together every creature in God's universe. In his typically analytical method he divides it into three graces: Gift Love, Need Love, and Appreciative Love. Each is a grace given by God, not inherent in human beings. Gift Love, of course, imparts eternal life to the human race through Christ. But Need Love is also a divine grace, for only through it can human need respond in love to the gift of life.

Of Appreciative Love or adoration he says very little. In *The Four Loves* he seems to promise a short discussion of this third grace and then finds that he has nothing to say about it. The last chapter of the book ends rather abruptly with the admission that for this "you must go to my betters" (160). Perhaps here again he felt that the inward or introspective look was an area with more pitfalls than he cared to encounter.

The grace called Gift Love, however, is one which he freely discusses in the apologetic works and illustrates in the fictional ones. Screwtape refuses to accept this ingredient in the divine character but admits that Hell has utterly failed so far to find out the real motive. "What does He stand to make out of them?" he asks in frustration. But he refers scornfully to what he calls "the cock-and-bull story about disinterested love" (97).

The Oyarsa of Malacandra speaks with awe "of more wonders than are known in the whole of heaven" when in the unrecorded conversation in *Out of the Silent Planet* Ransom tells him of the divine grace which reached from Heaven to Golgotha (160). *Perelandra* does not discuss the atonement directly because neither the King nor Queen has had any experience with sin. They do, however, know of the incarnation, the Queen telling Ransom that she knows a reason for the incarnation which she cannot tell him and he knows a reason which he cannot tell her. This statement hints at what Lewis says elsewhere, that perhaps God would have become man even if there had been no Fall.

But, of course, the story is replete with expressions by Tinidril of praise for Maleldil's gifts. The paradisal planet itself is an example of the Gift Love of God, and perhaps the young Queen's rapturous words of delight could be called Appreciative Love. So maybe we could say that Lewis illustrates this third grace even though he does not describe it.

But in addition to the divine grace of Gift Love to human beings and our response in Need Love, Lewis says that on the human level there is also gift love and need love—the love which humans show for the unlovely; the love for lepers, criminals, enemies, morons. This is a grace given whereby humans share the divine Gift Love: "Love Himself working in a man" (*The Four Loves* 146). And he says that we need divine grace also to receive the gift love of others—not the love which we think we deserve, but the human love that is bestowed upon our unloveliness. To respond with need love to this gift love takes grace.

Perelandra's chief contribution to the concept of grace is, perhaps, on this creaturely level—the grace which binds each of us in a web of vicarious debt. The key episode is in the last chapter of the story where Ransom asks the King about his own testing. In response, the King laughs, not a laugh of amusement but of joy. The contagious laugh causes all the others, without knowing why, to join in. Even the assembly of beasts and birds respond with wagging tails and clapping wings. For what the King is about to pronounce is an affirmation which touches them all.

The whole paragraph merits quoting:

> "I know what he is thinking," said the King, looking upon the Queen. "He is thinking that you suffered and strove and I have a world for my reward." Then he turned to Ransom and continued. "You are right," he said, "I know now what they say in your world about justice, and perhaps they say well, for in that world things always fall below justice. But Maleldil always goes above it. All is gift. I am Oyarsa not by His gift alone but by our foster mother's, not by hers alone but by yours, not by yours alone but my wife's —nay, in some sort, by gift of the very beasts and birds. Through many hands enriched with many different kinds of love and labor, the gift comes to me. It is the Law. The best fruits are plucked for each by some hand that is not his own." (241)

Lewis seems to be saying here that the universe is not built upon justice but upon grace. All is gift. In God's economy there are no rights. The merit of the individual is not a consideration, for even from his fellow creatures he receives infinitely more than his merits justify. In *The Great Divorce* the big ghost demanded his rights and finally went back to Hell because that was the only place where rights were handed out. But where Gift Love gives and Need Love receives, "the best fruits are plucked for each by some hand that is not his own."

Which brings me to my last point—which I have rather grandiosely called the nature of the universe. Lewis did not claim to be able to explain the nature of the universe, nor if he could, would I be able to explain his explanation. But one of his most poetic pieces of prose gives us a series of principles of God's creation. I am referring, of course, to what might be called the Hymn of the Great Dance, which appears at the close of the story. The King, Queen, Ransom, and the two tutelary spirits all contribute to the twenty paragraphs, although we cannot always identify the voice. But it would not be improper to call it a hymn, for we are told that the participants contributed "like the parts of a music into which all five of them had entered as instruments" (*Perelandra* 246).

It is important to remember that the statements are about God's creation, not about God's character. These paragraphs are not Lewis's attempt to present a literary theophany. More than once he refers to Lady Julian's vision of God in which God held in his hand a small object something like a nut. And she was told that that was "all that is made." In *The Four Loves* Lewis says that God's main function is not just to run the universe, to be its manager. It is no great matter to God to be its sovereign. At home in "the land of the Trinity" God "is Sovereign of a far greater realm" (144).

And so the twenty paragraphs of praise lay down some principles relative to God as we know God—as Creator and Giver of Grace, which may be among a multitude of other activities. The question, "What was God doing before he created the universe?" Lewis would say, is a moot point, deprived of practical consideration. Possible answers are infinite and unimaginable.

But the hymn has to do with things, from dust to archangels, and the question of what is at the center of the universe. In fact, this passage could be called the Song of the Center. It opens with the statement that the Great Dance is at the center and that it is eternal—not that creation had no beginning, but that each contributor that is produced by the Eternal Creator partakes of his nature. As George MacDonald said, "When a man is one with God, what should he do but live forever" (Lewis, *George MacDonald: an Anthology* 42).

By dance Lewis seems to mean the interlocking and constantly shifting relationship of all created things. Nothing moves at random. All are a part of the pattern and contribute in perfect harmony to the beauty of the whole.

Each contributor is not only eternal but also unique. There are no clones in God's pattern. What might be called the snowflake principle is fundamental to creation. God never repeats himself. Each individual also has a unique place in the universe — a place which no one else can fill, and for which each one was made. As Lewis says in *The Problem of Pain*, "Your place in heaven will seem to be made for you and you alone because you were made for it — made for it stitch by stitch as a glove is made for a hand" (135-36). Uniqueness is a fundamental principle of the universe.

But all are not equal. God's creation is hierarchical. The ground before the Cross may be level, but in the temple of God there are pillars and arches — stones that support and stones that cap the column. Or, as the hymn says, "All the patterns linked and looped together by the unions of a kneeling with a sceptered love" (*Perelandra* 250).

The question might arise, If each one is different and unequal and each place unique, are not some at the periphery, lost in the gloom of far frontiers? Where is the center? And so the Song of the Center answers the question by declaring that all creation rests with God, and God exists completely at every point of the universe, "not some of Him in one place and some in another, but in each place the whole of Maleldil, even in the smallness beyond thought. There is no way out of the centre save into the Bent Will which casts itself into the Nowhere" (*Perelandra* 249).

So, from the dust to the greatest eldil all are at the center. God is not a thinly distributed gas or ocean of existence. All of God exists in the smallest seed, and all of the universe lives within God who is in the seed. Dimensions do not define God.

But all are not only central, but also needful. If all have a place, the pattern would be incomplete without each contributor. All are necessary. "Love me my brothers, for I am infinitely necessary to you and for your delight I was made" (*Perelandra* 250).

And yet over against this principle is the paradox that all is superfluous. Nothing is needed by God—not a grain of dust nor an archangel. God's creation is pure gift and adds nothing to the Creator. Nor do those who have God need anything else, nothing of the rest of creation. "Love me my brothers, for I am infinitely superfluous, and your love shall be like His, born neither of your need nor of my deserving, but a plain bounty" (*Perelandra* 250).

So, Lewis says, the nature of the universe is eternal, unique, unequal, central, needful, and superfluous. But lest we think that he had tied it up neatly in a ribboned package, he adds one more. As a mirror of its Creator the universe is incomprehensible: "Lest if we never met the dark, and the road that leads no whither, and the question to which no answer is imaginable, we should have in our minds no likeness of the Abyss of the Father, into which if a creature drop down his thoughts for ever he shall hear no echo return to him. Blessed, blessed, blessed be He!" (*Perelandra* 251).

Works Cited

Barfield, Owen. Introduction. *Light on C. S. Lewis*. Ed. Jocelyn Gibb. London: Geoffrey Bles, 1965. ix-xxi.

Gibson, Evan K. *C. S. Lewis, Spinner of Tales: a Guide to His Fiction*. Grand Rapids: Eerdmans, 1980.

Green, Roger Lancelyn, and Walter Hooper. *C. S. Lewis: A Biography*. New York: Harcourt Brace Jovanovich, 1974.

Lewis, C. S. *The Four Loves*. London: Geoffrey Bles, 1960.

_____. *George MacDonald: an Anthology*. London: Geoffrey Bles, 1946.

_____. *The Great Divorce*. London: Geoffrey Bles, 1946.

_____. *Mere Christianity*. London: Geoffrey Bles, 1952.

_____. *Out of the Silent Planet*. London: The Bodley Head, 1938.

_____. *Perelandra*. London: The Bodley Head, 1943.

_____. *The Problem of Pain*. London: Geoffrey Bles, 1940.

_____. *The Screwtape Letters*. London: Geoffrey Bles, 1942.

_____. *Surprised by Joy*. London: Geoffrey Bles, 1955.

_____. *They Stand Together: the Letters of C. S. Lewis to Arthur Greeves*. Ed. Walter Hooper. New York: Macmillan, 1979.

III. LIVING THE RIDDLE:
THEIR SOCIAL THOUGHT

G. K. Chesterton,
the Disreputable Victorian

by Alzina Stone Dale

My title, "G. K. Chesterton, the disreputable Victorian," came from a cartoon in the John Bennett Shaw Collection at Notre Dame. Chesterton drew it for the *Juggler* when he was "artist in residence" there. In his drawing there are two groups on the page. At the top a stern, unsmiling Queen Victoria in widow's weeds points a finger at a knock-kneed, messy G. K. Chesterton. Beneath her is the caption "Just Indignation of Queen Victoria." On the lower half of the page, a top-hatted and frock-coated "True Victorian" stalks past "a disreputable author," who is a slinking Chesterton in slouch hat and cape.[1]

The joke—or perhaps the paradox—is that Chesterton was both a disreputable Victorian (by their standards) and a true Victorian (by his own). Not only at Notre Dame when he lectured to students on Victorians and their literature, subjects on which he was an expert, but whenever he considered serious matters—the first and last things, Chesterton knew himself to be a true Mid-Victorian. He was committed all his life to championing the

1. John Bennett Shaw Collection, Catalogue Item #4, University of Notre Dame.

ALZINA STONE DALE is a lecturer and the author of *The Outline of Sanity: A Life of* G. K. *Chesterton* and T. S. Eliot, *The Philosophical Poet.*

Victorian causes of those Victorians who rebelled against the complacency and what he called the "compromise" of the Victorian Age. As he said in *Chaucer*, he felt that "the real vice of the Victorians was that they regarded history as a story that ended well—because it ended with the Victorians" (28).

Superficially, of course, Chesterton's disreputable Victorianism came from his untidy appearance. He was a big, messy man who liked to eat and drink with gusto. Still worse, from the standpoint of Victorian propriety, he laughed at everything, especially himself, in an age whose queen made a habit of Not Being Amused. As any kind of Victorian, Chesterton was describing himself when he wrote "This is the last essential of the Victorian. Laugh at him as a limited man, a moralist, a conventionalist, an opportunist, a formalist. But remember also that he was really a humorist; and may still be laughing at you" (*The Victorian Age* 155).

Chesterton was actually reared to be both a "disreputable" and a true Victorian. His messy habits and bohemian disregard for money and respectability may be attributed to his sharp, clever mother; his old-fashioned liberal principles, his love of Victorian literature, and his sense of humor came from his genial, Pickwickian father.

Other "disreputable" attitudes were his open fondness for Fleet Street and ephemeral journalism instead of academia or the sedate role of a Man of Letters. Another was his social egalitarianism in class-conscious England, which Margaret Canovan called "radical populism." As she pointed out, despite being raised in the urban middle class, Chesterton always had faith in ordinary working people. He combined this belief with an anti-intellectual intellectual's "intense suspicion of metropolitan society, plutocrats, bureaucrats, and intellectuals" (Canovan 5-6). He also disapproved of the "jewel in the crown," or imperialism, which he called a child's game of painting the map red. He claimed he had caught this attitude from learning to sing the songs from Gilbert and Sullivan's *H.M.S. Pinafore* before he learned to sing "Rule Britannia." Socialism and imperialism Chesterton saw as equally remote from the Victorian caution and the Victorian idealism (*The Victorian Age* 250).

His family also, in spite of his charming disclaimers, helped to nurture the darker side of Chesterton's disreputable Victorian attitude—a sense of sin and evil—which led him to orthodox Christianity. His "return to religion" makes Chesterton one of us, who live in the insane asylum we call the modern world (Kirk).

At the same time, in both his life and work, Chesterton reflected his Victorian upbringing by insisting that there can be no art without morality. In his *Autobiography* he said he had never taken his books seriously, but he had taken his opinions quite seriously indeed (110). To him, as he wrote in *Heretics*, "the most practical and important thing about a man is still his view of the universe" (15).

Chesterton was a true, if "disreputable," Victorian in two important and interrelated ways. The first relates to his own experience of the Victorian loss of faith; the second is his interpretation of Victorian literature, which was his lifelong "academic" specialty.

First, it is necessary to describe what Chesterton meant by "Victorian." In *Cobbett*, his biography of the nineteenth-century Tory radical journalist, Chesterton gave a characteristic description of the Victorian Age. He said that when he heard the word "Victorian" it made him

> think of a time somewhere about 1837 when a change was passing over England. . . . [I]t was not exactly a creed or a cause, or even a spirit; the nearest description is to say that it was a silence. . . . There was a silent understanding in the new middle class that it would not really rebel against the aristocracy, while the latter would not really resist the invasion of the middle class. There was a silent alliance . . . that neither would really think about that third thing which moved in the depths; visible for an instant in burning hayricks and broken machines. It was an understanding that produced its own courtesy and culture, its own poets and painters, and its patriotism and historic pride; so that we who were born in the last days of that tradition can never treat it altogether without piety and gratitude. The atmosphere had then no name . . . but a few years afterward there was found for it a name and a figure and a national symbol; when a girl stood crowned. . . . We call it the Victorian Age. (258-59)

For most of us today the whole period from Victoria's ascension to World War I seems to be monolithic. We call it the "Good Old Days" and see it as old-fashioned as Barrie's *Peter Pan*; it evokes an unChestertonian sense of fairyland or critical nostalgia. But as Samuel Hynes pointed out in *The Edwardian Turn of Mind*,

> Nostalgia is a pleasing emotion, but it is also a simplifying one; to think of Edwardian England as a peaceful, opulent world before the flood is to misread the age. . . . Virtually everything that is thought of as characteristically modern already existed in England by 1914. (5)

Chesterton, therefore, found himself speaking as a Victorian in the modern world where the leading thinkers with whom he debated were largely "heretics" or "men whose philosophy was quite solid, quite coherent, and quite wrong" (*Heretics* 11-12). These men like H. G. Wells or G. B. Shaw, however modern their ideas, were also great "simplifiers."

Born in 1874, Chesterton grew up in the late Victorian period, which he later described as "the decadence of a great revolutionary period" which had begun with the French and American Revolutions. These revolutions ". . . had set up against the governing class and the government . . . the citizen, whose influence on the state depended upon his independence of the state."[2] This was the old liberal creed in which Chesterton was raised.

Young Chesterton did grow up within what seemed to be a secure family enclave, Kensington, the highly respectable home of the young Victoria herself. He paid tribute to what he saw as the good Victorian qualities when he wrote at the end of his life:

> I am actually old enough to remember the Victorian Age; and it is almost a complete contrast to all that is now connoted by that word. It had all the vices that are now called virtues: religious doubt, intellectual unrest, a hungry credulity about new things, a complete

2. G. K. Chesterton, speech made as candidate for Rector of Glasgow University, 1925, copyright 1981 by Chesterton Estate. In the Marion E. Wade Collection, Wheaton College, Wheaton, Il.

lack of equilibrium. It also had all the virtues that are now called vices: a rich sense of romance, a passionate desire to make the love of man and woman once more what it was in Eden, a strong sense of the absolute necessity of some significance in human life. . . .

But, as he added,

> The general background of all my boyhood was agnostic. My own parents were rather exceptional, among people so intelligent, in believing at all in a personal God or in personal immortality. . . . [A]gnosticism was an established thing. We might almost say that agnosticism was an established church. There was a uniformity of unbelief among educated people. . . . [A]ny number . . . proclaimed religions, chiefly oriental religions, analyzed or argued about them; but that anybody could regard religion as a practical thing . . . was quite . . . new to me. (*Autobiography* 143-45)

His parents were undogmatic liberals, who had retained simple beliefs derived from liberalism, which they held to be self-evident, like the Fatherhood of God and the Brotherhood of Man. Chesterton said that his father's generation "was the first that ever asked its children to worship the hearth without the altar . . . whether they went to church at eleven o'clock or were reverently latitudinarian, as was much of my own circle" (*Autobiography* 26-27).

Although Chesterton humorously apologized for having a family whose

> landscape . . . appear[s] so disappointingly respectable and even reasonable, and deficient in all those unpleasant qualities that make a biography really popular. I regret that I have no gloomy or savage father to offer . . . as the true cause of all my tragic heritage. . . . I cannot do my duty as a true modern, by cursing everybody who made me whatever I am. (*Autobiography* 29)

He found he could not believe as his father and uncles did "in progress and all new things." "All the more because they were finding it increasingly difficult to believe in old things" (*Autobiography* 24).

Beneath the pleasant surface of his family life, there also lurked his dimly remembered older sister Beatrice, whose death had had a drastic emotional effect upon his normally equitable

Alzina Stone Dale

father. After a stormy adolescence, marked by a very modern, existential anxiety and depression over the meaninglessness of existence, during which he flirted with suicide, Chesterton was converted as a young man to orthodox Christianity. Part of the external impetus came from the heretics' one-sided attacks upon Christianity; part from the example set by his future wife and her friends who "actually practiced religion."

Much later in *The Everlasting Man*, written to counter H. G. Wells's progressive *The Outline of History*, Chesterton described the nature of the attack on faith which had started before he was born and lasted all his lifetime when he said that

> the next best thing to being really inside Christendom is to be really outside it . . . . [But] the popular critics of Christianity are not really outside it. . . . their mood about the whole religious tradition [is that] . . . they are in a state of reaction against it. (9-10)

Chesterton came to disbelieve in progress because

> real development is not leaving things behind, as on a road, but drawing life from them, as from a root. . . . The ancient English literature was . . . European . . . it was something more than European. A most marked and unmanageable national temperament is plain in Chaucer and the ballads of Robin Hood. . . . [T]hat note is still unmistakable in Shakespeare, in Johnson and his friends, in Cobbett, in Dickens. (*The Victorian Age* 12-13)

He found the sources for his own adult beliefs in this past, too, a situation which brings us to the second major starting point for discussing Chesterton as both a true and a disreputable Victorian: his love of and defense of Victorian literature, which was also a legacy from his family. As he defended the values of the Victorian world against the Modernists, he was not being "medieval" in the late Victorian manner of the Pre-Raphaelites, but reaching back to the earlier Christian roots to be found in Victorian literature. Just as it had infected him with its loss of faith, so did the Victorian Age itself "convert" Chesterton to Christianity, precisely at the time when it was unfashionable to believe in much of anything. It did so by making Chesterton a "revolutionary" Victorian, or radical (Dale xxi-xvi; Hunt 37).

It was in *Orthodoxy*, which Chesterton described as a sloven-
ly autobiography, that he described the stages of his personal loss
of the faith he had been raised with, while continuing to stress
the family's deep, underlying, almost inarticulate, devotion to the
libertarian ideals of the French Revolution.

Chesterton was to discover that these ideals had been based
upon those of "Western Civilization," which was what Chesterton meant when he talked about "the Church" or "Christendom." He did not mean simply the Roman Catholic church, but
rather the whole, historic, European community of faith, once
symbolized by the sacred and secular power of the bishop of
Rome. His biggest anti-heroes, therefore, were the Teutonic war-
riors of the celebrated northern forests who were acclaimed in
his time as the creators of democratic government and the an-
cestors of the "Prussian" Zeitgeist or spirit of the time from
Nietzsche to Bismarck.

Chesterton found the English equivalent of the French
Revolution in the literature of the Victorian Age, especially after
the twentieth-century Liberal Party became infected with welfare
statism. To Chesterton, the significance of the French Revolution was that it stood for a dogma that was really another name
for Christianity. He came to see that the old Christian virtues of
faith, hope, and charity were simply the earlier names for liberty, equality, and fraternity (Bogaerts 175).

Chesterton's family was not only comfortably urban middle
class, but well educated. At home, English literature was his daily
bread, and he knew a great deal of it by heart "long before I
could really get it into my head" (*Autobiography* 110). He knew
it so well that by the time he was grown he could play with it;
to make a point he might casually translate a line from Robert
Browning into "Tennyson" or vice versa.

Victorian literature in particular became Chesterton's lifelong
study. He took English literature courses at the University of London and at thirty, having published *Robert Browning*, he was offered one of the newly established university professorships in
English literature. But, following in the footsteps of his favorites
Dr. Johnson, Cobbett, and Charles Dickens, he chose to remain
a journalist.

As a critic, Chesterton exhibited both an "unseemly" wit which helped keep his critics from taking him seriously and an Impressionistic style which made him appear disreputable to the literary establishment. He demonstrated his grasp of literary criticism's rules of the game by saying that

> the usual way of criticizing an author . . . who has added something to the literary forms of the world is to complain that his work does not contain something which is obviously the specialty of someone else. . . . [Thus] the right thing to say about *Cyrano de Bergerac* is that it may have a certain wit and spirit, but it really throws no light on the duty of middle-aged married couples in Norway. (*Robert Browning* 138-39)

His unorthodox theory about quotations was that they ought not be looked up, because literature ought to be a part of a man. His editor found 13 misquotations on one page of *Robert Browning* and had fits, but the biography was a huge success (Dale 88).

Although he had grown up feeding upon Victorian literature, it was largely thanks to reading and rereading Charles Dickens that Chesterton also grew up to be a Victorian radical (or revolutionary). More specifically, in regard to the literature of the Victorian Age or any age, Chesterton began with the proper Victorian premise that literature, like life itself, always had moral overtones. He derived this conviction from his education in Impressionism and the *fin de siècle* "art for art's sake" at the Slade School of Art. As an adult Chesterton stated his own artistic creed, saying that

> individual artists cannot be reviewed without reference to their traditions and creeds. It is enough to say that with other creeds they would have been, for literary purposes, other individuals. . . . It is useless for the aesthete (or any other anarchist) to urge the isolated individuality of the artist, apart from his attitude to his age. His attitude to his age is his individuality: men are never individual when alone. (*The Victorian Age* 8-10)

His approach to the literature of the Victorian Age was not strictly literary, but it has been said of him that

> no other writer of this century has been able to elucidate the central

ideas of the major writers with such clarity and wit, or to place those ideas so clearly against the broader perspectives of their cultural background. (Clipper, G. K. Chesterton 37)

In looking at literature Chesterton maintained his own sane and balanced outlook, seeing life whole instead of seeing it dark and dismal. In his talk on Chesterton and Dickens at Notre Dame in 1981, Lawrence Clipper commented that Chesterton was as sensitive to Dickens's psychological problems as Edmund Wilson with his theory of the "secret wound." But unlike Wilson, Chesterton did not feel that the total Dickens was summed up in the so-called "dark" Dickens. By using this stable, balanced approach, true "Victorian" Chesterton was reacting against the common problem noted by Northrup Frye that literary critics in our time find it more difficult to deal with comedy and think that an unhappy ending is more defensible (Clipper, "Chesterton on Dickens" 41).

Probably his best statement about the Victorian world was made in The Victorian Age in Literature, published in 1913. It was put out by one of the popular libraries aimed at the general public, and, according to Samuel Hynes and many other critics, is one of the several "minor masterpieces" written by this "master without a masterpiece" who wrote in the wrong mediums. As always, disreputable Chesterton wrote from such an original viewpoint that his editors published a disclaimer that "this book is not . . . an authoritative history of Victorian literature" (The Victorian Age frontispiece).

In the words of critic Garry Wills, this book marks one of the many times when Chesterton took stock of where he had come from to determine where he was going. Wills pointed out that the book is

> marked by great caution and fairness . . . [and is] a masterpiece of arrangement, of suspension, and counter-tension, whereby names are lifted in large webs of inter-reacting influence. . . . [It] illustrates the way Chesterton the critic goes to work.[3]

His main thesis about the Victorians is that their age repre-

3. 77-79. See also Hunter 107.

sented a compromise between the rising forces of rationalism and the waning influences of faith, belief, and sentiment. The high-water mark of the compromise had been his hero and mentor, the Mid-Victorian Charles Dickens. When this compromise was no longer stable, the Victorian period ended.

In discussing individual artists, Chesterton followed his usual pattern of emphasizing the artist's relationship to this central ideological struggle. He explained that he could not forgive the Victorians for their materialism, religious doubts, failure of traditions, enslavement of the worker, and triumph of artistic ugliness. He saw their underlying failure as a failure to use allegory and ritual to fuse matter and spirit with reference to an eternal authority. He felt that they did not use sacramental modes of expression because underneath they were still Puritans (Hunter 107). A generation later this critical argument was to be repeated, lock, stock, and barrel, by a Chestertonian critic turned admirer, T. S. Eliot.

Parenthetically, the term "Puritan" as used by Chesterton is also close to Eliot's use of it. Both were talking about historical Calvinist determinism, with its utopian doctrine of predestination. As Chesterton put it, "Puritanism" assumed that our earthly life was not the drama but the epilogue. "Puritans" like G. B. Shaw had rejected as superstition the likelihood of being judged after death but were still defending the doctrine that man is judged before he is born. By believing in this kind of fantasy, modern thinkers were denying the incarnational nature of this world which orthodox Christianity affirms.

The Victorian Age began, according to Chesterton, the moment a footman opened the door to an aristocratic Whig drawing room and announced, "Mr. Macaulay." Macaulay's literary popularity was both representative and deserved, but his presence among the ruling Whig families marked an epoch. It was his "wit and his politics (combined with that dropping of the Puritan tenets but retention of the Puritan tone which marked his class and generation), [that] lifted him into . . . [the] Whig world" (*The Victorian Age* 28-29).

At this moment the middle classes emerged in a state of damaged Puritanism, while the upper classes remained utterly pagan. Macaulay personified the decision of those middle classes (to which Chesterton belonged) to use their new wealth to back the Victorian Compromise. The compromise was that instead of guillotining the aristocrats, they joined them.

In their turn, the aristocrats compromised by recruiting more and more of themselves from these middle classes, by way of the public schools and universities. The aristocrats also accepted two middle-class positions as their own; they rejected immorality and accepted free trade.

Chesterton then asserted that to describe how the Victorian heirs of Macaulay stood in relation to one another was to describe

> the difficulty of keeping the moral order parallel with the chronological order. For the mind moves by instincts, associations, premonitions and not by fixed dates of completed processes. Action and reaction will occur simultaneously; or the cause actually be found after the effect. . . . Thus Newman took down the iron sword of dogma to parry a blow not yet delivered, that was coming from the club of Darwin. For this reason no one can understand tradition, or even history, who has not some tenderness for anachronism. (*The Victorian Age* 37-38)

At the center of the Victorian Age Chesterton set Jeremy Bentham who stood for the cold science of self-interest. His utilitarianism made possible the great victories of Darwin and Huxley, so that

> if we take Macaulay at the beginning of the epoch and Huxley at the end of it, we shall find that they had much in common. . . . The difference that the period had developed can best be seen if we consider this: that while neither [of them] was of a spiritual sort, Macaulay took it for granted that common sense required some kind of theology, while Huxley took it for granted that common sense meant having none. Macaulay . . . never talked about his religion; but Huxley was always talking about the religion he hadn't got. (*The Victorian Age* 39-40)

If rationalism held the stage during the Victorian era, the intellectual history of the period was a series of literary rebellions against it, and, as a disreputable or revolutionary Victorian, Chesterton was firmly in the camp of two out of the three rebellions.

The first came from the Oxford Movement; the second one was one man, Charles Dickens; and the third was a group which tried to create a new romantic Protestantism to fight both reason and Rome. This group was made up of Carlyle, Ruskin, Kingsley, and probably Tennyson.

The first Victorian revolution was the Anglican high church revival, called the Oxford Movement, which began in 1833. It was a movement away from the "frivolity of established religion and consisted mainly in taking Christianity seriously."[4] Its importance was the fact that it represented a hunger for dogma. For dogma means the serious satisfaction of the mind. Dogma does not mean the absence of thought, but the end of thought. The Oxford Movement was a rational movement, which made it sharply different from the blinding mysticism of Carlyle or the mere manly emotionalism of Dickens. It saw that the Victorians were trying to have their cake and eat it, too. It appealed to the reason which said that "if a Christian had a feast day, he must have a fast day, too. Otherwise all days ought to be the same." The movement centered around Newman, who was its one great writer, and it also broke up because of Newman, who left the Anglican for the Roman Catholic church. His great service was protesting the rationality of religion against the increasingly irrational comfort, or smugness, of the age.

The second great Victorian revolution was one man: Charles Dickens, the Victorian author who fueled most of Chesterton's social and ethical convictions, who, in turn, to paraphrase his own credo in *Orthodoxy*, taught him "how to find a way to contrive to be at once astonished at the [Victorian] world and yet at home in it." In Chesterton's words, Charles Dickens was:

> like the rising of a vast mob . . . not only because his tales are . . .
> as crowded and populous as towns . . . [but] also because he was
> the sort of man who has the impersonal impetus of a mob. . . .
> Dickens was a mob . . . in revolt; he fought by the light of nature;
> he had not a theory but a thirst . . . for things as humble, as human,
> as laughable as that daily bread for which we cry to God. He had

4. John J. Connolly, "Lecture Ten: Newman: October 27, 1930," in *The Chesterton Review*, Vol. IV, No. 1, p. 125.

no particular plan of reform . . . [but he] did know what he didn't like . . . the *mean* side of the Manchester [Utilitarian] philosophy. (*The Victorian Age* 79-82)

It was paradoxical, remarked Chesterton, that Charles Dickens was the most popular radical of his day. We might add that in defending Dickens against the twin accusations of being popular and revolutionary, Chesterton was also defending himself as a disreputable Victorian.

Chesterton saw that Dickens attacked the Victorian compromise between rationalism and faith because the compromise was cold. He included Dickens among his fighters, or revolutionaries, not the storytellers, insisting that we will get the Victorian perspective wrong if we do not see that

> Dickens was primarily the most successful of all the onslaughts on the solid scientific school; because he did not attack from the standpoint of extraordinary faith, like Newman, or the standpoint of extra-ordinary inspiration, like Carlyle; or the standpoint of extraordinary detachment . . . like [Matthew] Arnold, but from the standpoint of quite ordinary and quite hearty dislike. (*The Victorian Age* 86-87)

Chesterton explained that Dickens's work was to be reckoned always by characters, sometimes by groups, oftener by episodes, but never by novels, " . . . for they are simply lengths cut from the flowing and mined substance called Dickens." He added that Dickens "did not simply exaggerate his characters . . . ; he blows up his readers . . . [with] the true Dickens atmosphere in which clerks are clerks and at the same time, elves" (Wills 68-69). It is intriguing to remember that Chesterton and his favorite sparring partner, socialist G. B. Shaw, were both ardent Dickens fans in a post-Victorian period when Dickens was ignored by intellectuals. Margaret Canovan said that much of Chesterton's political background derived from Dickens. She felt that Chesterton's "triumphant vindication of Dickens as the great democratic genius was one of his most successful enterprises" (Canovan 32-34). By contrast she pointed out that G. B. Shaw defended Dickens's grotesque characters with the idea that he showed how ordinary people seem to geniuses.

153

While Lawrence Clipper feels that it is an exaggeration to say that Chesterton saved Dickens "from oblivion" or proved that Dickens is *the* Victorian writer (the judgment of critic Edmund Wilson in his essay "Dickens: the Two Scrooges"), Clipper readily acknowledged the seminal importance of Dickens's ideas for Chesterton. He further insisted that Chesterton did not present just a "Santa Claus or Christmas Dickens" but showed a well-rounded Dickens, larger than life, which he celebrated with all his creative genius (Clipper, "Chesterton on Dickens" 39). Clipper succinctly stated the main objections to Chesterton as literary critic: instead of minute textual analysis a la New Criticism, Chesterton used a broader Impressionist method in order to make moral criticism. (At the same time, however, Chesterton not only insisted upon a pragmatic relationship between life and art, he called Dickens "a mythologizer," now a very contemporary critical term.)

In "Dickens' Influence on Chesterton's Imaginative Writing" Peter R. Hunt also paid tribute to the "all-pervasive Dickensian elements in [Chesterton's] writing . . ." which he, too, saw as the source of Chesterton's "life-long social vision and his dedication to revolutionary reform of industrial capitalism" (Hunt 36). Hunt pointed out the important fact that the Pickwickian Dickens provided Chesterton with his "foolery and fantastic sense of the absurd," what Michael Mason called his "centre of hilarity." Hunt saw Dickens's work as the nurturing agent for Chesterton's own humorous literary tone and discursive style; he reminded us that Dickens also shared Chesterton's sense of wonder at the world. Hunt then suggested that there is much of Mr. Pickwick in Father Brown (Hunt 42).

Chesterton's third and last revolution against Victorian complacency was the one to which he attributed the break-up of the Victorian compromise with its stable but materialistic ways. This revolution sprang from those whom he called the new romantic Protestants, whose leader was Thomas Carlyle. Chesterton knew that he owed much to the Oxford Movement, whose twin heirs in his time were the Anglo-Catholic, Christian Social Union wing of the Church of England, and the pro-Boer Liberal Party. He also took vast pride in being Charles Dickens's disciple; but

Chesterton had almost nothing in common with this third group of "late" Victorians. Instead, he saw them as the progenitors of the worst intellectual evils of his own day.

The two things he found in Carlyle were his early Scotch education, which was excellent, and his later German culture, which was despicable. He called Carlyle more of a poet than a writer of prose because, "though his general honesty is unquestionable, he was by no means one of those who will give up a fancy under the shock of a fact" (*The Victorian Age* 53).

He praised Carlyle for attacking Bentham's cold utilitarianism, for being the first to see that the wealth of the state is not the prosperity of the people, but he criticized Carlyle for his reckless optimism which assumed that all human affairs were "a clouded but unbroken revelation of the divine . . . [because this] practically comes to saying that God is on the side of the big battalions . . ." (*The Victorian Age* 58-59).

He called Carlyle the ancestor of both socialism and imperialism which developed in the late Victorian era. These were the two leading "heresies" of the modern age, represented by Shaw on the one hand and Kipling on the other. Carlyle's young lieutenant, John Ruskin, fought utilitarianism, too, but Ruskin

> did not . . . set up the romance of the great Puritans as a rival to the romance of the Catholic Church. Rather he set up and worshipped all the arts and trophies of the Catholic Church as a rival to the Church itself. . . . It is not quite unfair to say of him that he seemed to want all parts of the Cathedral except the altar. (*The Victorian Age* 63-65)

From Ruskin, Chesterton passed on to Pater, whom he classed with Rossetti and Swinburne, saying they all wanted to see paganism through Christianity, with the incidental amusement of seeing through Christianity itself.

One more of his Victorian "fighters" was not of the school of Ruskin or Carlyle but one who fought many of their battles and worked the hardest at convincing bourgeois [Victorian] England that it was priggish and provincial. This was Matthew Arnold. Chesterton said that Arnold was chiefly valuable as a man who knew things. For instance, he knew that England was part of Europe, that it was ruled by an oligarchy, and that the Catholic church was not a sect.

> He was not so much the philosopher as the man of the world. . . . [While his] enemies might say that he was . . . trying to . . . endow Agnosticism. . . . It is fairer . . . to say that unconsciously he was trying to restore Paganism. . . . But [in his commentary] Arnold kept a smile of heartbroken forbearance, as of the teacher in an idiot school, that was enormously insulting. (*The Victorian Age* 75, 77-78)

In the next two sections of *The Victorian Age in Literature*, Chesterton first discussed the great novelists, then the great poets, always in terms of his own Victorian roots. Both are brief summaries of authors and ideas that Chesterton discussed at greater length in his other writings, but the thesis of these chapters is important because it contains his idea of what broke up the Victorian compromise.

Chesterton said that the "Victorian novel was a thing uniquely Victorian because the greatest Victorian novelists are women . . . [whose books] overhaul . . . that part of human existence which has always been the woman's province . . . the play of personalities in private" (*The Victorian Age* 93). He went on to explain that "only where death and eternity are intensely present can human beings fully feel their fellowship. Once the divine darkness against which we stand is really dismissed from the mind (as it was very nearly dismissed in the Victorian time) the differences between human beings become overwhelmingly plain . . ." (*The Victorian Age* 96).

To him neither George Eliot nor Charlotte Bronte is as great as Jane Austen, because they live in a world where "women had a sort of unrest in their souls. And the proof of it is that . . . it began to be admitted by the great Victorian men" (*The Victorian Age* 115). Chesterton sensed in their writing the approach of the modern age of anxiety, and he claimed that the tragedy of these Victorian women was not that they were allowed to follow men but that they followed them far too slavishly. The Victorian novel also showed the growth of "unEnglish" class distinctions: Thackeray's Pendenis would never have gone riding with a cook, but Chaucer's knight did so quite naturally.

Perhaps the most famous capsule comments he ever made on English writers were about a pair of novelists who were intellectually moral enemies, George Meredith and Thomas Hardy. Meredith

> was perhaps the only man in the modern world who has almost had the high honor of rising out of the low estate of a Pantheist into the high estate of a Pagan . . . a person who can take Nature naturally. . . . Hardy went down to botanise in the swamp, while Meredith climbed towards the sun . . . [so that] Hardy became a sort of village atheist brooding and blaspheming over the village idiot. (*The Victorian Age* 138-39, 143)

Together, Meredith and Hardy represented the end of the Victorian compromise. The only good thing that was left was the Victorian talent for nonsense, found in Lear and Carroll and Gilbert and Sullivan —and their disreputable heir, Chesterton.

In his discussion of the Victorian poets, Chesterton took more of a debater's stance, pushing his arguments to extremes to counter the prevailing wind (or Zeitgeist). Chesterton had no desire for an end to Christendom; he merely wanted to restore it to its democratic roots. As a result, he took umbrage at Swinburne and Tennyson, Ruskin and Browning for being parochial, spiteful, and priggish about the Irish, the Roman Catholics, the French Revolution, and the South African Boers. He defended Elizabeth Barrett Browning not only for her poetry, which he admired, but also because she was "by far the most European of all the English poets of that age; all of them, even her own much greater husband, look local beside her" (*The Victorian Age* 178).

In his discussion of the break-up of the Victorian compromise Chesterton said that the old spiritual theory and the new material theory ended in a deadlock that has endured.

> It is still impossible to say absolutely that England is a Christian country or a heathen country. . . . It has driven [religion] . . . into the power of the religious people . . . [who are] much more extravagantly religious than they would have been in a religious country . . . [while skeptics are] equally driven back on being irreligious; that is, on doubting things which man's normal imagination does not necessarily doubt. (*The Victorian Age* 204-5)

157

Like most historians, Chesterton dated the crack-up about 1880 when the two great enthusiasms of western Europe, Christianity and the French Revolution, had exhausted each other, "killing off both belief and democracy; so that religion and politics were ruled out of all the later Victorian debating clubs [like Parliament] . . . denying the dignity of man and the dignity of God" (*The Victorian Age* 210).

Then came the period of Chesterton's own adolescence, a cold emptiness known as the *fin de siècle*, like "one long afternoon in a rich house on a rainy day" (*The Victorian Age* 217). During this interregnum two writers epitomized the best and worst of literature: Henry James, who is in the "deepest sense of a dishonored word" a spiritualist if there ever was one; and Oscar Wilde, in whom we have a "perpetually toppling possibility of the absurd; . . . of just falling too short or just going too far" (*The Victorian Age* 222).

Then socialism and imperialism finished off the compromise. Shaw trod out the last ember of the equality of the French Revolution, while Kipling taught Victorian England to paint the map red ". . . in an attempt to reform England through the newer nations . . . [who were] equally remote from the Victorian caution and the Victorian idealism" (*The Victorian Age* 250).

As a disreputable Victorian, Chesterton told his audience of young American Roman Catholic college students in 1930:

> the curse came upon the Victorians when they began to apply their ideas. . . . Both *Alice in Wonderland* and the Lady of Shalott were typical Victorian ladies in that they did not see the realities of life [except] through a mirror; . . . the Victorians lived in a doll's house, but they lived a life that was balanced, sane, humane, reasonable, and tolerable. It was, however, only a doll's house . . . not a home.[5]

As a disreputable Victorian today, Chesterton would still remind us to reestablish the "Home of Jones," where the ordinary man can be himself to paint his walls purple or grow dandelions in his yard. At the same time, Chesterton the true Vic-

5. John J. Connelly, "Lecture Eighteen: Kipling, Shaw and Wells, November 14, 1930," in *The Chesterton Review*, Vol. IV, No. 2, p. 298.

torian would admire Allan Bloom's *The Closing of the American Mind* for its insistence upon our need to regain our historic roots and for its call for intellectual virtues and moral virtues.

Works Cited

Bogaerts, Anthony Mattheus Adrianus. *Chesterton and the Victorian Age.* Hilversum: Rozenbeck en Veneman, 1940.

Canovan, Margaret. *G. K. Chesterton, Radical Populist.* New York: Harcourt Brace Jovanovich, 1977.

Chesterton, G. K. *Autobiography.* London: Hutchinson & Co., 1936.

_____. *Chaucer.* London: Faber & Faber, 1932.

_____. *The Everlasting Man.* New York: Doubleday & Co., 1955.

_____. *Heretics.* New York: Dodd, Mead, & Co., 1923.

_____. *Robert Browning.* London: Macmillan Co., 1904.

_____. *The Victorian Age in Literature.* New York: Henry Holt, 1913.

_____. *William Cobbett.* New York: Dodd, Mead & Co., 1925.

Clipper, Lawrence J. *G. K. Chesterton.* New York: Twayne Pub., 1974.

_____. "Chesterton on Dickens, A Closer Look." *A G. K. Chesterton Celebration.* South Bend: University of Notre Dame, 1982.

Connelly, John J. "Lecture Eighteen: Kipling, Shaw and Wells," November 14, 1930. *Chesterton Review,* Vol. IV, No. 2, p. 298.

_____. "Lecture Ten: Newman: October 27, 1930." *Chesterton Review,* Vol. IV, No. 1, p. 125.

Dale, Alzina Stone. *The Outline of Sanity.* Grand Rapids: Eerdmans Pub. Co., 1982.

Hunt, Peter. "Dickens' Influence on Chesterton's Imaginative Writing." *The Chesterton Review.* Vol. VII, No. 1, p. 37.

Hunter, Lynnette. *G. K. Chesterton: Exploration in Allegory.* New York: St. Martin's Press, 1979.

Hynes, Samuel Lynn. *The Edwardian Turn of Mind.* Princeton: Princeton University Press, 1968.

Kirk, Russell. "Chesterton, Madmen and Madhouses." *Myth, Allegory and Gospel.* Minneapolis: Bethany Fellowship, 1974. 33-53.

Wills, Garry. *Chesterton, Man and Mask.* New York: Sheed & Ward, 1961.

G. K. Chesterton and
C. S. Lewis:
The Men and Their Times

John David Burton

> *I tell you naught for your comfort;*
> *Yea, naught for your desire,*
> *Save that the sky grows darker yet*
> *And the sea rises higher.*
>
> (Chesterton, *Ballad of the White Horse*)

What doomsday mood in Chesterton prompted "Naught for your comfort" in 1911, forty-four years before the Anglican Trevor Huddleston used the words as a title for his own book, published on leaving his twelve-year mission in South Africa? The priest was grieving for the land of which Jan Christiaan Smuts, on leaving South Africa, said, "Look your last on all things lovely." For what was Chesterton grieving? Against what in Victorian England or in the world was Chesterton giving a warning? Within "the jolly journalist," amid the paradoxes, there was the conviction that each age needs an Alfred to "fight for the Christian civilization against the heathen nihilism" (prefatory note to *Ballad of the White Horse*). No one had to conscript Chesterton for the fray. He volunteered and reenlisted time and time again. What

THE REV. JOHN D. BURTON is a pastor, poet, and formerly Visiting Fellow at Princeton Theological Seminary.

or whom does he see as enemy or enemies under the banner of "heathen nihilism"?

Trying to see Chesterton in relation to his age tempted me to similar inquiry with C. S. Lewis. From Chesterton's birth in 1874 to Lewis's death in 1963, earth and empire shook and shifted to Darwinism, the Fabian Society, industrial capitalism, and socialism. War was frequent, with "that sceptre'd isle" twice the line of defense against the nihilism threatening to put out the lights all over the world. My intention with Lewis, as with Chesterton, is to see him apart from his familiar role as defender and interpreter of the faith. I want to see him in his relation to the so-called "secular world," how he speaks, writes, and acts in connection with the events political, economic, and social amid which he lives and writes, believes and bears witness.

Out of my curiosity comes my premise, which is that Lewis and Chesterton, disciples and apostles to be sure, are as well men of their age, on occasion seeing clearly peril and promise in events of their times, at other moments seeing "through a glass darkly," with limited understanding. I want to end with a sanctified, "so what?" How is my own life as a Christian and citizen in my time to be shaped by seeing Chesterton and Lewis as Christians and citizens in their day? If this seems a self-serving purpose, I remind you that Chesterton claims that a man should be allowed to laugh at his own humor, that an architect may pray in a cathedral of his own design (Ffinch 3).

If a man be known by his enemies as well as by his friends, Chesterton needs no introduction. He goes forth, "fighting for the Christian civilization," throwing down a gauntlet to whatever, whomever is there in public view. The Fabian Society, Calvinism (at least Chesterton's slight grasp on the Gospel via Geneva), the landed aristocracy, industrial capitalism, the Jewish community at home and abroad, you name it and Chesterton tackles it. He lives the Roman proverb, "I am a man and nothing human is foreign to me." His eccentric life-style and what seems at times to be a "hit and run" literary style may tempt some to see him as a shambling crusader seeking to slay a dragon a day to earn a knight's pay. To read Chesterton again and again, particularly the nonfiction prose, is to see that he intends to take seriously and to be taken seriously on the public issues of his day, some of which are with us still. Consider, as examples, two facets of Chesterton's world wherein he seeks change. The first issue is what Chesterton terms "industrial capitalism."

When Chesterton puts a label on what is wrong with his world (indeed, he authors an entire book under the title of *What's Wrong with the World*), he sees the agony of his day as caused by "industrial capitalism": that is, control of persons and processes to produce and distribute goods needed for sustenance of life. Owners, employers, and managers make up a small percentage of the population, but this small company is in charge of conditions of employment, wages, and setting of prices for goods. Thus the few manage life for the many. The "industrial capitalists" keep wages low for those who produce and prices high for those who consume. Chesterton sees this ownership of resources and control of production and distribution as a major cause of misery in England. "Misery in England" in the mid-nineteenth century is more than a windmill for tilting. The historian of economics, Robert L. Heilbroner, writes of what he calls "The Victorian World and the Underworld of Economics":

> The boys and girls (working in factories) —all about ten years old— were whipped day and night, not only for the slightest fault, but to stimulate their flagging industry. (It was) a social climate in which practices of the most callous inhumanity were accepted as the natural order of events and, even more important, as nobody's business. (102-3)

By Chesterton's time there had been improvement, but Chesterton saw beneath the veneer of industrial society the demons ready to be let loose at any time the capitalists thought they could get by with it. As Chesterton saw it, what industry was doing to persons was God's business, therefore Chesterton's business, and he challenged the "callous inhumanity" of his day, writing:

> The modern state and commercialism . . . hampers human character at its best . . . has restrained respectable marriage . . . threatens to destroy domesticity. (*The Quotable Chesterton* 331)

At the heart of Chesterton's criticism of industrial capitalism is his concern with ownership of property.

The word, 'property,' has been defined in our times by the great
capitalists. It is the negation of property that the Duke of Suther-
land should have all the farms in one estate, just as it would be the
negation of marriage if he had all our wives in one harem. (*What's
Wrong with the World* 60)

In his autobiography Chesterton allies himself with William Butler Yeats, writing, "I was fighting with Willie Yeats and his farmers
against the urban mechanical materialism" (147).

Chesterton sees also the need for renewal of crafts, which,
he believes, have served well for livelihood in time past and which
could be used again to earn a living and to supply human needs.
In an essay "A Return to the Land," he writes: "The tragedy in
our time can only be cured by a return to practical crafts like
carpentry and thatching and ploughing, and getting a living from
the land" (71).

One alternative to industrial capitalism was socialism.
Chesterton scorns the idea that state ownership of resources,
property, production, and distribution of goods would be in any
way an improvement over private ownership. In January 1908,
his article "Why I Am Not a Socialist" appeared in the *New Age
Magazine*. A recent biographer, Michael Ffinch, writes that

Chesterton believed strongly in the mass of common people who
were "caught in the trap of a terrible machinery, harried by a shameful economic cruelty, surrounded by an ugliness and desolation
never before endured by men." As imperialism had been foisted
upon them by the interests of commerce and international banking, so socialism would be imposed on them by the interests of intellectuals . . . "Oxford dons and journalists and Countesses on the
spree." (Ffinch 157)

In company with others, Chesterton sought a way out of the
slavery imposed on masses by both capitalism and socialism. That
way was in a system called "Distributism." Ffinch writes:

From 1926 onwards it (Distributism) was Chesterton's constant concern. Quite simply, Distributism meant a system by which
as many people as possible were owners of property and their means
of livelihood. In a Distributist state the wage system based on

employers and employees would be replaced by an economy of owners. It had its roots . . . in the encyclical letter of Pope Leo XIII, *Rerum Novarum*, which had been sent out to the whole Church in 1891. The Pope had offered an alternative to both the capitalist system and the emerging socialism, which was unjust because, to use the Pope's own words, "every man has, by nature, the right to possess things, not merely for temporary and momentary use . . . but in stable and permanent possession." "Man," said the Pope, "precedes the state." (305)

How many of us think it worthwhile to give to Chesterton's view on land reform, control of property and of production, and distribution of goods the same loyalty we give to his theology and apologetics? How do we manage when the champion of the church, our comforter in Christ, turns economist, political activist, and social reformer? I showed this paper to a man who traces his conversion to Chesterton's witness. My friend, a man pious and profane, said,

Distributism? You are claiming that Chesterton was into that? Distributism! For God's sake!

Chesterton would have accepted the oath as an accolade. There is every evidence that, in the holiest sense of calling, Chesterton looked in mercy and love on the human situation and set out to do "for God's sake" what he could do to change the world for the better and to improve life for the poor whom God loves. Chesterton's "Distributism" may or may not have been a viable alternative to capitalism and socialism. In retrospect, for those of us who have the benefits of capitalism and of socialism, "Distributism" may seem simplistic, an easy answer to a hard question. It remains that Chesterton saw before him a human situation calling for change, and he attempted to do something. He was there, to do the best he could do at the time he had to do it.

Another issue of the day with which Chesterton engages himself is what was called "the Jewish problem." Unhappily, our hero emerges as an anti-Semite. W. H. Auden acknowledges Chesterton's most grievous fault by quoting Chesterton's own words:

I [Chesterton] said that a particular kind of Jew tended to be a tyrant and another particular kind of Jew tended to be a traitor. (Auden 11)

Auden then attempts to exonerate Chesterton:

> I [Auden] . . . blamed his [Chesterton's] brother, Cecil, and Hilaire
> Belloc [and] . . . Eliot and Pound . . . but it [Chesterton's views
> on the Jews] remains a regrettable blemish . . . on a man who was
> generous of mind and decent of heart. (12)

Auden's defense of Chesterton, however well meant, fails in light
of Chesterton's own words on what came to be called "the Jewish
problem." Christopher Hollis, devoted to Chesterton, declines to
let his love blind him to the beam in Chesterton's eye. Hollis writes:

> Chesterton argued that the Jew in England was not an Englishman,
> the Jew in France was not a Frenchman . . . . "Where, then, should
> the Jews go?" (137)

To this question Chesterton's answer was Zionism. Jews, by their
nature, as Chesterton saw it, could not be loyal and participat-
ing citizens of any nation. Therefore, let the Jews go to their own
country. It speaks for Chesterton's stature, if not his discipleship
to Jesus the Jew, that Chesterton was, finally, commended by the
American, Rabbi Wise, for his — Chesterton's — eventual de-
nouncement of Hitler and the Holocaust (Hollis 140).

In fairness to Chesterton, perhaps as well to Hilaire Belloc,
it may be claimed that the two men express rather than create
the anti-Semitism of their day. They embrace Zionism as a way
for the Jews to be safe even before some of the Jewish community accept the idea of a "Jewish homeland." It is worth a wonder
that Chesterton and Belloc, before the Holocaust, see for the
Jews a persecution and massacre on a scale beyond anything
known, even in the ages when Christians were competent at killing Jews. Chesterton and Belloc contend that, since some Jews
could not be loyal citizens of other nations, either there would
be found a place, a homeland, for the Jews or the Jews would
be subject to terror and attempted extermination. Admittedly,
the support of Zionism was to get the Jews out of the way, especially out of the field of international banking, in order for the
Gentiles to go on with their proper part in the building of a
grander England. In this Chesterton, as each of us, is haunted by
T. S. Eliot's line in *Murder in the Cathedral*:

The last temptation is the greatest treason:
To do the right deed for the wrong reason.

There is no way to deny, nor any acceptable explanation of, Chesterton's anti-Semitism. In his anti-Semitism Chesterton is a man of his age. Worse for him, he is one of us, a fallen person in a fallen world, well out of the Garden now. In theory he wants to help the Jews have a place of their own. In reality he and we partake of the savagery to God's people, Israel, which marks the dark and bloody history of the church of Jesus Christ.

I come now to Lewis and his times. It is awkward for me, in my tradition of "pro testare" ("to testify for," thus to be "Protestant") to face the matter of Lewis and his engagement with his world. While Chesterton is a "political animal," a public figure, at times Lewis intends to be neither political nor public. The difference in Chesterton and Lewis may be due to the habitat of each man. Fleet Street, the world of the London journalist, is a public arena, a latter-day Coliseum. Chesterton, champion of "the Christian civilization," goes forth to meet whatever foes are there. For Lewis, the cloisters of Cambridge and the tutorial rooms of Oxford make possible his passion for privacy, scholarly pursuits, and personal witness borne primarily through his writing. Yet there is enough information on Lewis's views on some issues for us to see how he sees his world, at least on modern industry and war.

As late as 1944 Lewis maintains that he knows nothing about "Modern Industry," known in Chesterton's vocabulary as "Industrial Capitalism." Moreover, Lewis makes it clear that what he does observe fills him with despair. Speaking at the head office of Electric and Musical Industries, Middlesex, April 18, 1944, Lewis says:

Modern Industry is a subject about which I know nothing at all. . . . My own idea is that modern industry is a radically hopeless system. You can improve wages, hours, conditions, etc., but all that doesn't cure the deepest trouble: i.e., that numbers of people are kept all their lives doing dull repetition work which gives no full play to their faculties. How that is to be overcome I do not know . . . . I don't know the solution: that is not the kind of thing Christianity teaches a person like me. (48)

After claiming total ignorance, Lewis goes on to describe what he sees as happening to persons under the system of which he has no knowledge! He says that he has no view on what could improve the situation and that Christianity has no information on the matter for a person like himself. I find it interesting, perhaps indicative of a "tunnel vision" on Lewis's part, that he makes the statement in 1944, when "modern industry . . . , a radically hopeless system," is mustering strength to stand against, indeed to overcome, the Nazi darkness, bastard child of "the heathen nihilism" seen aright by Chesterton. Modern industry, of which Lewis despairs, guarantees a world in which Lewis is free to despair.

Elsewhere, Lewis moves in sympathy with Chesterton's concept of Distributism:

> I believe man is happier . . . if he has a freeborn mind. . . . I doubt whether he can have this without economic independence, which the new society is abolishing. Economic independence allows an education not controlled by government; and in adult life it is the man who needs, and asks, nothing of Government who can criticize its acts and snap his fingers at its idealogy. Read Montaigne; that's the voice of a man with his legs under his own table, eating the mutton and turnips raised on his own land. (Lewis 314)

Lewis is as doubtful as Chesterton about the chance that modern industry may allow men and women to grow and to become the persons God intends. The difference is that Chesterton plunges headlong into the effort to organize a Christian state via Distributism, and Lewis goes on with his life, explaining that "Christianity does not teach a person like me" what to do to change matters. He does observe, with some interest and favor, an "Amana Colony" type of venture on the part of his friend Griffiths and two other persons. Lewis writes:

> They felt that their only course of action was to retreat to an earlier century and live without all the products of the industrial revolution. They picked a plain little village at the bottom of a valley with a small stream running through it, Eastington: they thought it had the simple beauty of everything that was in harmony with nature. They bought a four-room cottage built of solid Cotswold

stone with Cotswold tiling, but without water, drainage or lighting of any sort. Daily life approached the idyllic. They milked cows, herded sheep, and grew their own vegetables. In the evenings they lit tallow dips, stuck them into an iron candelabrum, and read poetry and philosophy. (Griffin 81)

Lewis, like Chesterton and many another wearied of industrial society, dreams of a world where, in the words of the prophet Micah,

They shall sit every man under his vine and under his fig tree, and none shall make them afraid. (Micah 4:4)

The difference between Chesterton and Lewis is that the former flails away at organizational efforts to bring his vision to reality, while Lewis, seeing no hope for industrial society, moves on with his life as a scholar and—eventually—takes his hope and offers hope to others in a vision of the City of God, to arrive after disappearance of the world as the world is now.

Another aspect of his time which Lewis cannot escape is war. In this he is a staunch if reluctant son of the empire. At officers' training camp, getting ready for service in World War I, he writes:

I have no patriotic feeling for anything in England . . . except Oxford, for which I would live and die. (Griffin 7)

He is wounded in France in 1918, at the same battle that claimed the life of his friend, Paddy Moore. Lewis, fulfilling a promise made to Moore, takes care of Moore's mother for more than thirty years. This commitment must be seen as a major factor in the way Lewis uses his time, money, energy—indeed—his life.

Never a pacifist, Lewis is nonetheless unwilling to glorify World War II. Moreover, he will not let his pupils evade their work with the excuse that wartime is an abnormal time. In October 1939, preaching in University Church, Lewis says:

We are mistaken when we compare war with "normal life." Life has never been normal. Even those periods we think most tranquil, like the nineteenth century, turn out, on closer inspection, to be full of crises, alarms, difficulties, emergencies. . . . [Humans] propound mathematical theorems in beleaguered cities, conduct metaphysical arguments in condemned cells, make jokes on scaffolds, discuss the last new poem while advancing to the walls of Quebec and comb their hair at Thermopylae. (Griffin 164)

Underlying Lewis's way of being, or not being, in relation to his time seems to be a resolution to stand apart from issues which occupy others. A pupil, John Lawlor, tells Lewis that he, Lawlor, is involved in refugee funds, collecting money for the support of the monarchy during the Spanish Civil War. Griffin, Lewis's recent biographer, records the way Lewis responds to Lawlor.

> No, he did not want to contribute, said Lewis before he was asked. He had a rule about not contributing to "anything that had a directly political implication." (137)

Lewis's detachment stands in contrast to Belloc's interview with Franco just before the fall of Catalonia. The fact that Belloc misinterprets Franco's intention regarding Islam in Spain does not alter the fact that Belloc at least is aware that a dress rehearsal for World War II is happening in Spain. Lewis goes along in splendid isolation, observing his "rule about . . . anything . . . directly political." Recently I listened to the eighty-six-year-old Douglas Steere, an American Quaker, tell of Oxford dons who in the mid-1920s went to do relief work amid the terrible depression in Wales. Lewis was at Oxford at that time but there is, as far as I know, no record of Lewis knowing that his colleagues were involved in such work.

In contrast to his detachment from organized efforts at relief work or anything political is the remarkable personal generosity of Lewis with regard to time, money, and energy used for those around him. The man simply gives himself away. Scarcely a week goes by, hardly any mention of monetary income from speaking, without reference to his wish that the money be given to this or that person, because, in Lewis's words, "He / she is having a hard time." In days after World War II Lewis accepts in good grace the food and other supplies sent to him from abroad, most of it from admirers in the U.S. Typically, Lewis then hands on the gifts to those known to him to be in need and lacking the friends from abroad who have sent gifts on to Lewis. In keeping with this "losing life to find it" is Lewis's care of Mrs. Moore, a matter which must have called for the proverbial "patience of a saint." Indeed, Lewis refers to himself as a "tethered man." If organized group efforts political or charitable do not appeal to him, in his personal stewardship of time, money, and energy he is consistently generous.

Chesterton and Lewis engage the world to change the world, not because they despise the world but because God loves it. Chesterton attempts beachheads, storms ramparts. Lewis, as though dropped behind enemy lines, fashions holy resistance to paganism in society, academia, and in the church itself. One suspects that Lewis survives as an academician because of the brilliance of his scholarship and the "secular" popularity of his writing. For academia to have one of its own a professed believer may have been a greater hazard for Lewis than Chesterton endured in London town. It remains that each man, in his own domain, lived and acted as though we have limited choices with regard to Jesus of Nazareth — to follow him or to lock him up or, better still, to kill him. God loving the world as the world is, called Lewis and Chesterton, and calls us still, to be in the world for as much of God's purpose as we may decipher in our time.

I gather from Chesterton and Lewis a second clue for my own use, which is that the spirit of our witness may be as important as the strategy or content of that witness. I am aware of Chesterton's thesis, echoed by Lewis, that sincere pessimism is the unpardonable sin. They did not, in Blake's words, build "Jerusalem/In England's green and pleasant Land," but neither do the two men "cease from Mental Fight . . . [nor let] Sword sleep in . . . hand." Chesterton and Lewis live as though it is better to fail in that cause which finally will succeed than to succeed in all other causes which, finally, must fail.

Lastly, Chesterton and Lewis speak to me that, when one has done the best one may, all efforts at work and witness are commended to God and left there. The issues with which Lewis and Chesterton reckon and wrestle are as old as Eden and as new as the Senate hearings (1987) which tell of spiritual wickedness in high places in these United States. Chesterton's poem "A Hymn" phrases what he and Lewis hoped for their times and what we may hope for and trust in our time.

O God of earth and altar, Bow down and hear our cry,
Our earthly rulers falter, The people drift and die,
The walls of gold entomb us, The swords of scorn divide,
Take not Thy thunder from us, But take away our pride.
From all that terror teaches, From lies of tongue and pen,
From all the easy speeches That comfort cruel men,
From sale and profanation Of honor and the sword,
From sleep and from damnation, Deliver us, good Lord.

Chesterton and Lewis, in their times, believed in a God able to hear the cries of the people, a God able to act, indeed, to act through Chesterton and Lewis, among others, to go on with the saving of the world. Let us so believe and so live.

Works Cited

Auden, W. H. G. K. Chesterton: Selections from His Non-Fictional Prose. London: Faber, 1970.

Chesterton, G. K. Autobiography. New York: Sheed and Ward, 1936.

_____. Ballad of the White Horse. New York: John Lane Company, 1911.

"A Hymn." The Collected Poems of G.K. Chesterton. New York: Dodd, Mead and Company, 1932. 136-37.

_____. The Quotable Chesterton. Eds. G. J. Marlin, P. Rabatin, and J. L. Swan. San Francisco: Ignatius Press, 1968.

"A Return to the Land." Avowals and Denials: A Book of Essays. New York: Dodd, Mead and Company, 1935.

_____. What's Wrong with the World. New York: Dodd, Mead and Company, 1910.

Eliot, T. S. Murder in the Cathedral. New York: Harcourt Brace Jovanovich, 1935.

Ffinch, M. G. K. Chesterton: A Biography. San Francisco: Harper and Row, 1986.

Griffin, W. Clive Staple Lewis: A Dramatic Life. San Francisco: Harper & Row, Publishers, 1986.

Heilbroner, Robert L. The Worldly Philosophers. New York: Simon and Schuster, 1972.

Hollis, C. The Mind of Chesterton. London: Hollis and Carter, 1970.

John David Burton

Huddleston, Trevor. *Naught for Your Comfort*. Garden City, NY: Doubleday, 1956.

Lewis, C. S. *God in the Dock*. Grand Rapids: Eerdmans Publishing Co., 1970.

The Chesterbelloc and Modern Sociopolitical Criticism

Jay P. Corrin

Gilbert Keith Chesterton and his friend and collaborator, Hilaire Belloc, were two of the best-known writers of the early twentieth century. It was Chesterton's intellectual sparring partner, George Bernard Shaw, who coined the term the "Chesterbelloc," a portmanteau that stuck in the popular mind and suggested a unique literary and political partnership devoted to reforming all that was wrong with the modern world.[1]

Undergirding Chesterton's and Belloc's writings was a special sociopolitical vision known as Distributism, a concept difficult to define, especially since it was never spelled out definitively in any single piece of writing. Distributism essentially was an approach to life itself, a middle road between the inequities

---

1. Contrary to general opinion, Shaw did not intend the "Chesterbelloc" to represent a common worldview. Rather, it was meant to be a symbol of an unnatural beast representing the mistaken union of the two men. Shaw believed that Chesterton, a "colossal genius" in his opinion, was inadvertently following the lead of the lesser man. Shaw's "Chesterbellocisms" were Belloc's opinions which Chesterton delivered without having discovered them for himself.

JAY P. CORRIN is associate professor of social science at the College of Basic Studies, Boston University, and the author of *G. K. Chesterton and Hilaire Belloc: The Battle Against Modernity*.

of monopoly capitalism and statist collectivism. Distributism emphasized the importance of widely distributed private proprietorship and a restoration of worker control in commerce, agriculture, and industry along the lines of medieval guilds. The Distributist ideal was a balanced or mixed economy of independent farmers and small industries owned and operated by those who toiled. Political power in the Distributist state was to be decentralized, a sort of New England town hall democracy, offering the maximum opportunity for full participation of each citizen at the local level. At the core of Distributist values was a genuine love and admiration for common, ordinary people. Here was the ultimate creative source of civilization, and, in Chesterton's mind, it was imperative that the common man remain free to fulfill his religious and social needs in the confined sanctity of his family and home. Distributism stood in opposition to Shaw and his fellow Fabian imperialists, who had the expansionist's penchant for great growing and groping things, like trees. As Chesterton put it,

> I believe in the flower and the fruit; and the flower is often small. The fruit is final and in that sense finite; it has a form and therefore a limit. There has been stamped upon it an image, which is the crown and consummation of an aim; and the medieval mystics used the same metaphor and called it Fruition. And as applied to man, it means this; that man has been made more sacred than any superman or supermonkey; that his very limitations have already become holy and like a home; because of that sunken chamber in the rocks, where God became very small. (*Autobiography* 232).

Although this sociopolitical vision of Chesterbelloc failed to capture the imagination of Chesterton's and Belloc's generation, Distributism was based on enduring principles that are particularly relevant to our own times. As seen in a broad historical and sociological context, Chesterton and Belloc shared much in common with a small number of intellectuals who refused to accept what the German sociologist Ferdinand Toennies called the emergence of *Gesellschaft*. Toennies's well-known book, *Gemeinschaft und Gesellschaft* (1887 and 1912), formulated a typology of social relations designed to measure change. The book has had immense influence on subsequent sociological research.

The terms *Gemeinschaft* and *Gesellschaft* were employed by Toennies as ideal types or models to describe two polar ways in which people organize themselves. *Gemeinschaft,* meaning community, is a tightly integrated organic unity. Individual interaction is intimate and based on trust, but there is a high degree of social control and conformity. One usually finds such organizations in rural areas or in small communities. Historically, they prevailed before the advent of the industrial revolution. Relationships within *Gemeinschaft* settings are what sociologists call "primary": this is the type of association that prevails between parent and child, husband and wife, guildmaster and apprentice, and between friends. The most perfect representation of *Gemeinschaft* is the family, seen by anthropologists as the essential kernel of social order out of which all community life arises. Just as the family derives from the physiological and psychological constitution of man, so does *Gemeinschaft*:

> Being together, so to speak, is the vegetative heart and soul of
> *Gemeinschaft*—the very existence of *Gemeinschaft* rests in the consciousness of belonging together and the affirmation of the condition of mutual dependence which is posed by that affirmation. . . . Regarding being together it is descent (blood), regarding living together it is soil (land), regarding working together it is occupation (*Beruf*) that is the substance . . . by which the wills of men . . . are essentially united. (Toennies 69)

Gesellschaft is the opposite of this, a type of arrangement in which relationships are largely "secondary," that is, impersonal, formal, designed for a particular purpose, and extrinsic of the individual. People in this type of organization are not joined organically to one another. Separated from the matrix of communal life, each individual is free to pursue his or her own ends. What is significant here is exchange value: social relations are determined by calculation and speculation. To a degree, everyone in *Gesellschaft* is considered a merchant. Society gives prominence to commerce, buying and selling, which is relegated not only to commodity exchange but to ideas and people as well. The social order of *Gesellschaft* is founded on contract and can be integrated and legitimized only through the coercive power of the state. One finds this kind of organization and its accompanying secondary-type relationships in the large urban communities that proliferated during and after the industrial revolution. *Gesellschaft*, then, is notably a characteristic of modern society.

Chesterton and Belloc, much like the Frenchman Emile Durkheim, one of the founders of modern sociology and with whose writings they were probably not familiar, became vitally concerned about the disruptive and alienating effects of the transformation to *Gesellschaft*. An essential fact of modern society which preoccupied Durkheim was the release of the individual from social ties and the loss of norms. Although it emancipated the individual from the strict ties of the community, industrialism imposed a heavy burden on modern people, that of being totally responsible for their lives, yet without strong connections to the community. The result was frequently a sense of alienation, which Durkheim called "anomie," meaning "without norms or without roots to the community."[2] The rootlessness and despair which Durkheim labeled anomie were qualities of modernity which Chesterton and Belloc had quickly identified. Their social and political philosophy was designed, in large part, to battle the corrosive anomic forces that accompanied *Gesellschaft*. Distributism was a plea to return to a small-scale society in which the individual could experience a close sense of involvement with the community, where one could reach one's full potential as a creative being by working with both hands and mind. In short, Distributism beckoned a return to the intimate, personalized world of *Gemeinschaft*.

A major fear of Chesterton's and Belloc's was the infatuation of their contemporaries with a collectivist society. Collectivism was best illustrated during Chesterton's day in the writings of Sidney and Beatrice Webb, two stalwarts of the Fabian Society, an organization of middle-class socialists which, it was

2. For a detailed elaboration of anomie and social pathology, see Emile Durkheim, *Suicide: A Study in Sociology*, trans. John A. Spaulding and George Simpson. Glencoe, IL: Free Press, 1951.

once said, seemed more aggrieved by the world's mess than hurt by its wrongs. The Fabians, for their part, saw themselves as latter-day philosopher-kings replete with the requisite expertise, sociological theories, and precise statistics to rectify all of Britain's social ills. For them what society needed was rational administration for the "common good" under the direction of a Platonizing and efficient elite. In what he saw as a ceaseless struggle for the survival of the fittest, Sidney Webb spoke of a "higher freedom" of corporate life in which "the perfect and fitting development of each individual is not necessarily the utmost and highest cultivation of his own personality, but the filling, in the best possible way, of his humble function in the great social machine" (58).

Chesterton and Belloc had strong objections to collectivist methods because they approached the social problem from the perspective of the state, not the individual. In the process, as Chesterton put it, the socialists aimed to alter the human soul to make it fit desired social conditions rather than to alter artificial conditions to fit the human soul (*What's Wrong with the World* 37). Regardless of how well planned and intelligently administered, Chesterton and Belloc were convinced that massive reforming schemes imposed from above via the engines of the state could never achieve lasting success. They insisted that lasting reform would need popular support, commitment to change among ordinary people being necessary from a moral and practical standpoint. Reform from above was wrong because it would stifle creativity and remove the common people from positions of responsibility for their own affairs. Initiating and carrying out reform from outside the community also would have an enervating effect on democracy itself, since the state would be taking the initiative in areas of local concern. Furthermore, collectivism contributed to the construction of big, bureaucratic government which could potentially exercise totalitarian control over its citizens. Basically, Chesterton and Belloc were convinced that the collectivist emphasis on efficiency and the rationalization of centralized planning were contrary to human nature.

In *What's Wrong with the World*, a seminal statement of his sociological vision, Chesterton highlighted the family as the starting point of understanding man as a political animal. Only within the web of family life, a true *Gemeinschaft* setting based firmly on the ownership of private property, did individuals initially satisfy their primary socialization needs. Here was the wellspring of personality and cognitive development, for it was from the family unit that one first encountered the wonders of the outside world. For Chesterton, the home was the initial sphere of liberty, the source of one's first chance for personal expression and creativity:

> The average man cannot cut clay into the shape of a man; but he can cut earth into the shape of a garden; and though he arranges it with red geraniums and blue potatoes in alternate straight lines, he is still an artist; because he has chosen. The average man cannot paint the sunset whose colours he admires; but he can paint his own house with what colour he chooses; and though he paints it pea green with pink spots, he is still an artist; because that is his choice. Property is merely the art of the democracy. It means that every man should have something that he can shape in his own image as he is shaped in the image of Heaven. (47)

For Chesterton, the state was no more than a human contrivance to protect the family as the most fundamental of social mechanisms, and, in his opinion, the integrity of this important vehicle of primary socialization could best be protected by the state's guarantee of private property, which Chesterton recognized as the mainspring of liberty and the source of creativity. Socialists, on the other hand, were intent upon strengthening and renewing the state, the shell of society, but were not particularly concerned about abetting the family, the very substance of society. Nor were socialists sensitive about basic familial relationships. Collectivism displayed no firm understanding of either the private (family life) or the public (government) aspects of human nature. Nowhere was this fact better exemplified than in the call for turning private property over to the state, which, in Belloc's view, was a truly "novel proposal—to do something new and as yet untried by men of our descent with our inherited instincts and ways of looking at things" (*The Alternative* 41).

It was Belloc who in 1912 with the publication of the *Ser*-

vile State first articulated the alternative to socialism and capitalism called Distributism. In this work Belloc prophesied that the socialists' attempts at wholesale nationalization would prove too difficult, and that there would be a compromise with capitalism, in which the owners of industry would be allowed to hold the means of production provided they accept the responsibility of keeping their workers in a tolerable living condition. The potentially revolutionary worker would be given security—in short, be bought off by bread and circuses—and thus, for all practical purposes, would become a slave to the capitalists and state bureaucrats. The remedy to this system of slavery (the "servile state") which Chesterton and Belloc demanded was restoration of the system of general property holding (i.e., Distributism) in place of the present scheme in which a large proportion of property was concentrated in the hands of a few capitalists.

In order to popularize their ideas the Chestertons and Belloc published a weekly journal which lasted under various names for nearly forty years. A Distributist League with branches all over Britain and throughout the world was set up in 1926. The League was designed to parallel the work of G. K.'s *Weekly* and to put Distributist ideas into practical application. The major objectives of the Distributist movement were the restoration of self-sufficient agriculture based on small holdings, the revival of small businesses, and the transfer of management and ownership of industry to workers. The Distributists worked out a trenchant critique of large-scale industrialism. Their objection was that mass production demeaned the laborer, made work itself drudgery, eroded the quality of craftsmanship, and led to the alienation of the worker. In their preoccupation with efficiency and profit, the economies of large-scale production destroyed the humanity of the individual laborer. It must be pointed out, however, that, contrary to the claims of its detractors, official Distributist policy was not anti-industrial. The league never called for a return to a purely agrarian subsistence economy reminiscent of medieval times. Instead, the ideal was a balanced economy where neither agriculture nor industry was based on large-scale organization, an economy in which those who labored owned the means of production.

Throughout the early years of its publication, G. K.'s *Weekly* gave steady support to working-class efforts to improve their position through the trade union movement, and, despite Chesterbelloc's hostility to the party system, recognized the possibility of reforming economic and social life via parliamentary politics. From 1925 through 1929, Chesterton's journal threw its support to the fledgling Labour Party, since it seemed to be the only parliamentary group battling plutocracy and the amelioration of the poor by servile devices. G. K.'s *Weekly*'s parliamentary correspondent, Henry Slesser, was convinced that Labour could be persuaded to accept the Distributist version of guild socialism, which might ultimately instill a belief in private ownership within the labor movement. By the autumn of 1927, however, G. K.'s *Weekly* and the Distributist movement began to question the wisdom of their support for trade unionism and for reform through parliamentary politics. This shift in attitude appears to have been caused by labor's growing willingness to collaborate with industrial capitalism and the governing establishment. Throughout 1928 and 1929 a group of Britain's major industrialists, inspired by Sir Alfred Mond, chairman of Imperial Chemical Industries (in Distributist opinion a model "monopoly capitalist") and major trade union officials undertook what was known as the "Mond-Turner" talks. The purpose of these deliberations was to overcome long-disputed differences between management and labor and to arrive at some compromise in the interest of industrial harmony. The discussions were purposely kept secret for fear of raising the wrath of extremists in both camps. In July 1929, the group published a report which indicated that the employers were willing to make concessions, including the recognition of trade unions as the sole bargaining agencies for workers and accepting changes in the unemployment insurance in favor of labor. Most importantly, the Mond-Turner report recommended the establishment of joint consultative machinery by the Trades Union Congress (TUC), the Federation of British Industries, and the National Confederation of Employers' Organizations. These proposals were bitterly attacked by Distributists, for they considered this closer understanding and cooperation between employers and workers to be the foundation of the servile state. The TUC's willingness to participate in these talks was, for Distributists, an indication that the trade unions had relinquished their struggle for ownership of the means of production. The trade union movement had forsaken the guild idea for the promise of security. From this time on, the Distributists moved further away from conventional politics and sought to gain support for their schemes through a variety of other expedients.

How relevant were the social, economic, and political views of G. K. Chesterton and Hilaire Belloc? Until recently it has been easier to recognize the validity of the Chesterbelloc's social and economic critique than their political analyses. Chesterton's and Belloc's political commentaries asserted that the electorate had no real power to control politicians and bureaucrats; in short, both the vote and the Member of Parliament in twentieth-century Britain were useless. This critique, which highlighted a plot, veiled in secrecy, to eliminate class and party conflict in the interest of an industrial and financial plutocracy, has been frequently dismissed as the ravings of bitter men obsessed with conspiracies.[3] However, two recent historical studies cast the Chesterbelloc's political critique in a different light; both these works should alter substantially the way scholars examine political practice in twentieth-century Britain. Major changes in the Official Secrets Act (modifying the ban on examining state documents from fifty to thirty years) have brought information into the public domain which substantiates arguments developed in these two books.

The more detailed of these two studies, Keith Middlemas's *Politics in Industrial Society: The Experience of the British System since 1911*, argues that by the early 1920s Britain's nineteenth-century political system had broken down under the weight of industrial conflict, the Irish problems, and World War I. What took its place was a government of "corporate bias," that is, government not by Parliament, but by a corporate triangle con-

3. For example, see Patrick Braybrooke; the writings of Henry Somerville, leader of the Catholic Social Guild and editor of the *Christian Democrat* during the 1920s; Wilfrid Sheed; and Michael Mason. Two of Chesterton's biographers, Maisie Ward and Dudley Barker, also have been critical of Chesterton's political obsessions.

Jay P. Corrin

sisting of the chief representative bodies of business, labor, and, on the government's side, officials of the state. The other study, *The Challenge of Labour: Shaping British Society, 1850-1930* by Keith Burgess, corroborated Middlemas's argument, though instead of accepting the latter's triangular model, Burgess identifies a series of "power blocs" which had a similar function. Unlike Middlemas, Burgess sheds more light on the role of bureaucrats who, though supposedly disinterested, had special connections and status-group ties with the various worlds of Oxbridge, industry, and finance. Burgess confirms the emergence of a power bloc by the 1930s that would successfully control British life for the next forty years. This power bloc was dominated by the bureaucrat: "The more 'progressive' sections of big industrial capital . . . a new managerial elite in the highest echelons of administration in commerce, industry, and government" (Burgess 248).

A major figure in this political transformation was David Lloyd George, the *bête noire* of the Chesterbelloc. Lloyd George was one of the first politicians to recognize the necessity of a managerial concept of government to overcome party and class differences and to create a special administrative body, or center group of power brokers, to regulate political and economic life. What particularly frightened Lloyd George and the moguls of industry were the anarcho-syndicalist activities of 1911-14, in which Chesterton and Belloc were leading figures.[4] This phenomenon clearly revealed that the official labor leadership was unable to control the extreme fringes of the working class movement by fusing it with parliamentary democracy. Syndicalist activity had potentially disastrous consequences for industrial production and political order, a situation all the more serious because of worsening diplomatic relations with Germany.

The attempts to formulate a coalition government during the constitutional crisis of 1911, together with David Lloyd George's efforts after the war to create a National Industrial Convention

4. For a detailed discussion of the role of the Chesterbelloc in these activities see Jay P. Corrin, "Labour Unrest and the Development of Anti-Statist Thinking in Britain, 1900-1914," *The Chesterton Review*, August 1982, February 1983, August 1983.

composed of government officials, business, and labor leaders which would discuss industrial problems, were, in Middlemas's thesis, the first attempts to create a formal, triangular power bloc. It was hoped that a special tripartite national body, through consensus among its leadership, would guide Britain away from class antagonism and political crises and thereby insure the kind of harmony required for steady economic growth. In the words of W. Milne-Bailey of the TUC Research Department, a leading proponent of the new cooperation theory as a means of ending economic conflict, Britain's traditional political institutions were not fit for the task: "A Parliament of the ordinary democratic kind, elected on a territorial basis, is largely ignorant, and is bound to be ignorant of industrial needs and problems, and to that extent is a very unsatisfactory authority for industrial regulation and legislation" (Middlemas 213). What Milne-Bailey, Lloyd George, and others had in mind was a managerial concept of government, and this process was capped, according to Middlemas, by the Mond-Turner talks of 1928.

In February 1929, the National Confederation of Employers Organizations, the Federation of British Industries, and the TUC agreed to undertake permanent discussions on fundamental questions of industrial legislation, unemployment, and national economic policy. Due to the fact that the TUC and employers associations had not succeeded in making their institutions fully representative, and because their new alliance with the state was vulnerable to revolt from below, it became official policy from the very beginning to keep this triangular relationship shrouded in secrecy. Middlemas asserts that by the 1930s this new institutional collaboration had supplemented the parliamentary system and was largely responsible for the relative harmony of the interwar years. During this period the function of the political parties changed, and henceforth, under the tutelage of the triangular bloc, ideological differences and substantive discussions largely disappeared from party warfare. Thus, long before 1945, Parliament had ceased to be the supreme governing body in Britain. It subordinated itself to the managerial powers of the state's bureaucratic apparatus. Parliament's function was to be an electoral source of the majority which provided the party element in government, though, according to Middlemas, the electoral cycle itself had no effect whatever on economic and political decisions (Middlemas 22). If anything, the old political system was used by the corporate leaders to win popular mandates for decisions they either had already arrived at or would soon make.

Both Middlemas and Burgess describe a process in the consolidation of power away from Parliament and popular democracy that, at the time, was identified with exquisite precision in the political criticisms of the Chesterbelloc. The formation of Middlemas's corporate triangle was called "Mondism" by G. K.'s Weekly. The paper frequently remarked on the interlocking interests and relationships between government officers, bankers, industrial magnates, and trade union leaders. Indeed, Mond himself was referred to in G. K.'s Weekly as the "Apostle of Rationalization," an appellation that in the Weberian sense accords perfectly with the Middlemas thesis.[5]

As early as September 1928, G. K.'s Weekly told its readers that it did not make any difference which party won power at the next general election, because all three parties were pledged to obey the governmental and industrial bureaucracies. As for the Mond-Turner conferences, the paper accurately identified them as marking the accession of the official trade union leadership into the political establishment, thereby completing what Middlemas identified as the corporate triangle. In 1935 Belloc wrote that Parliament had fallen under the dictatorial control of an oligarchy, a group of wirepullers far beyond the sway of public opinion. What was left of the old parliamentary system, argued Belloc, was bound up with all the "forces of the state": the lawyers, industrialists, the bankers, the civil service, and the new bourgeoisie of the labor leadership.

The studies of Middlemas and Burgess demonstrate the relevance of the Chesterbelloc's political analysis. Rather than being an exaggerated or distorted description of political practice, Chesterton's and Belloc's critique seems to have identified accurately a series of circumstances and events which brought about a substantial shift in power away from the locus of

5. For example, see the January 3, 1931, issue of G. K.'s Weekly.

legitimate authority—Parliament—to special interest groups and bureaucrats. The acuity of the Chesterbelloc's political analysis has not yet been recognized by most historians of modern British politics.

The present relevance of the Chesterbelloc's social and economic message is substantiated by a number of significant contemporary thinkers who assume positions and arguments similar to Chesterton's and Belloc's. One noteworthy writer who stands out here, a man who has won wide acclaim for his fresh insights and ideas, is the French social historian Jacques Ellul. In *The Technological Society*, Ellul argues that the western infatuation with mechanics and technology has led us, unconsciously, to reconstruct social institutions, in particular the state, on the model of machines. In the process, individuals themselves unwittingly have been turned into interchangeable parts to fit the engine of state. Besides destroying what is human in humanity, this model has led to an enormous increase in the dominion of government, a tendency which evolved out of peoples' blind faith in the power of political action to solve all problems. Ellul recognized one of Marx's greatest failings: that revolution, rather than dissolving the superstructures of government and state, has done exactly the opposite. Each revolution since 1789 has led to the enlargement of the state.

The modern "political illusion," argues Ellul, is that people in democracies think that they really control the state. Although people have increased their dependency on the state and choose others to represent them in government, elected officials in practice have no way of controlling the sprawling administrative complex of which they are a part. Professional politicians, therefore, perform two basic tasks: to manipulate information to influence public opinion, and to prevent the emergence of nonconforming political forces. Real decision-making is done by those who understand the technical complexities of administering the state apparatus, namely experts and bureaucrats. Ellul believes that modern democratic political organs have no other purpose than to endorse decisions already made by technocrats and special interest groups (*The Political Illusion* 138). Much like Chesterton and Belloc, Ellul also calls for a revolution against the entrap-

Jay P. Corrin

ment of statism which, in merging with technology, has produced massive alienation and dehumanization. In *Autopsy of Revolution*, Ellul argues for a cultural revolution which, unlike all other revolutions, will not succumb to the expedient of organization that is required for efficiency and only serves to strengthen the state. Ellul's revolution requires a "decreased efficiency" in all areas, a lowered standard of living, a reduction in large-scale organization of all kinds, and, most importantly, a new kind of culture that will reawaken the virtues of individualism and personal responsibility.

Ellul is not alone in calling for a basic moral transformation of contemporary society. Perhaps the best-known spokesman for decentralization, a man whom Theodore Roszak has called the "Keynes of post-industrial society," was the late E. F. Schumacher. Schumacher's best-selling book, *Small Is Beautiful*, could easily be called a manual for Distributist economics. Like those of Chesterton and Belloc, Schumacher's concerns start with people. In his view it is morally imperative that the economic system serve the long-range needs of ordinary people, not the immediate gratifications of elite interest groups. Instead of continuing to rely on large-scale industrialization which consumes the foundation upon which it is based, unrenewable resources, Schumacher urges us to develop new methods of production and consumption that will permanently serve the community. The alternative to total preoccupation with growth ("more, further, quicker, richer") is a balanced economy based on agriculture and small-scale industry utilizing methods of production that are biologically sound. Schumacher also sees it necessary to change our whole approach to work. Rather than continuing to enslave ourselves to technology, we need to utilize a new kind of technology, "technology with a human face," in order that people have a chance to enjoy themselves while working, so that labor, once again, can become meaningful and creative for the individual worker. Much like the Distributists and guild socialists, Schumacher also sees the efficacy of developing new forms of partnership between management and labor, even demonstrating the practical success of new experiments based on common ownership of the means of production. In his commentary on work as a means of developing human character, Schumacher reveals a close affinity to one of the most perceptive of all Distributist thinkers, the artist-craftsman Eric Gill.

Similar concerns are voiced in the writings of Ivan Illich, a scholar who has brought Distributist-type analysis to the Center of Intercultural Documentation in Guernavaca, Mexico. For years the center has done research on industrial society and has tried to develop alternative modes of production for the post-industrial age. Illich's research demonstrates that the industrialization of any service agency—whether it be education, compulsory insurance, or public transport—leads to negative effects analogous to the corrosive results brought by overproduction of goods in the market place. Illich concludes that any institution or service has a limit to its growth beyond which the scale of operation frustrates the end for which it was originally developed. Such a condition can even threaten society itself. This destructive process occurs any time the scale of operation isolates people from one another and undermines the texture of the community through the necessary introduction of specialization in services. Growth which accelerates faster than traditional institutions can guide society will ultimately transform the individual into an unthinking automaton whose only purpose is to serve the machines of bureaucracy.

The views of Illich, Schumacher, and Ellul, although they run against all conventional economic wisdom, are gaining international attention and respect. They have received kudos from those who recognize the need for fresh approaches to the chaos of contemporary social and economic ills. Peter Barnes, for example, reviewing Schumacher's *Small Is Beautiful* in the *New Republic,* recommended the author for a Nobel prize in economics. Previous Nobel winners have been "measurers," "tinkerers," and "growth addicts." Barnes concluded that it was "time to turn the spotlight around, to start digging out some subterranean wisdom before we are all buried under a billowing cloud of madness and sledge."

The writings of Illich, Ellul, and Schumacher highlight the relevance of Chesterbellocian social and economic criticism within certain contemporary intellectual circles. A host of other people in business, labor, and politics, almost too numerous to catalogue, also have begun to approach economic and social issues along these lines. Note, for instance, the ideas of the student counter-culture of the late 1960s and, more recently, those associated with the Green Movement in Germany. Both have rejected the unlimited technological growth of an acquisitive society that is ecologically unsound in favor of a simpler standard of living. Being distrustful of the due process of administrators and bureaucrats, they have tried to curb the power of these groups by bringing ordinary citizens back into the political process. Although few of these people acknowledge a debt to Chesterton and Belloc, the fact that they are now looking at life from the perspective of Distributism is testimony to the timeliness of the Chesterbelloc's message.[6]

In Chesterton's and Belloc's own day, Distributism did not capture sufficient attention. Chesterton and Belloc had been effectively boycotted by the predominant media brokers of the most influential newspapers as far back as 1918. Both were also seen chiefly as Catholic apologists, indeed militants of the faith. In countries such as France or Italy this attitude might have presented no problem, but in Britain, with its almost unbroken tradition of anti-Catholicism, the Chesterbelloc's Roman connection seriously prejudiced their cause. The pervasive Whig-Protestant bias within English intellectual circles forced Chesterton and Belloc to assume especially tendentious approaches in their writing of history. Belloc, in particular, seems to have exaggerated his ideas just to attract some public attention, a situation which only served to highlight the Chesterbelloc's public image of unrespectable political extremism. Furthermore, some stalwart advocates of Distributism in assuming rather intolerant,

6. A number of important post–World War II writers and publications have developed social, political, and economic critiques of modernity that are Distributist in tone. Many have acknowledged their debt to Chesterton and Belloc. In particular, see the work of F. A. Hayek; Max Eastman; Wilhelm Roepke; Garry Wills; William Chamberlain; Henry Hazlett; Hazel Herderson; Jane Jacobs; and the Report for the Club of Rome's Project on the Predicament of Mankind, Dennis L. and Donella Meadows, et al., eds., *The Limits of Growth.*

self-righteous positions tended to obfuscate the essence of the Distributist message. As Christopher Derrick has written, "Chesterton was accused of wild exaggeration: he talked about the seed as though it were a tree." But Chesterton did so because he had the perspicacity to recognize what kind of tree was going to grow. Few in his day had the foresight to see that the tree would bear poisonous fruit (Derrick 228). The Distributist message in the 1920s and 1930s seemed irrelevant because of the increasing success of the welfare state and the recognition of a need for a bigger and more interventionist government which would not only have the power to increase its control of society but also to shepherd its industrial growth.

The most salient feature of western societies in the twentieth century, and a phenomenon generally welcomed by public opinion, has been the expansion of the state. The state has grown not only for purely mechanical reasons, but also because this century has witnessed an almost uninterrupted series of crises and emergencies which, in themselves, encouraged the concentration of political power. With the exception of the Chesterbelloc and a minority of others (in Britain, the guild socialist and the so-called "pluralists," John Neville Figgis, Harold Laski, et al.), the rest of the western world did not appreciate the evils of statist tendencies until after the horrors of Nazi Germany and Stalinism in the Soviet Union. In the 1920s and 1930s, the promises of *Gesellschaft* had not yet turned into nightmares. Here, as elsewhere, Chesterton and Belloc were ahead of their times. In the first four decades of the twentieth century, the evils which they forecasted were still largely abstract issues for the majority of Britons. Since then, however, the old ideals of industrialism, growth, technology, bigness, and so on, have come down to earth, and today the message of Distributism seems far more relevant.

Nevertheless, Distributism failed in its day as a political movement, and it continues to fail to attract the imagination of the common people. This failure may spring from an incorrect assumption of its defenders about human nature. Distributism, being a voluntarist movement, is dependent on individuals who must will its existence. The dilemma for Distributists was that they worked to maximize the individual's liberty, but the majority of people have persistently preferred the security of a fixed income, a guaranteed job, and health care to the risks associated with self-employment. Perhaps humans naturally seek security before liberty. After all, the burden of making freedom work, the immense responsibility of wielding true liberty, may possibly be beyond the strength of everyman. Such was the fear of both Durkheim and Toennies. A more recent argument along these lines can be found in the work of the late Erich Fromm. In his monumental study *Escape from Freedom*, Fromm explained the social and psychological attractions of totalitarian movements. The absence of security and the constraints of preindustrial communities did cause many to experience isolation, anxiety, and powerlessness. To escape from the burden of freedom, modern humanity submits to larger movements, organizations, or governments which remove the difficulties of liberty, yet at the same time provide security. This attraction of a "false *Gemeinschaft*" works against the Distributist promise to return freedom and responsibility to modern life. As long as modern people desire only material success, maintain their Faustian quest for growth, and continue their worship of mammon, the social and economic propositions of Gilbert Keith Chesterton and Hilaire Belloc, though clearly relevant, will never succeed.

Works Cited

Barnes, Peter. Review of Schumacher's *Small Is Beautiful* in the *New Republic* (June 15, 1974).

Belloc, Hilaire. *The Alternative*. London: Distributist Books, 1947.

Braybrooke, Patrick. *Some Thoughts on Hilaire Belloc*. London: Drane's, 1923.

Burgess, Keith. *The Challenge of Labour: Shaping British Society, 1850-1930*. New York: St. Martin's Press, 1980.

Chesterton, G. K. *The Autobiography of G. K. Chesterton*. New York: Sheed & Ward, 1936.

_____. *What's Wrong with the World*. London: Cassell & Co., 1910.

Corrin, Jay P. "Labour Unrest and the Development of Anti-Statist Thinking in Britain, 1900-1914." *The Chesterton Review*. Aug. 1982, Feb. 1983, Aug. 1983.

Derrick, Christopher. "Chesterton and the Pursuit of Happiness." *The Chesterton Review*. Spring/Summer, 1980: 228.

Durkheim, Emile. *Suicide: A Study in Sociology*. Trans. John A. Spaulding and George Simpson. Glencoe, IL: Free Press, 1951.

Eastman, Max. *Reflections on the Failure of Socialism*. New York: Grosset & Dunlap, 1955.

Ellul, Jacques. *Autopsy of Revolution*. Trans. Patricia Wolf. New York: Knopf, 1971.

_____. *The Political Illusion*. Trans. Konrad Kellen. New York: Vintage Books, 1972.

_____. *The Technological Society*. Trans. John Wilkinson. New York: Knopf, 1964.

Fromm, Erich. *Escape from Freedom*. New York: Farrar & Rinehart, Inc., 1941.

F. A. Hayek; Wilhelm Roepke; Garry Wills; William Chamberlain; Henry Hazlett.

Henderson, Hazel. *Creating Alternative Futures: The End of Economics*. New York: Berkeley Pub. Corp., 1978.

Illich, Ivan. *Tools for Conviviality*. New York: Harper & Row, 1973.

Jacobs, Jane. *Cities and the Wealth of Nations*. New York: PUBL, 1984.

Mason, Michael. "Chesterbelloc." *G. K. Chesterton: A Half Century of Views*. Ed. D. J. Conlon. New York: 1987.

Middlemas, Keith. *Politics in Industrial Society: The Experience of the British System since 1911*. London: A. Deutsch, 1979.

Report for the Club of Rome's Project on the Predicament of Mankind, Dennis L. and Donella Meadows, et al., eds., *The Limits of Growth* (New York: PUBL, 1974).

Schumacher, E. F. *Small Is Beautiful: Economics As If People Mattered*. New York: Harper & Row, 1975.

Sheed, Wilfrid. *The Morning After: Essays and Reviews*. New York: Warner Paperback Library, 1972.

Somerville, Henry. Ed. *Christian Democrat*.

Toennies, Ferdinand. "The Concept of Gemeinschaft." *Ferdinand Toennies on Sociology: Pure, Applied, and Emipirical*. Ed. Werner J. Cahnman and Rudolf Heberle. Chicago: University of Chicago Press, 1971.

Webb, Sidney. *Fabian Essays*. London: The Fabian Society, 1889.

IV. PROCLAIMING THE RIDDLE: THEIR APOLOGETICS

Chesterton in Debate with Blatchford: The Development of a Controversialist

David J. Dooley

In an article entitled "Chesterton's Landmark Year: The Blatch-ford-Chesterton Debate of 1903-1904" (*Chesterton Review*, November 1984), Stanley L. Jaki expressed surprise that little attention had been paid to what Chesterton referred to in his *Autobiography* as "a landmark in my life"—his lengthy controversy with Robert Blatchford, editor of a very influential Socialist paper, the *Clarion*. Near the end of the dispute, Chesterton wrote three articles for the *Clarion* in defense of Christianity; but his argument with Blatchford had been going on for a year and a half before that, and Jaki did not have room in his article to analyze some of Chesterton's earlier contributions — especially some long letters he wrote to the paper. Chesterton's early contributions to the debate are worth looking at in detail, especially because of what they tell us about Chesterton's methods of conducting an argument at this phase of his career.

In a preface to Robert Blatchford's *My Eighty Years*, his longtime friend Alexander M. Thompson called Blatchford a great man; declared that in his "fighting period" between 1890 and

---

DAVID J. DOOLEY is professor emeritus of St. Michael's College, University of Toronto. He has written several books, as well as edited volume one of *The Collected Works of G. K. Chesterton*.

1920 he had done more to improve the lot of the British people than any statesman, general, or man of letters; and quoted a tribute to the combative journalist from Chesterton:

> Very few intellectual swords have left such a mark on our time, have cut so deep or remained so clean. . . . His case for Socialism, as far as it goes, is so clear and simple that anyone would understand it, when it was put properly; . . . his triumphs were triumphs of strong style, native pathos, and picturesque metaphor; his very lucidity was a generous sympathy with simple minds. . . . For the rest, he has triumphed by being honest and by not being afraid. (Blatchford, *My Eighty Years*, 1931)

As Thompson explained in a lengthy article in the *Clarion* for July 22, 1904, on January 23 of the previous year Blatchford had published an enthusiastic review of Haeckel's *The Riddle of the Universe*. In his "unreasonable and uncalculating way," as Thompson put it, he concluded that the book demolished the entire structure upon which the religions of the world were built: "There is no escape from that conclusion. The case for science is complete." The members of the *Clarion* staff uttered a collective gasp at the thought of such an uncompromising attack upon circulation; the cashier "wrapped himself in his Returns Book as in a garment, and disparagingly whistled Strauss' waltzes through clenched teeth." In any event, however, the series of articles which Blatchford subsequently wrote attracted a great deal of attention; they were published as a book under the title *God and My Neighbour*; and Thompson's article was occasioned by the appearance of a sixpenny edition of this book, after the original edition had sold out.

To all reproaches that he was undermining the great work which the *Clarion* was called upon to do, Blatchford replied that it had to be done: "My object is not so much to help to destroy an obsolete religion, as to help to build up a better religion in its place. It will be a big job, and I shall be tired before it is through. But I shall do it" (*Clarion*, July 22, 1904). His views on religion, as Thompson described them, complemented his views on philosophy and politics. His philosophy said, "The time to be happy is now"; his politics, "The place to be happy is here — in

England"; and his religion, "The way to be happy is to make others happy" (*Clarion*, July 22, 1904). Believing that the old religion forgets about the "neighbor" part of the commandment to love, he argued that "to build a cathedral, and to spend our tears and pity upon a Saviour who was crucified nearly two thousand years ago, while women and little children are being crucified in our midst, without pity and without help, is cant, and sentimentality, and a mockery of God" (*Clarion*, July 22, 1904).

His was no wanton attack on the faith of others, Thompson said. In order to establish his socialistic claims on behalf of the world's failures, he had to begin by showing that social failure is not owing to individual sin but to heredity and environment: "Before we can propagate our religion of Determinism and Humanism, we must first clear the ground of Free Will, of Sin against God, and of the belief in the divine inspiration of the Bible" (*Clarion*, July 22, 1904). Even as his pamphlet "Merrie England" (which sold over a million copies) was the concrete expression of new economic and social theories and sentiments, so *God and My Neighbour* was the concrete expression of the twentieth century's assimilation of the divine with the secular.

On page five of the *Clarion* for January 2, 1903, there appeared a long article by "Nunquam" (a pseudonym Blatchford used) on "Christianity and Socialism." In reply to a letter of objection, Blatchford contended that for centuries the organized Christian church had put dogma ahead of truth and had fiercely, even cruelly, opposed any new discovery which controverted its dogmas. He stated his preference for an older and more tolerant faith—Buddhism.

The religious controversy began in earnest, however, when Blatchford praised a new cheap edition of Haeckel's book *The Riddle of the Universe*, translated by Joseph McCabe, in his "In the Library" column for January 23. "If any reader still imagines that the theory of evolution is incomplete," he asserted, "let him read this book of Haeckel's." The conclusion he came to was one which he was to repeat again and again: "A religion which will not bear the truth will have to go, no matter how dear to some of us it may be."

In the next issue, the whole of his "In the Library" column on page five was devoted to the controversy he had aroused. He gave answers especially to three letters, concluding with one question, "Is religion *true?*" For weeks afterwards, his own articles on religion and science kept appearing, together with some rejoinders. On February 20, for example, there was an article, "Religion and Science," by Nunquam on the first page, occupying five columns, and five more columns on page eight in which two clergymen responded to his arguments.

While Blatchford was continuing his attacks on Christianity, Chesterton began a running rebuttal of them in his regular Saturday column in the *Daily News* and in six articles in the monthly *Commonwealth* published between July and December, 1903. Blatchford referred to one of the pieces in the *Clarion* for March 27:

> Mr. G. K. Chesterton, who gave a column to me and my "rationalism" in the "Daily News," takes the same erroneous view of my position. His article is witty and brilliant, but it amounts to little more than a statement that Mr. Chesterton believes in some form of spiritual life because nearly all other men believe in something of the kind.
>
> I do not challenge Mr. Chesterton's belief, nor does his belief touch mine.
>
> I maintain that if there is a God, Christians have not found Him. Mr. Chesterton's essay is delightful, it is friendly, it is clever; but, so far as my argument is concerned, Mr. Chesterton might just as well have let off a catherine wheel as his brilliant article. A catherine wheel is a pleasing firework. But one cannot argue with a catherine wheel. And, pretty, and sparkling, and surprising as a catherine wheel may be, it cannot be seriously regarded as a contribution to a theological debate.

These comments give a good indication of the tone the two opponents were to adopt to each other. In fact, Blatchford shows more humor here than he usually does; his articles are filled with dogged reiteration of a few main points, but if he disagrees with Chesterton he has no animus against him. As for Chesterton, in his *Daily News* column for March 14, he said that it had been a great mistake to cease talking about our religious differences; he welcomed the end put to this nonsense by "one of the most genuine men alive, Mr. Blatchford." Yet Blatchford could not have been entirely pleased by Chesterton's reference to "his childlike emphasis — as if he had heard of Christianity for the first time" ("The Return of the Angels," *Daily News*, March 14, 1903).

In his paper for July 31, 1903, Blatchford mentioned that he had received heaps of letters about his attack on free will, but he spent almost all of his three full-length columns dealing with "Mr. Chesterton, who has honored me by writing a delightful, but wholly unconvincing reply in the 'Daily News.'" In this reply, which Blatchford quotes almost *in toto*, Chesterton had left himself open to rebuttal in surprising ways. For example, he had defended another article in the *Commonwealth*, which Blatchford had called brilliant and paradoxical, by saying that he had the advantage of youth and spoke for his generation. Collect any seven or eight really cultivated young men in London, he said, and the chances are that three or four of them will believe in the reality of supernatural or preternatural phenomena ("The Return of the Angels," *Daily News*, March 14, 1903). Naturally, Blatchford raised an eyebrow at this claim; was not Chesterton going too far when he spoke for the first seven or eight cultivated young men one met in London? "I do know a good many men of education and intelligence," he said, "and my experience is the very reverse of his."

Chesterton also appeared vulnerable in something else he said: "When we read sentences like 'No, Mr. Chesterton, we shall not cease our war against Christianity. We have got rid of hell, we have got rid of the devil,' and so on: 'before long we shall have destroyed the belief in miracles' — we only murmur sadly, '1860.'" ("The Return of the Angels," *Daily News*, March 14, 1903). Was it very sensible of Chesterton to adopt the blasé attitude of someone who had seen it all before, who had lived through the arguments surrounding *Essays and Reviews* in 1860 and the appearance of Darwin's *Origin of Species* shortly before — controversies which had occurred years before he was born?

Yet in a sense, as A. L. Maycock brings out in his *The Man Who Was Orthodox*, Chesterton did have a valid point to make. The main ground of Blatchford's attack "was that the Church

David J. Dooley

was indifferent to social injustice and was no more than the subservient ally of capitalism" (a selection from the uncollected works of G. K. Chesterton, in Maycock, London: 1963, 55). When it came to discussing Christian belief, it was very apparent that Blatchford had no idea what historic Christianity really was. The object of his strictures was something quite provincial and ephemeral — that same Victorian Calvinism against which the new theologians were reacting so strongly.

Chesterton was not merely defending Christianity, therefore, but a purer form of Christianity than the materialized version which he and others had thought existed in the high Victorian era. Much of what Blatchford said was true, Maycock wrote, and could have been written by a convinced Christian. In support he quoted a summing up of the controversy by an Anglican clergyman, Chesterton's good friend Conrad Noel, in the *Daily News* for September 23, 1904:

> We must always remember that the main object of rationalist attack is the popular theology of fifty years ago, and not the religion of today nor the religion of the Gospels, nor of the first centuries, nor of what are called the "Dark Ages." . . . Everyone knows of this curious theology and nobody believes it or reckons with it, except the very ignorant and conservative agnostics who still fuss and chatter round it and preach about it and treat it as of the utmost importance. The thinking, living Christian has outgrown it, forgotten it. (Maycock 56).

There is no objection to any Christian reading the works of Blatchford and his ilk, he continued, except that he will find the religion which these gentlemen attack much more effectively demolished by the leading Anglican, Roman, and Presbyterian theologians.

If it could be argued that Chesterton was not presuming too much when he murmured "1860," he was very much in error when he adopted, or seemed to adopt, a patronizing attitude to his adversary. The world is young and youth always appears paradoxical to its elders, he said: "We cannot help going forward and being happy—in the new spring of belief. No, Mr. Blatchford, you will not cease your war against Christianity; but Christianity

200

(being otherwise employed) will cease its war against you." Now, it was quite in order for Newman to say that he was in a train of thought far above petty slanders and to say, "Away with you, Mr. Kingsley, and fly into space." But Chesterton deserved, and got, a trenchant reply: that the assertion that Christianity is otherwise engaged "comes oddly from a writer who is engaged in writing a series of articles against me; and it sounds peculiar at a time when the Christian Social Union has announced a campaign against me, and when sermons and articles attacking my views are coming in every post." Let us be candid, and not pretend, Blatchford went on: "To pretend that you are mobilizing your forces because the enemy is beneath contempt is absurd."

This incident taught Chesterton a lesson he was not to forget. The first of his letters to the *Clarion*, published on August 7, 1903, began with an apology:

> Dear Mr. Blatchford,—I should be genuinely grateful if you would insert this letter in the CLARION, but chiefly because this would give me the opportunity of publicly correcting what appears to be a possible interpretation of my personal tone. If any phrases of mine have been so clumsy as to convey the idea that I thought you, or pretended to think you, "incompetent and stupid," they expressed the very reverse of my thoughts. I think of you what I have always thought—that you are an honor to England and to journalism, and that I am proud to be of the same people and the same trade.

In "Pope and the Art of Satire," which appeared in *Five Types*, Chesterton showed how well he had learned the lesson Blatchford taught him. We are not generous enough to write great satire, he said: to attack a man so that he feels the attack and half acknowledges its justice, it is necessary to have a certain intellectual magnanimity which realizes the merits of the opponent as well as its defects (Freeport, NY: Books for Libraries Press, 1969 [1911], 20-22). There may be some exceptions, but again and again in controversy, and certainly in the Blatchford debate, he did demonstrate that magnanimity himself.

In his column of July 31, Blatchford had contended that if God is omnipotent God was responsible for Adam's sin. He reinforced the point with a series of sharp hammer blows:

Now, then, did God make Adam? He did. Did God make the faculties of his brain? He did. Did God make his curiosity strong and his obedience weak? He did. Then, if this man Adam was so made that his desire would overcome his obedience, was it not a foregone conclusion that he would eat that apple? It was. In that case, what becomes of the freedom of the will?

Finally, he crystallized his argument into one sentence: since God is responsible for human existence, God is responsible for all human acts. "If any reader can show me any way of escape from that conclusion," he wrote, "I shall be glad to hear from him."

Naturally, after his preliminary apology Chesterton had a try. ". . . I had got a notion, from your earlier remarks," he said, "that you did admit that blame could attach to one man for his conduct to another. The passage which misled me occurred in the article of March 20, and ran: 'But he (man) can be un-just and cruel and base and mean towards his fellow man, and he often is. He can sin against his fellow man, and he often does'" (*Clarion*, Aug. 7, 1903). Given this marvelous oppor-tunity, Chesterton exploits the self-contradiction fully, playing with it in the way Meredith describes as typical of the comic spirit:

> For Folly is the natural prey of the Comic, known to it in all her transformations, in every disguise; and it is with the springing delight of hawk over heron, hound after fox, that it gives her chase, never fretting, never tiring, sure of having her, allowing her no rest. (George Meredith, *An Essay on Comedy*, Wylie Sypher, ed. Gar-den City, NY: 1956, 33)

"Allowing her no rest" certainly applies in this case; Chesterton pursues his victim through one lengthy paragraph after another, amounting in all to about 1500 words.

The Comic Muse employs many rhetorical flourishes — a great deal of parallelism, a series of questions, repetitions with variation building up to a decisive climax; in fact Chesterton is here employing his best platform manner, which can best be il-lustrated by a somewhat extensive quotation:

> The Christian fantasy crops up in the most unlikely places. Even

202

in the CLARION, for instance, I have seen writers distributing a grave and tender blame to their political opponents and to those who adulterate milk and butter and rack-rent slums. But you, on your principle, hold all these men guiltless. Why do you not come to their rescue? Why this immersion in the Garden of Eden? Why this exaggerated tenderness for the reputation of Adam, a gentleman who has been dead some time, and left only distant relations living? Shake off this exaggerated respect for the Old Testament. Clear yourself, Mr. Blatchford, from these Hebraic mists. You have discovered something infinitely more sensational and modern than any dusty Bible criticism: you have discovered this lucid and interesting fact—that whether Lord Penrhyn starves himself to save his men, or saves himself by putting poison in their beer, he is equally spotless as the flowers of spring.

As we would expect, Chesterton takes special delight in paradox and antithesis and in turning an argument upside down. Blatchford, he says, is not attacking Christianity at all, but the whole of human civilization, Europe, the *Clarion*—and himself. Two other points need to be made, however, about the nature of Chesterton's argument. One is that, even though he seems to be giving rein to a wild and exuberant fancy, some of his illustrations are very concrete:

> What is the point of insisting that a man cannot say that Adam fell, when by the same argument a man cannot even say, "Please pass the mustard"? For "please" means "if you please," and this is free will: the Blatchfordian formula would be "if God has so constructed your psychology."

The other point is that, for all his rhetorical flourishes, for all the verbal pyrotechnics which left Blatchford bewildered and not sure whether or not his opponent was a mountebank, Chesterton went straight to the heart of the matter. Claiming that Blatchford's rationalism would mean the end of all civilization, he went on in his concluding paragraph to say that the strength of Christianity has nothing to do with controversial ingenuity. It is simply that Christianity is indispensable: those who attack it wind up in positions which no sane mass of people have ever held, such as Schopenhauer saying that life is a delusion, or Nietzsche saying that charity is a delusion, or Nunquam saying that human goodness and badness are delusions. So Christianity guards, through the ages, an eternal sanity.

Blatchford responded on August 14 by saying that he had never denied the existence of a will, but that he had raised questions concerning its origin. He admitted that he had been inconsistent in saying that man can sin against man; given a certain frame of mind and a certain environment, an intolerant and abusive man cannot be blamed for being so. But even if we do not blame the man who burns a house down any more than we blame a shark which devours a baby, we take steps to resist him; similarly, the editor of the *Clarion* can give a clerk a scolding, as part of the educational process.

Chesterton seized with delight on these and similar statements in his reply of August 28. This letter was fully two columns long—two newspaper columns, in eight-point type, type almost indecently small. In fact, he apologized for the length of his letter, saying that he had a fancy it might end the matter on his part, and that one long letter would be better than many short ones. But he began by writing, "I am sure you are enjoying this argument as much as I am, and it was like your chivalry to answer me at such length." His own chivalry, of course, did not prevent him from attacking Blatchford in a forceful, if paradoxical way: "You talk as if you were amputating a malignant growth when you are only cutting off your nose to spite your face."

Again the way in which Chesterton builds up his argument is very interesting to watch. His paragraphs are long — one of them contains about 600 words — and the thought in them is developed at length, with a good deal of repetition and parallelism, as when he suggests that one cannot harpoon a vicar who has become a public nuisance in the way you might harpoon a whale—regarding the one as being just as innocent as the other:

> Who expects to harpoon vicars? What is the use in this real and living world of people who will do nothing against public nuisances but knock them down or lock them up? What is the use of saying that society is a garden and the wicked are weeds? You cannot grub up selfish brothers with a spade. You cannot go about with a rake weeding out hypochondriac old gentlemen. You cannot scatter Keating's powder and find the ground strewn with the corpses of

interfering aunts. These are the real problems of society, and if they are to be resisted, they must be blamed.

As we have seen, Blatchford had said that it would be appropriate to scold a clerk, if not to blame him, and Chesterton was at his best in inquiring how you could do one without the other. He imagines the situation in very graphic terms:

> On your principles, you would say, "My blameless Ruggles, the anger of God against you has once more driven you, a helpless victim, to put your boots on my desk and upset the ink on the ledger. Let us weep together." If that is the way clerks are scolded in the CLARION office, gaily will one I now apply for the next vacancy in that philosophical establishment.

Even then he is not finished with the scolding of the clerk: he carries the idea on, plays with it, teases Blatchford with it, for another twenty-two lines.

He still has two major points to make, one on the modern ignorance of philosophy, the other on the difference between Christian and Oriental mysticism. Physical discussions can be definitely ended, he writes, but philosophical ones can only be reduced to their first principles. So "when you say that man cannot sin and add that hate is a crime, I can stop you at the contradiction." On the second question, one Chestertonian paradox followed another. Blatchford seems to think that Christianity has taken up its position only against skepticism and materialism; he does not realize that it has also to defend itself against religious fanaticism. For example, Christianity has to defend itself against the fatalistic fanaticism of the Oriental mystic, the dehumanized piety of the man who says "God is angry" when he is struck on the face by a tyrant. So Chesterton describes how the Blatchford religion came out of the East, scimitar in hand, and rocked the civilization of free will on its throne, until it was driven back across the Danube, "leaving us progress and free will." It is the position of Blatchford, therefore, which is inimical to progress and to scientific inquiry, as Chesterton implies, leaving for once the implication to be drawn. But he does conclude by turning the tables neatly on Blatchford, making him seem allied with quietism and passivity.

"And Christianity has always seen afar off this symbolic Blatchford, who, in his religious monism and utter consciousness of God, froze all human effort, and insulted all human dignity." It is Blatchford, paradoxically, not Chesterton himself, who is made to seem a religious fanatic: the so-called infidel is really a believer, in fact too fanatical and rigid a believer.

In the article "Clerical Logic," on November 13, Blatchford expressed astonishment at one of Chesterton's *Commonwealth* articles: he quoted a long passage in which Chesterton listed many of the indictments Blatchford brought against Christianity and then said, "He is perfectly right in all these assumptions. That is he is perfectly right in everything, except in not following them to their obvious Christian deduction." Blatchford then took up two questions raised by his opponent. To the comment that the killing of heretics by Christians was hardly worse than the persecution under the last reform movement, the French Revolution, he replied that at least the revolutionists did not torture their enemies or burn them alive. To the assertion that the infinite world of the solar systems could not be nobler than that revealed by Genesis, he answered, "If Mr. Chesterton does not regard the universe of science as a grander and nobler, as well as a larger, scheme than that of Genesis, I can only say that I do not agree with him." He also accused Chesterton of undue haste —"He is in such a hurry"—and of flippancy: "Mr. Chesterton can think clearly enough and write clearly enough; it is only because he finds it cheaper, and easier, to show off than to reason that he descends to the levity of which he is too often guilty." Then he came back to the fact about Christianity which, he said, all the King's bishops and all the Pope's men could not disprove: "It is not true."

In his reply (November 20 — only a column and a half) Chesterton dealt with the question of whether the French revolutionaries were less cruel than Christians in the treatment of their enemies and moved on from this to the question of persecution in general. He said that he did not understand why one human being should want to torture another: "The real truth is that we are in this matter in the presence of one of the permanent riddles of human nature—the sort of riddles which you entirely ignore." Of two possible explanations, his own is that there is a certain dreadful impatience sleeping in men which can break out as cruelty when it is thwarted. Blatchford's explanation, he asserts, is that when a man gets the doctrine of the Trinity inside his head he may suddenly start cutting up people with a great knife. "And this, with all respect, seems to be so ridiculous as to be indiscussible by men of the world."

"I should simply say," Chesterton continues, "that whenever men are enormously concerned, whether for creed or a government or a social system, they have a temptation to persecute." Blatchford had said this was not true of the American revolutionaries. Chesterton replied that of course they did not, because American loyalists were not a problem, but that since then, having found in their midst a black race which does not understand their civilization, they have behaved quite otherwise. Describing their behavior, in fact, he uses a much heavier irony than he has usually employed in this controversy:

> And having these strange people in their midst, what do the advanced, enlightened American democrats do to them; how humanely do they educate their ignorance; how tenderly do they train their barbarity; in how Blatchfordian a manner do they deal with the real problem of these human beings? The answer is very simple. They roast them alive.

As to Blatchford's admiration for the immensity of the cosmos, Chesterton responds in a characteristic way. He calls this a spiritual imperialism, a mere worship of size, and goes on to say, ". . . I do not think it in the least magnanimous not to be interested in small things."

Lastly he twits Blatchford about his display of assurance:

> Just as I send this off, I discover that my explanations are superfluous. . . . I find that you have got into communication with that absolute truth which Agnostics have hitherto failed to reach. You have a supernatural assurance, an assurance beyond argument, one "which I cannot dispose of in a hundred columns." It is "It [Christianity]—is—not—true."

Two weeks later, on December 4, in "A Few Arrears," Blatchford replied to Chesterton, among others. At the end of this column, he invited the champions of Christianity to occupy space in his newspaper:

> They shall have a fair field if they will come forward. I will find good men to answer them, and one side shall have the same space as the other, and no member of the CLARION Staff shall interfere.

Out of this fair offer to his adversaries came the series of defenses of Christianity which George Haw edited under the title *The Religious Doubts of Democracy*. Haw began the series himself on January 29; Chesterton concluded it with three articles (which became four in the book): "Christianity and Rationalism," which appeared on July 22; "We are All Agnostics until we discover that Agnosticism will not work" the following week; and "Mr. Blatchford's Religion. Is Nobody to be Responsible for Anything?" on August 5. In spite of his much-praised magnanimity, Blatchford was not going to let the Christian responses to his attack go unanswered. On August 12, the week following Chesterton's last article, he announced that he had asked some of the ablest of the freethinkers to reply—and they did so, the first of them being one of the best-known, Joseph McCabe. These articles were also published in book form, under the title *Christianity and Rationalism*.

The controversy obstinately refused to die down; the November issues of the *Clarion* were full of discussions of free will and determinism, even though another debate was going on over Shaw and socialism. Chesterton came back into the fray on December 23, with a letter headed "The Inconsistency of Robert Blatchford." It is perfectly logical, from a determinist point of view, he maintained, to kill a man as a nuisance, much as we kill a viper, but it is not logical to reproach him and urge him to a nobler choice. "As long as you continue, in the face of every actual problem," he said to Blatchford, "to act in flat contradiction to all your principles, you will continue to be the very jolly person you are. But the world might contain some day a logical Determinist: and he would be a lunatic."

With what abiding impressions does this debate leave us? One, of course, is Chesterton's enjoyment of it; he often says to

Blatchford, "I hope that you are enjoying this as much as I am." One day a head waiter in a Fleet Street cafe said of Chesterton to Charles Masterman, "Your friend, he very clever man. He sit and laugh. And then he write. And then he laugh at what he write" (*The Georgian Literary Scene*, London: 1938 [1935], 96). Frank Swinnerton, who tells the story, adds, "It has always been essential to Chesterton that he should be amused by what he wrote, and by what he said in public. I have heard him laugh so much at a debate that he gave himself hiccups for the rest of the evening" (96).

A second impression is of his dedication to the cause he was supporting. It is regarded as unprofessional in the trade, a journalist friend has told me, to write letters to the newspapers: you are supposed to be paid for what you write. Yet Chesterton, who during this period was writing books on Browning and G. F. Watts and *The Napoleon of Notting Hill*, together with columns and articles for the *Speaker*, the *Daily News*, the *Commonwealth*, *Black and White*, and the *Bystander*, was still prepared to write extraordinarily long letters for publication in the *Clarion*, because it was important to him to defend religion against the attacks of skeptics and agnostics.

Third, he took his stand on human nature and human experience; frequently he sets Blatchford's ideas against the general experience of humankind. Even before this debate began, he had written in the *Speaker* in 1900 that "Christianity stands for a simplification of the heart and a reliance on the most indestructible sentiments," and again, "Christianity seeks after God with a most elementary passion it can find, the craving for a father, the hunger that is as old as the hills" (*The Speaker*, Nov. 17, 1900, as quoted in Maycock, 180-81). Time and again, he insists that society cannot operate on Blatchford's principles. Flannery O'Connor was later to write, "I don't think literature would be possible in a determined world. We might go through the motions but the heart would be out of it" (*The Habit of Being: Letters Selected and Edited by Sally Fitzgerald*, New York: 1980, 489). For Chesterton, determinism would take the heart out of everything; the fortunate thing about Blatchford, he said, was that he did not follow his own professed principles.

Behind Chesterton's view of human nature and of religion was not a well-worked-out philosophical system but at least a metaphysical assurance. As always, he emphasized in his controversy the wonder of being. He is awed, not like Blatchford by the immensity of the cosmos but at the existence of anything whatsoever, be it ever so small.

Eventually Blatchford asked for straightforward answers to four straightforward questions ("A Few Arrears," *Clarion*, Dec. 4, 1903, 5). Naturally the answers Chesterton gave were not without their humorous side, but to the first question, whether he considered himself a Christian, he answered straightforwardly enough: "Certainly" ("On Irrelevancy," *Daily News*, Dec. 19, 1903, 8).

Yet many of his opponents remained unconvinced. In his December 4 column, Blatchford had made it clear that though he admired the brilliance of his antagonist, he was never going to accept his arguments:

> What is Mr. Chesterton trying to do? Is he trying to defend Christianity? If he is, I can only express my respectful astonishment. He is a brilliant man. And I have read many columns of his Christian apologetics, and the only impression they have left on my mind is the impression of a brilliant man making brilliant efforts to evade the issues in debate. (*Clarion*, Dec. 4, 1903)

This, he said, was not only his own impression but the impression of many others, Christians included, who had commented on the controversy to him.

As Father Jaki points out, Blatchford, to the very end of a long life—he did not die until 1943, at the age of 92—regarded Chesterton as a consummate actor who played the role of believing Christian so well that he became convinced in the end that he believed in Christian dogma. "Like you," he wrote to his friend Thompson much later, "I don't understand Chesterton turning a Catholic. But he was a subtle thinker, and I have noticed that your subtle thinker often loses his way in his own intricacy. He spins a kind of web round his own brain" (L. Thompson, *Robert Blatchford: Portrait of an Englishman*, London: 1951, 170-71).

In the heat of this debate, Jaki again relates, Chesterton first became aware that he was suspected of insincerity, a suspicion which was to follow him to the end of his life. "What was the most likely reaction," Jaki asks, "to this fearless demolition of science as the chief ideal of secularism, and of the no less courageous erecting in its place the statue of Christ?" (420). Chesterton describes the reaction himself, in two passages of his *Autobiography*. The first makes it clear that half the bright young men in London did *not* believe in the supernatural:

> Very nearly everybody, in the ordinary literary and journalistic world, began by taking it for granted that my faith in the Christian creed was a pose or a paradox. The more cynical supposed that it was only a stunt. The more generous and loyal warmly maintained that it was only a joke. It was not until long afterwards that the full horror of the truth burst upon them; the disgraceful truth that I really thought the thing was true. (London: 1936, 178)

In the next paragraph of his *Autobiography*, Chesterton describes how he first made this discovery at a *Clarion* dinner.

> But I remember that there was, sitting next to me at this dinner, one of those very refined and rather academic gentlemen from Cambridge who seemed to form so considerable a section of the rugged stalwarts of Labor. There was a cloud on his brow, as if he were beginning to be puzzled about something; and he said suddenly, with abrupt civility, "Excuse my asking, Mr. Chesterton, of course I shall understand if you prefer not to answer, and I shan't think any the worse of it, you know, even if it's true. But I suppose I'm right in thinking you don't really *believe* in those things you're defending against Blatchford?" I informed him with adamantine gravity that I did most definitely believe in those things I was defending against Blatchford. His cold and refined face did not move a visible muscle; and yet I knew in some fashion it had completely altered. "Oh, you *do*," he said, "I beg your pardon. Thank you. That's all I wanted to know." And he went on eating his (probably vegetarian) meal. But I was sure that for the rest of the evening, despite his calm, he felt as if he were sitting next to a fabulous griffin. (178-79)

Others might utter a polite "Oh" and pass on, but Joseph McCabe, in the *Clarion* for October 21, 1904, delivered a devastating attack on Chesterton's methods of argumentation. Its title indicated its character — "Christianity Defended by Sleight of Hand." He said he wanted "to strip Mr. Chesterton's case for Christianity of all its literary tinsel and its sparkling paradoxes." After deprecating Chesterton's habit of turning things upside down, he said that if Chesterton was really as serious as he himself about the issues, why then did he desert serious methods of conducting inquiry? In a long paragraph, he quoted a number of Chesterton's more reckless statements and more sweeping generalities — such as that "religions almost always arise out of skeptical civilizations" — and asked how such statements could possibly be defended. To his mind, Chesterton was serving up a case which was intellectually despicable.

Chesterton's answer to this attack was to come in chapter sixteen of *Heretics*, "Mr. McCabe and a Divine Frivolity." The Blatchford controversy was in fact an important preliminary to the writing of both *Heretics* and *Orthodoxy*. Even by this time, however, as we have seen, his critics were saying that he was too fond of paradox. Instead of replying to his opponent's arguments in detail, he often amused himself by turning these arguments upside down — by saying, for example, that Blatchford's assaults on Christianity provided him with reasons for believing in it, or by declaring that Blatchford was a better Christian than the Christians themselves. Normally he seized upon one or two central issues to which he gave his imagination play; he would elaborate on them and expand on them, until he might very well give rise to the accusation that he was fonder of the embroidery upon the stuff of controversy than of the material itself. He was not likely to convince Blatchford, the dedicated socialist who thought that human progress depended upon the development of science and the extermination of traditional forms of religion, and he was not likely to convince McCabe, an ex-priest who had already written *Why I Left the Church of Rome* and who was to direct many more attacks at Catholicism, including eventually, in 1941, *The Pope Helps Hitler to World-power*; but he might have been able to say to a Blatchford bewildered by his rhetorical ingenuity, "I *have* answered you — but you do not know it."

The cultivated young gentlemen were not, in fact, likely to

be influenced strongly by him, and he was not going to expect very much of them. He got a good reception when he delivered a "Reply to Mr. Bernard Shaw" at Cambridge in 1911, but he was reported as saying, "We had got into a world in which the majority of the governing classes believed in no religion. He had known many editors and newspaper proprietors, but he had yet to meet one who believed in religion. The overwhelming mass of the governing body of the State was un-Christian" ("The Future of Religion: Mr. G. K. Chesterton's Reply to Mr. Bernard Shaw," *Chesterton Review*, Vol. XII, No. 3, Aug. 1986, 287). During his lifetime, he was to see one *trahison des clercs*, one betrayal by the intellectuals, after another. He was often called a populist, and it is noteworthy that he made his reputation, not in some highbrow journal, but in the popular press, the *Daily News*. Siding with the common people against the intellectuals, he was able to deliver a strong rebuke in his last *Clarion* article to Blatchford, the dedicated reformer whose whole life had been changed by his experience of viewing the slums of Manchester. Far more shameful than anything done to the poor in a material way, Chesterton says, is what you are trying to do to them in a mental and spiritual way — take away their hope, with your so-called "scientific determinism" ("Mr. Blatchford's Religion," *Clarion*, Aug. 5, 1904). In setting himself against the intellectual currents of his day, he reminds us of Newman, who wrote an astonishingly prophetic letter to his mother in 1829, well before the start of the Oxford Movement, in which he virtually said that he was siding with the prejudiced and unenlightened against the so-called enlightened minds of the age, for "the talent of the day is against the Church" (Henry Tristram, ed., *The Living Thoughts of Cardinal Newman*, London: 1948, 42-44).

In *The Georgian Literary Scene*, the eminent English man of letters Frank Swinnerton described how when he was about sixteen (around 1900) he used to tramp around London to listen to Chesterton lecturing on any subject under the sun, from Puck to the Dreadful Danger of Liberalism. While Belloc and Chesterton never knew him, he said, he could testify to their former grandeur in the eyes of the young. But he referred to their progressive failure to impress younger skeptics and gave a reason for it—which may itself be a matter of some controversy. Declaring that the world was in a very bad way, they asserted that it had once been in a good way; Belloc deliberately, and Chesterton with misgiving, set up a version of what had happened in England long before, and this version was not accepted by Protestants, scientific historians, or skeptics. And the past, as Chesterton admitted, was no easy subject: "I can make the future as narrow as myself; but the past is obliged to be as broad and turbulent as humanity" (99). This was the time futurology was getting off to a good start with Wells's *Anticipations* in 1900 and *Modern Utopia* in 1905 and many similar books extolling the marvelous things which the scientific outlook was going to accomplish in the twentieth century. Belloc and Chesterton seemed to stand outside the stream of current opinion, to occupy a backwater; and when all is turmoil, Swinnerton wrote, it is too much to expect that the occupants of a backwater will receive any acknowledgment of their literary genius (106-7). Only in time, after their deaths (he was writing in 1935), would their great gifts be appreciated. Is it too much to say that the time for such appreciation is now?

C. S. Lewis:
Some Keys to His Effectiveness

Lyle W. Dorsett

A few men and women have the remarkable ability to change lives. Either personally or through their writing, they inspire us, edify us, and spur us on to worthy endeavors. These people are spiritually magnetic. They draw us in, touch us, and then send us on our way profoundly altered.

Certainly C. S. Lewis was such a man. Indeed, few people in this century have helped more seekers find the way to Light than this Belfast-born writer. Lewis's books were instrumental in my conversion from agnosticism to faith in Jesus Christ, and since then I have met scores of people who told me how Lewis's writings pointed them to Christ. Countless others have explained to me how Professor Lewis became their spiritual guide when they could find no one else to help them along the pathway of discipleship — a route often slippery, craggy, and intersected with dangerous crossings. Some of our most influential Christian writers testify that this author of nearly forty books assisted them onto the Calvary road. The names of Os Guinness, Rebecca Pippert, Charles Colson, Chad Walsh, Sheldon

LYLE W. DORSETT is curator of the Marion E. Wade Collection, Wheaton College, and the author of *And God Came In: The Extraordinary Life of Joy Davidman*.

Vanauken and Joy Davidman are a few names that come immediately to mind.

Lewis's role in changed lives can never be quantified, but one bit of data is suggestive. In 1954 an administrator in the largest mainline American Presbyterian denomination surveyed all of the career missionaries at home and abroad. One of the questions asked was "What person most influenced your decision to become a missionary?" Fifty percent wrote "C. S. Lewis" in the space provided.

Lewis's extraordinary effectiveness in touching the spiritual lives of so many people has intrigued me for several years. Consequently, I have read hundreds of his letters, studied his books, and interviewed numerous people who knew him. I am still doing research on Lewis's life and influence, so my findings to date are preliminary. These limitations notwithstanding, my goal in this article is twofold. First, I want to suggest some reasons for C. S. Lewis's effectiveness with which students of his life and writings may not be familiar. Second, I am confident that those of us with only ordinary gifts and advantages, who nevertheless are seeking to live more effective lives as disciples of Christ and fishers of men, can be edified and instructed by this light on C. S. Lewis — the way he lived and worked.

Of course I am not the first person to raise questions about Lewis's effectiveness. Several able scholars, among them Richard Purtill, Clyde Kilby, Thomas Howard, Walter Hooper, Peter Kreeft, and Chad Walsh, have set forth many illuminating and persuasive reasons for Lewis's wide range of influence. For the most part, however, these authors have focused on Lewis's literary task. They have stressed, and rightly so, Lewis's ability to think critically and analytically; and they have noted his superb skill as a stylist, especially his keen ability to tell stories and encode his messages in metaphor, allegory, symbol, and myth.

Of all of the students of Lewisiana, none has gone further than Professor Purtill in trying to plumb depths beyond the technical tools and imaginative gifts employed by this best-selling author. Although Purtill agrees with some well-meaning biographers that Lewis taught truth in the power of the Holy Ghost, he correctly suggests that this is not particularly illuminating. Professor Purtill points out that other writers have lifted up the same truth and evoked the blessing of the same Spirit, but with markedly less success. In short, there must be other reasons why Lewis was "an extraordinarily effective conductor of the message." In *C. S. Lewis's Case for the Christian Faith*, chapter one, "Some Reasons for Lewis's Success," Purtill contributes much to our understanding by underscoring Lewis's intellectual and imaginative qualities, his enthusiastic love for many things, his humility, and his ability to sympathize with people who suffer.

I am grateful for Purtill's suggestions. My own thoughts have been stimulated by his work. Continuing down the pathway he opened, I want to offer a few more factors that strike me as important.

First of all, it is important to remember that C. S. Lewis was a convert. It is true that he was baptized in the Church of Ireland, but he was outside the faith for at least a quarter century before he embraced Christianity with confidence. His mother's early death, his long periods of separation from his brother, and his father's melancholia, all conspired to convince him that God was either cruel or dead. His experience with an atheist tutor in the 1910s, followed by the horrors of World War I, did little to change Lewis's mind about God's indifference toward human affairs. In brief, Lewis kept a distance between himself and the Christian church for nearly two and a half decades, and this kept him in touch with pagans, materialists, and unbelievers of all varieties. Association with a non-Christian culture became a marked asset once he became a Christian with missionary zeal. He knew the doubts of the people he hoped to reach. He asked their questions; he spoke their post-Christian language; he understood their emptiness; he knew from experience what might awaken them.

Once Lewis became a Christian, he employed his considerable writing skills to communicating the Christian story in the clearest and simplest way. In "Version Vernacular" he wrote, "Any fool can write *learned* language. The vernacular is the real test. If you can't turn your faith into it, then either you don't understand it or you don't believe it." A practitioner of his own advice, he presented the faith in the words of the people, and he did it well.

But now I want to move beyond this generally well-known and well-studied side of Lewis — his skill as a writer and communicator — and focus on another area altogether. Increasingly, I am convinced that the power and lasting attraction of Lewis's work comes from his spirituality. Furthermore, as I sift through his letters and interview people who knew him, I am rather certain that the wellspring of his charisma (in person and through his books) is the manifestation of a deeply devotional life. To be sure, all of us who read the published primary and secondary literature are aware of glimpses of this, but no one has made a careful survey of the subject. What follows are some of my findings in this area.

Underlying C. S. Lewis's strength and persistence in touching his readers' spirituality was his prayer life. Lewis had a remarkably full and disciplined prayer life, and I am confident that this is a source of much of his power — an element lacking in so many other authors. An examination of this influential writer's prayer life reveals a wide range and scope. Indeed, it is so comprehensive that I calculate he must have spent a minimum of an hour to an hour and a half a day in prayer. This would be remarkable devotion in any person's life, but Lewis was an exceptionally busy man. He published nearly forty books, 125 essays and pamphlets, sixty-eight poems, two short stories, and three dozen book reviews; he edited or wrote prefaces to another eleven books as well. To this massive writing effort he added a full schedule of tutorials and lectures, an enormous reading list, and he answered dozens of fan letters each week.

Lewis's prayer life was not haphazard and sporadic; it was well disciplined and neatly arranged. From the time of his conversion in 1931, corporate prayer was always high on his list of priorities. We have his Anglican *Book of Common Prayer* in the Marion E. Wade Center. This black, leather-bound volume is floppy and worn, and the end papers contain pencil jottings of his meditations on grace. Always a faithful communicant in the Church of England, he used his prayer book during services at his local parish church, Holy Trinity, at Headington Quarry, Oxford, and he faithfully attended Dean's Prayers from 7:45 to 8:15 each morning during the academic term at the Magdalen College Chapel.

Regular attendance at mass and Dean's Prayers does not particularly set Lewis apart from countless others in the band of the faithful, but he parts company with the crowd in other ways. He made a routine pilgrimage to one of the Cowley Fathers at the Society of Saint John the Evangelist, and there he sought guidance from a spiritual director. He made regular confessions as well.

Sitting under the direction of a spiritual counselor was certainly out of the ordinary for a busy author and academician, and so was his one-on-one prayer time with a layman. It is impossible to know just how often Professor Lewis prayed with others, except to offer thanksgiving for a meal. But he did pray with his hired driver, Mr. Clifford Morris. A low churchman and an evangelical, Morris is accustomed to praying extemporaneously in small groups. However, I was astounded to learn that Lewis joined Clifford Morris in this style of praying. Although the two men never made this a regular habit, Morris told me that after Joy Davidman Lewis's death the two men spent considerable time together in prayer.

Beyond the boundaries of corporate worship and an occasional prayer with a man like Morris, Lewis devoted much time to private prayer. Despite his reticence to discuss his personal life, we learn of this from letters to a few deeply devout people. Lewis apparently prayed for the conversion of souls who were outside the faith, and he asked others to join him in this endeavor. He continually prayed for the health and economic needs of friends and acquaintances, and he meditated on portions of Scripture when difficulties entered his own life.

The private prayer closet was a focal point of Lewis's devotional life, and he evidently spent more time there than he did in corporate prayer on Sundays and early morning during term. One friend of the Oxford don recalled that Lewis was in private prayer each morning before he left home, and that when an emergency occasionally interrupted the discipline, he made time for prayers in some other way.

It was in the solitude of the inner chamber that Lewis interceded for others; it was there that he confessed sins, sought ways to serve others, and prayed to bear the pain of his wife's cancer in her stead. In fact, during one period of Joy's convalescence, she was relieved of the bone cancer's excruciating pain, and Lewis himself (unbeknownst to her) developed a painful case of osteoporosis.

The quiet of the inner chamber did more than give Lewis an opportunity to intercede for the lost and hurting people in his life; it provided crucial times of revelation. It was in prayer about the need to be freed from interruptions in order to get more work done that Jack Lewis felt God revealed to him that these very invasions of his privacy were his real work. In private prayer he felt directed to see everyone who wrote to him as someone to minister to. Indeed, because of this revelation Lewis determined, to the extent it was possible, to answer personally all of his mail.

To Lewis's view, one of the most important revelations he received was regarding grace. He acknowledged faith in Jesus Christ in 1931, and for the next twenty years he "*believed that* [he] *believed* in the forgiveness of sins." Nevertheless it was not until 1951 — and, he assumed, in part because of the intercessory prayers of a friend — that he finally "believed it with [his] whole heart" (Moynihan 37).

Lewis's correspondence with several other people suggests the importance he ascribed to intercessory prayer. Like St. Paul and the early body of believers, Lewis had a prayer network in place and functioning. With regularity he prayed for others and in turn asked them to pray for him. His perception of his own need for the prayers of others is clearly manifested in one of his early letters to an Anglican nun, Sister Penelope: "Though I am forty years old, I'm only about twelve as a Christian, so it would be a maternal act if you found time to mention me in your prayers" (Unpublished letter, Wade Center, July 9, 1939). In another revealing letter over a decade later, Lewis implored, "Pray for me; I am suffering incessant temptations to uncharitable thoughts at present" (*Letters of C. S. Lewis* 222).

Prayer was not the only key to C. S. Lewis's effectiveness as a communicator of spiritual truth, but it was an impetus behind some other causes. Lewis's prompt dealings with sin in his own life are revealing, and they help explain his ability to maintain spiritual freshness and alertness. When he found himself tempted to judge others, or when he harbored a resentment against a man who wronged him, Lewis prayed for the ability to repent and forgive, and he sought intercession from others. He also took radical action to remove obstacles that caused him to sin. Money, for example, was a stumbling block to Lewis's reliance upon God. One of the ways he wrestled with this recurring temptation was to give away his royalties rather than save or invest them. In this way he avoided temptations to build his security on such an unbiblical foundation.

Lewis did more than take bold steps to overcome temptations. He decided to obey God along whatever lines the Lord's will could be discerned. For example, Jesus commanded his disciples to partake of Holy Communion. Lewis neither understood the Eucharist nor felt particularly edified after he had partaken. Nevertheless, he obeyed because Jesus gave the command. As a consequence, several years after his conversion Lewis realized he gradually gained strength from the sacrament, but he never would have received this blessing if he had obeyed only in the wake of understanding or on the strength of positive feelings.

In another instance where obedience was required, Lewis discerned through prayer that it was his duty to answer the letters sent to him by fans, regardless of their age, nationality, level of intelligence, or spiritual maturity. Eventually, especially after the publication of the Narnian chronicles in the early 1950s, so many letters arrived at The Kilns that it took two or three hours a day to write careful answers. Occasionally the busy author questioned God's will, wondering why the Sovereign Lord allowed him to get bogged down in so much correspondence rather than writing another book that would edify the saints and point lost people to the Christ. Again, however, Lewis chose to be obedient rather than demand understanding. Consequently, because he was faithful, he unknowingly wrote what became some of his best books — e.g., Letters of C. S. Lewis, Letters to an American Lady, and Letters to Children.

Many other factors account for Lewis's effectiveness, and one of these is his courage to be honest. Lewis, like every believer or seeker I have met, was sometimes plagued by doubts. Rather than deny or ignore the corners of darkness, Lewis discussed these openly in print. For would-be disciples who are weary of clergy and theologians who either ignore the difficult questions or rationalize them by asking more questions, Lewis's determination to battle through darkness is refreshing. A man who raises and attempts to answer the toughest questions on the efficacy of prayer is bound to attract attention, and so is the writer who courageously tackles *The Problem of Pain* or writes honestly about his struggles with God in the face of his wife's death from cancer. Writing on such elusive topics as miracles, the second coming of Christ, and human grief and pain conspires to give Lewis relevance in an age of doubt.

Some of C. S. Lewis's critics, and I'm thinking particularly of an early writing of Peter Kreeft and John Beversluis (see *C. S. Lewis: A Critical Essay* and *C. S. Lewis and the Search for Rational Religion*, respectively), illuminate still more reasons for Lewis's extraordinary effectiveness. Lewis is criticized for being philosophically inconsistent in his arguments for the existence of God, arguing from morality in *Broadcast Talks*, from reason in *Miracles*, and from experience or longing in *Surprised by Joy* and *Pilgrim's Regress*. Kreeft put it this way: "Lewis never fully resolved his youthful dilemma between rationalism and romanticism. Each of these two forces in him is so strong that it would take a giant to fuse them: Lewis is an elf, but not a giant. Though his rational apologetics do not lack imagination and his imaginative novels do not lack rationality, yet the two elements are not fully fused in either medium" (43). Kreeft's argument that "Lewis is the victim of his many-sidedness," and Beversluis's thesis that Lewis cannot decide whether he is an Platonist or Ockamist, suggest that there are apparent inconsistencies that bother some academicians. Nevertheless, what is a weakness to a few readers probably creates a wider audience in the last analysis. The general reader does not ponder the philosophical problems in *Miracles* versus *Surprised by Joy*. What I detect, in fact, is that the audience that prefers the rational approach to religion tends to read *Miracles* and similar works, whereas those who experience *Sehnsucht* are more drawn to the autobiography and romantic literature. In brief, he has two different audiences rather than one. And the number of people he might alienate because of his perceived lack of synthesis is small, in any case, because most readers have an insufficient understanding of the entire Lewis corpus to pass such judgments.

Professor Paul Holmer and Dr. Kenneth Harper have hit upon a crucial reason for Lewis's profound and lingering effectiveness among legions of thoughtful people. Holmer argues in *C. S. Lewis: The Shape of His Life and Thought* that Lewis is effective because he provides a schema that explains all of life. Harper puts a fine point on this in his unpublished dissertation entitled "C. S. Lewis As a Paradigm for Pastoral Apologetics": "If Christianity is both true and also capable of explaining all other truth, then that is tremendously liberating. One can enter any field of inquiry confident that one's faith can openly seek all truth. We can have the same attitude as that taken by Lewis's mentor, George MacDonald, 'Truth is truth, whether from the lips of Jesus or Balaam.' Gone is the fearful attitude that too much knowledge will overturn one's faith" (110-11).

Lewis, of course, has helped many a seeker see this freedom in the Christian faith. Maintaining that Christianity is capable of building a scaffolding that supports all truth is precisely what Lewis has done, and this approach wins converts to his point of view as well as to Christianity.

Another factor that helps account for Lewis's growing audience is his focus on the essentials of the faith that unite us rather than on the tangents that divide. Like John Wesley two centuries before, Lewis would say, "In essentials unity; in nonessentials liberty." To be sure, Lewis has been criticized by a few of his fellow sacramentalists for presenting "mere" Christianity without the Eucharist. Also, Roman Catholics like Father John Willis have raised questions about leaving the Magisterium out of any basic presentation of the faith. Likewise some fundamentalists have been disturbed by Lewis's refusal to be more exclusive and dogmatic, especially over literal interpretations of Scripture. This latter factor illuminates a comment made to me by Professor Lewis's friend, Harry Blamires. A former pupil of Lewis's, Blamires noted that one of his tutor's assets was his ardent desire to instruct rather than hurt. This was Lewis's posture in the classroom and the tutorial, and it carried over into his books. In short, he was not out to do battle with pagans; rather, he hoped to instruct those with an honest desire to learn.

Lewis was certainly inspired by more than an interest in teaching or learning for its own sake. Indeed, his underlying motive was revealed to Dr. Norman Pittenger in "Rejoinder to Dr. Pittenger." There Professor Lewis admitted that "most of my books are evangelistic." Whether it was in his fictional creations of Narnia or outer space, in his B.B.C. talks or his lectures to R.A.F. crews, in his papers at Socratic Club debates, or his sermons at an Oxford church, Lewis was always up to the same thing — pointing people to Jesus Christ. He was a man with a strikingly purposeful life. He was, as Dorothy L. Sayers phrased it in one of her letters, "God's terrier" — a man with "missionary zeal."

In conclusion, it is obvious that numerous factors have contributed to make C. S. Lewis so extraordinarily effective in touching lives. Nevertheless, all of these factors appear to be enlivened by his unceasing focus on Jesus Christ. "Look for yourself," he wrote in *Mere Christianity*, "and you will find in the long run only hatred, loneliness, despair, rage, ruin and decay. But look for Christ, and you will find Him, and with Him everything else thrown in" (175). Those who knew him well and were able to sympathize with his spirituality saw clearly that Lewis looked for Christ rather than himself, influence, or fame. In the end he found the Christ he sought, and everything else was thrown in as well.

Works Cited

Beversluis, John. *C. S. Lewis and the Search for Rational Religion.*

Harper, Kenneth. "C. S. Lewis As a Paradigm for Pastoral Apologetics." Unpublished dissertation. San Francisco Theological Seminary, 1986.

Holmer, Paul. *C. S. Lewis: The Shape of His Life and Thought.*

Kreeft, Peter. *C. S. Lewis: A Critical Essay.*

Lewis, C. S. *Letters of C. S. Lewis.*

———. *Letters to an American Lady.*

_____. *Letters to Children.*

_____. *Mere Christianity.*

_____. "Rejoinder to Dr. Pittenger." *Christian Century*, November 16, 1958.

_____. Unpublished letter, Wade Center, July 9, 1939.

_____. "Version Vernacular." *Christian Century*, December 31, 1958.

Moynihan, Martin. *The Latin Letters of C. S. Lewis.*

Purtill, Richard. *C. S. Lewis's Case for the Christian Faith*, Chap. 1, "Some Reasons for Lewis's Success."

Sayers, Dorothy L. *Letters* (or something) to G. E., July 10, 1947.

The Sweet Grace of Reason: The Apologetics of G. K. Chesterton

Kent R. Hill

Conversion is the acceptance of truth, not just its discovery. The task of a Christian apologist, therefore, must be to go beyond education to exhortation. But before an individual can consider whether to accept Christian truths, a plethora of modern misunderstandings and distortions regarding orthodoxy must be dispelled. The task of dispelling common myths about Christianity has been made more difficult as contemporary education has become increasingly vacuous. Religion and values have been pushed further and further to the periphery in order to advance an allegedly neutral agenda of pluralism. Of course, such education is anything but pluralistic; the creeds of Christianity and of natural reason may well face dogmatic and rigid opposition precisely because they are in conflict with the creed of relativism.

If indeed conversion is properly understood as a two-stage process—the confrontation with truth and then the acceptance of it—and if in the contemporary world the confrontation with Christian truth has been rendered particularly difficult because

---

KENT R. HILL is executive director of the Institute for Religion and Democracy in Washington, D.C., and formerly a member of the History Department, Seattle Pacific University.

its central claims are not even understood, then a modern apologist will have to give specific attention to this obstacle to the acquisition of faith.

My analysis of Christian apologetics is based on a practical, "common sense" approach. This kind of apologetics is not devoid of some of the critical elements of technical, formal apologetics; yet it includes arguments and methods more accessible to the majority of people and is enhanced, above all, by a spirit of civility in the advancing of one's positions. Both the rationality *and the character* of the apologist are involved here, and a life of integrity is a witness—often a far more eloquent witness than that traced in words and logic.

The central thesis of this paper is that G. K. Chesterton ought to be considered one of the preeminent "practical" Christian apologists of modern times. To be sure, a more typical description of Chesterton might focus on his gifts as a fine mystery writer, a scintillating essayist, a penetrating biographer, and an insightful Christian thinker. To the extent he is acknowledged to have engaged in apologetics, it is sometimes understood to be something which does not include the early period when he wrote *Heretics* (1902-05).[1] A contention of this paper, however, is that the task of recapturing realism and reestablishing a notion of truth is an indispensable early stage in apologetics. The fact, furthermore, that such a task involves the use of natural reason, something obviously not limited to Christian thinking, only confirms the existence of common grace, not the absence of Christian truth (see CW [*Collected Works*] 4:227-90).

In his classic work *Orthodoxy* (1908), Chesterton claims that his purpose is spiritual autobiography, not apologetics (6). We would do well here, however, to give greater credence to Etienne Gilson, who hailed it as the best apologetic the century had yet produced (Dooley 34). Nevertheless, Chesterton is persistently reluctant to don the apologist's mantle. To be sure, part of

1. David Dooley, "Introduction," *The Collected Works of G. K. Chesterton*, Vol. 1 (San Francisco: Ignatius Press, 1986), ed. George Marlin et al., p. 22. Garry Wills, for example, makes a distinction between Chesterton's attempt to reassert philosophical realism and certitude, and his Christian apologetics, which he wants to date to a much later period.

Chesterton's protest is simply a self-deprecation of his work—
something often encountered in his writing. But the record is
quite clear. Much of what Chesterton wrote clearly functioned
as apologetics in the broad meaning of the term, and he was all
the more effective for not appearing to focus on achieving conversions.

There was in Chesterton a certain disdain for the more formal, philosophical, and narrow apologetics. Indeed, in *Orthodoxy*
Chesterton brags: "I never read a line of Christian apologetics. I
read as little as I can of them now" (CW 1:288). He goes on to
observe that it was his reading of Huxley, Herbert Spencer, and
other Victorian freethinkers which sowed in his mind his "first
wild doubts of doubt" (CW 1:288). But this is precisely the point.
As A. L. Maycock has noted, Chesterton pioneered "a completely new approach to the proclamation of Christian truth"—one
which "wrestled the initiative from the skeptics and presented
the historic faith upon a note of triumphant challenge" (quoted
in Dooley 26). This new challenge often centered on demonstrating just how silly or inadequate were those alternatives cham-
pioned by those skeptical of Christianity.

Countless readers, both Christian and secular, love Chesterton for his Father Brown short stories. The quaint Father Brown,
who seems at first to belong to an earlier century, goes about
his business solving mysteries with uncanny insight and irrepres-
sible humor. Alzina Stone Dale has observed that "intuition,
based on common sense rather than on logical deductive reasoning, is the keynote of Father Brown's method" (158). To suggest that both his insight and his humor are by-products of his
orthodox Christian faith would be most distressing to many of
his readers. Yet, it is precisely his understanding of the nature
of man and the nature of God which sets Father Brown apart
from a society ignorant of both. For those able to make the connection between Father Brown's success as a detective and his
beliefs, the door has opened for a consideration of Christian
truth. To many modern people, Original Sin may appear at first
a repugnant theological concept, but if it accounts for reality
better than alternative theories, honest people will have to take
it seriously.

Another splendid example of Chesterton's ability to engage the reader on nontheological turf is the wonderfully imaginative novel *The Man Who Was Thursday*. Readers are immersed in an adventure fantasy which centers on the question of the nature of God. Chapter fourteen, "The Six Philosophers," illustrates especially well the author's ability to weave profound theology into the tapestry of an exciting novel. In this form, Christian truths may seem not only understandable, but even irresistible. An apologist without imagination is like a foot soldier in God's army—serving the right cause, but without vision. G. K. Chesterton, in contrast, is a high-ranking officer. From his elevated vantage point, much more of the terrain is visible. His vision of using fiction as a vehicle for conveying eternal truths is one which was caught by Charles Williams, Dorothy L. Sayers, and C. S. Lewis. It is not surprising that after Chesterton died, Williams lamented: "The last of my Lords is dead" (quoted in Dale 252).

Is Chesterton an apologist in his mystery and fantasy fiction? Yes, and he is probably a far more effective one than if he had written a theological treatise entitled "Original Sin." It is revealing that Chesterton was working on *The Man Who Was Thursday* and *Orthodoxy* simultaneously. Both were published in 1908. Many who read the former would never read the latter. Yet, Christian truths are defended and communicated in both.

What is particularly obvious to most who read very much Chesterton (and this is part of the reason they become addicted to reading more) is that he cuts to the heart of any issue and lays it out in ways plain for all to see. There are so many moments of genius and insight that no one pays much attention to errors of fact or occasional overstatements.

Chesterton's incisive analysis is applied to almost any topic imaginable. For example, consider his critique of the modern notion that evil resides in the environment, rather than in individuals. Chesterton first notes that if what the determinist socialist asserts is true, then democracy is foolish, and the poor should be disenfranchised until the environment can be improved. He continues:

> If better conditions will make the poor more fit to govern them-
> selves, why should not better conditions already make the rich more
> fit to govern them? On the ordinary environment argument the
> matter is fairly manifest. The comfortable class must be merely our
> vanguard in Utopia. (CW 1:322)

The accumulative effect of having Chesterton expose time
and again obvious weaknesses and absurdities in notions which
are so often accepted without question is to convince the reader
that here at last is one source which deserves to be trusted.
Furthermore, Chesterton was ingenious in finding ways to communicate Christian truths even while discussing the mundane.
As A. G. Gardiner, a liberal publisher of the *Daily News*, put
it: "You may tap any subject you like, he will find a theme on
which to hang all the mystery of time and eternity" (quoted in
Dale 78).

For nonbelievers, contact with Chesterton can be distressing. C. S. Lewis encountered Chesterton's works while in a hospital during World War I. He later remarked about this pre-faith
period in his life, "A young man who wishes to remain a strong
atheist cannot be too careful of his reading" (*Surprised by Joy*
191). Lewis was not sufficiently vigilant, and in the mid-1920s
he read Chesterton's *The Everlasting Man*. The result, according
to the young Oxford teacher, was that for the first time the whole
span of Christian history made sense to him.

Too often the art of apologetics is defined exclusively in
terms of the fluidity and power of intellectual argument.
However, apologetics broadly understood is also dependent on
the spirit of the apologist. Here Chesterton had few equals. Highly revealing is the deep affection in which he was held by three
with whom he frequently crossed intellectual swords: H. G.
Wells, George Bernard Shaw, and Robert Blatchford. As
Lawrence J. Clipper has observed: "There has probably never
been a gentler, kinder opponent in debate" (CW 27:30). But
Chesterton did not sacrifice conviction on the altar of civility.
On the contrary, he demonstrated that clear thinking is all the
more potent when combined with humor and compassion. Even
those who were not known for their optimism about life found

something contagious in G. K. Chesterton. As Franz Kafka observed, "He is so gay, one might almost believe he had found God" (quoted in Dale 113).

Why have so many come to trust Chesterton? He earned that trust by speaking with integrity and common sense about the world in which people live. It is not surprising that this is the same reason Chesterton gives for his own willingness to believe what the church says in areas where he did not have immediate knowledge. "I do it because the thing [the church] has not merely told this truth or that truth, but has revealed itself as a truth-telling thing" (CW 1:362). For thousands, Chesterton has revealed himself as a "truth-telling thing," and consequently the way is opened for Chesterton to be listened to when he touches on Christian doctrine. Once again, Chesterton emerges as an apologist, though he often arrives there unannounced through the back door.

Chesterton's Understanding of Reason

Chesterton's success as an apologist is in no small measure a product of his insightful understanding of reason. Although Chesterton had a profound appreciation for reason, he also recognized that reason at the level of "common sense" is not omnipotent:

First, reason presupposes faith. The modern predisposition to try to divorce reason from faith and view them as in perpetual conflict is "idle" to Chesterton.

> It is idle to talk always of the alternatives of reason and faith. Reason is itself a matter of faith. It is an act of faith to assert that our thoughts have any relation to reality at all. (CW 1:236)

In his brilliant biography of Aquinas, Chesterton takes issue with modern critics who charge that St. Thomas did not devote enough effort to the epistemological question of the correspondence between our perceptions and reality. Chesterton retorts:

> St. Thomas recognized instantly, what so many modern skeptics have begun to suspect rather laboriously; that a man must either answer that question in the affirmative, or else never answer any

231

> question, never ask any question, never even exist intellectually, to
> answer or to ask. . . . Most fundamental skeptics appear to survive,
> because they are not consistently skeptical and not at all fundamen-
> tal. (CW 2:515-16)

In other words, to utilize reason at all requires a certain fundamental faith in a human being's ability to know something
about the objective world; all intellectual endeavors, not just
those involving Christians, depend on this faith.

Second, reason is finite. Reason is always smaller than the
reality which it seeks to encompass. Few make the point so elo-
quently as Chesterton.

> Poetry is sane because it floats easily in an infinite sea; reason seeks
> to cross the infinite sea, and so make it finite. The result is men-
> tal exhaustion. . . . The poet only asks to get his head into the
> heavens. It is the logician who seeks to get the heavens into his
> head. And it is his head that splits. (CW 1:220)

Reason can accomplish much, but it is still finite.

Third, reason must accept the strangeness of some truths.
According to Chesterton, the world is "nearly reasonable, but
not quite" (CW 1:220). In a sense this point is directly related
to the last one and accounts for why some truth "seems" strange.
He contends that average people are quite able to maintain ideas
side by side which on the surface seem to contradict each other.
For example, a simple laborer often believes in both fate and free
will. For Chesterton this is a mark of the sanity of the ordinary
man — that "he has always cared more for truth than for
consistency" (CW 1:230).

It is this recognition that truth sometimes appears out of step
with reason which allows Chesterton to accept the paradoxes of
Christianity. In fact, he insists that "whenever we feel there is
something odd in Christian theology, we shall generally find that
there is something odd in the truth" (CW 1:286). Chesterton is
not saying that these paradoxical truths are irrational, only that
at first glance (often before experience has been able to test them)
they irritate rationality.

What are these paradoxical Christian truths to which

Chesterton is referring? One example is "He that will lose his life, the same shall save it." Chesterton contends that this

> is not a piece of mysticism for saints and heroes. It is a piece of everyday advice for sailors or mountaineers. . . . A soldier surrounded by enemies, if he is to cut his way out, needs to combine a strong desire for living with a strange carelessness about dying. He must not merely cling to life, for then he will be a coward, and will not escape. (CW 1:297)

Other difficult truths which Christians accept include: hate crime but love the criminal; celibacy has its place, but so does the family; pacifists and Crusaders both belong in the church (CW 1:299-303). The point is not that reason is opposed to these truths, only that reason will not be able to come to terms with such realities immediately or without a struggle.

Chesterton is aware that in the modern world some would dismiss as "mysticism" any acceptance of a reality which does not fit into purely objective, empirical boxes. This mysticism is then falsely contrasted with "rationalism," narrowly understood as empiricism. But Chesterton dismisses this notion as a false dilemma:

> It is not a question between mysticism and rationality. It is a question between mysticism and madness. For mysticism, and mysticism alone, has kept men sane from the beginning of the world. (CW 1:384)

When Chesterton talks of sanity, he means an ability to face reality squarely. Narrow empiricism is inadequate for this task.

Fourth, reason alone cannot compel religious faith. This particular fact about reason flies in the face of what so many in the nineteenth and twentieth centuries have wanted to believe, namely, that there is some kind of direct correlation between knowledge and morality, between knowing the truth and following it. History and current events, however, do not support such optimism, and orthodox Christian doctrine lines up squarely with the facts. There is an old adage that "you can lead a horse to water, but you can't make him drink." Chesterton always appreciated the wisdom contained in such sayings of the "common man."

An effective Chestertonian apologist very quickly learns that reason alone will not make converts; the will of the individual must be involved as well. Many questions are simply an intellectual smokescreen to hide the unwillingness of the nonbeliever to acknowledge the truth and to recognize his proper relationship to the Creator.

Just as some arguments by nonbelievers reflect a struggle against the truth rather than for it, Chesterton recognized that madness often clothes itself in rationality. He identifies madness with a fixation on one idea at the expense of common sense. The obsession of some with the material world may be infused with rationality, but their intellectual cosmos is smaller than the world we live in (CW 1:224-25). Regarding those who insist on their own rationality, Chesterton realizes that valid reasons may not break through the barriers at all. As he put it, "curing a madman is not arguing with a philosopher; it is casting out a devil" (CW 1:224). Reason gone mad requires a doctor, not a logician.

According to T. S. Eliot in his 1936 obituary for Chesterton, he "did more than any man of his time . . . to maintain the existence of the [Christian] minority in the modern world" (quoted in Dale 262). This comment accurately describes the importance of Chesterton in our day. His effectiveness is related directly to his nuanced understanding of reason, an understanding that reason is finite and reality sometimes irregular, and the recognition that reason alone is not sufficient to bring the nonbeliever into the Christian fold. However, Chesterton never denigrated reason; on the contrary, it is precisely reason as "common sense" which points the honest nonbeliever to the truths of the Christian church.

Limited as reason may be, Chesterton insists that it is quite sufficient to demonstrate to the honest nonbeliever three propositions: modern views are bankrupt from a rational standpoint, the attacks on Christianity are unfair and often untrue, and the beauty of Christian orthodoxy is that it is the key which fits the lock of reality. This triad of positions, infused with Chesterton's careful use of reason, forms the basis of his "common sense" apologetics. Let us now consider these three propositions in greater detail.

The Inadequacy of Modern Ideas

In seeking to convince modern secular thinkers that their views
are bankrupt, it is imperative that the apologist begin in the
nonbeliever's front yard, rather than in his own backyard. This
point cannot be overemphasized, since it is the violation of this
principle which accounts for the dismal record of so many would-
be apologists today. Chesterton, however, understood instinctively that there could be no effective apologetics apart from
honoring this tactic.

Chesterton points to Aquinas as one who recognized this
principle as well. In a famous dispute with Siger of Brabant over
the nature of truth, Aquinas exclaimed: "Behold our refutation
of the error. It is not based on documents of faith, but on the
reasons and statements of the philosophers themselves" (CW
2:475). Chesterton's commentary is highly revealing:

> Would that all Orthodox doctors in deliberation were as reasonable
> as Aquinas in anger! Would that all Christian apologists would remem-
> ber that maxim; and write it up in large letters on the walls, before
> they nail any theses there. At the top of his fury, Thomas Aquinas
> understands, what so many defenders of orthodoxy will not under-
> stand. It is no good to tell an atheist that he is an atheist; or to charge
> a denier of immortality with the infamy of denying it; or to imagine
> that one can force an opponent to admit he is wrong, by proving that
> he is wrong on somebody else's principles, but not on his own. After
> the great example of St. Thomas, the principle stands, or ought always
> to have stood established; that we must either not argue with a man
> at all, or we must argue on his grounds and not ours. (CW 2:476)

According to Chesterton, Aquinas is as relevant to the twentieth century as he was to the thirteenth, because Aquinas

> is arguing for common sense. He is arguing for a common sense
> which would even now commend itself to most of the common
> people. He is arguing for the popular proverb that seeing is believ-
> ing; that the proof of the pudding is in the eating; that a man can-
> not jump down his own throat or deny the fact of his own exis-
> tence. (CW 2:522)

Chesterton's method is to begin where modern thinkers are and

235

then to compare their conclusions with those of elementary common sense — the same common sense which it is impossible to escape in everyday life. The pain and tension which results from this juxtaposition of modern beliefs and common sense can lead to the birth of more sane positions, which also just happen to be orthodox Christian doctrines. As Chesterton puts it, common sense "often comes to us in the form of tradition" (CW 2:163).

The modern skeptic, for example, judges the Christian notion of Creation to be untenable and instead argues for an evolution in which everything comes from something smaller. Chesterton bristles:

> It is absurd for the Evolutionist to complain that it is unthinkable for an admittedly unthinkable God to make everything out of nothing, and then pretend that it is more thinkable that nothing should turn itself into everything. (CW 2:534)

Those interested in evolution continually insist that "every great thing grows from a seed, or something smaller than itself. They seem to forget that every seed comes from a tree, or from something larger than itself" (CW 2:219).

Chesterton is quick to point out that though there may be some evidence for the evolution of the body, there is not similar evidence for the evolution of the incorporeal aspect of the human being (CW 2:174). In other words, the sorts of conclusions one often hears about humans being simply a part of the animal world are not based on solid evidence. In fact, the evidence points dramatically in the other direction. The celebrated cave paintings of reindeer by early men indicate that humanity is rather different from other animals. We have yet to find a cave with drawings by reindeer of humans. Nor have we encountered birds who erect little clay statues of birds in front of their nests. Yes, humans have much in common with the animals, but they are also unique. It is only by twisting empirical facts that the modern critic is able to assert that humanity is just another animal (CW 2:155-71).

Modern thinkers, under the guise of science, dogmatically insist on materialism. Chesterton, however, contends that

> the materialist theory of history, that all politics and ethics are the expression of economics, is a very simple fallacy indeed. It consists

simply of confusing the necessary conditions of life with the normal preoccupations of life, that are quite a different thing. It is like saying that because a man can only walk about on two legs, therefore he never walks about except to buy shoes and stockings. (CW 2:269)

To put it another way, just because one must have food to live does not mean one lives only to eat (CW 2:270). The Christian position is a far more flexible stance than that of determinist materialism.

> The Christian is quite free to believe that there is a considerable amount of settled order and inevitable development in the universe. But the materialist is not allowed to admit into his spotless machine the slightest speck of spiritualism or miracle. (CW 1:227)

Chesterton delights in turning the tables on his adversaries, on those who make fun of Christian dogma. In *What's Wrong With the World* he wryly points out that "though Mr. Shaw and his friends admit it is a superstition that a man is judged after death, they stick to their central doctrine, that he is judged before he is born" (CW 4:154). All of a sudden it becomes clear to the reader that it is the modern notion which is insulting to human dignity, for at least the Christian position recognizes a measure of human freedom.

Modern thinkers assert that scientific findings and belief in miracles are incompatible. Chesterton, however, once again finds that it is dogma, rather than empirical evidence, which is at the root of skepticism about miracles. He quips:

> Somehow or other an extraordinary idea has arisen that the disbelievers in miracles consider them coldly and fairly, while believers in miracles accept them only in connection with some dogma. The fact is quite the other way. The believers in miracles accept them (rightly or wrongly) because they have evidence for them. The disbelievers in miracles deny them (rightly or wrongly) because they have a doctrine against them. (CW 1:355)

In other words, modern skeptics are so dogmatically committed to the notion of unalterable natural law that they are willing to ignore evidence to the contrary. Nor is Chesterton dissuaded by evidence of forgeries. "A false ghost disproves the reality of ghosts exactly as much as a forged banknote disproves the existence of the Bank of England . . ." (CW 1:358).

Modern thinkers often have shown a deep antipathy towards what has preceded the present age, imagining progress to be the inevitable product of the passage of time. Chesterton, however, points out that "all the men in history who have really done anything with the future have had their eyes fixed upon the past" (CW 4:54). In defense of tradition, in fact, he penned one of his most memorable passages.

> Tradition means giving votes to the most obscure of all classes, our ancestors. It is the democracy of the dead. Tradition refuses to submit to the small and arrogant oligarchy of those who merely happen to be walking about. All democrats object to men being disqualified by the accident of birth. Democracy tells us not to neglect a good man's opinion, even if he is our groom; tradition asks us not to neglect a good man's opinion, even if he is our father. (CW 1:251)

One final example of Chesterton's exposure of the flaws of modern thought involves the modern thinker's frequent rebellion against political systems and morality. This reflects shallowness of thought, as if it is really possible to get "beyond good and evil." Regarding the revolutionary, Chesterton observes:

> In his book on politics he attacks men for trampling on morality; in his book on ethics he attacks morality for trampling on men. Therefore the modern man in revolt has become practically useless for all purposes of revolt. By rebelling against everything he has lost his right to rebel against anything. (CW 1:245)

Once again the modern skeptic is shown to be short-sighted, naive, and inconsistent. And Chesterton has arrived at this judgment simply by using the tools of modern critics: empirical data and logical analysis. They stand condemned by the light of their own understanding, though Chesterton has deliberately turned up the wattage to show them more clearly where they are and where they are headed.

The remarkable thing about Chesterton is that he has the capacity to examine so-called "common" modern truths, which seem to be inviolable simply because they have been repeated so often, and to reveal them for what they truly are—shoddy pieces of analysis based far more on dogma than fact. In the process of critically examining modern thought, Chesterton transforms uneasy, slightly nervous Christians, uncomfortable with their minority status in twentieth-century culture, into bold believers who, if anything, feel a certain genuine pity for those latter-day pagans who defend silly and inconsistent positions. But it is not intellectual or spiritual arrogance which is called for, rather a firm and loving reason which will show the modern prodigal the error of his logic and his ways.

Religious dogmas are out of fashion in the twentieth century. They are considered the sure sign of the narrow mind, a certain source of intolerance. Christians who yet profess belief often prefer a Sunday worship service, where they can whisper their credal affirmations amid the safety of other timid believers. Paul's spirited, firm affirmation, "I am not ashamed of the Gospel, because it is the power of God for the salvation of everyone who believes," today might well be derided as religious imperialism, for dogma is the dreaded enemy.

Not so with G. K. Chesterton. Consider his bold challenge to modern wisdom found in *Heretics* (1905):

> Man can be defined as an animal that makes dogmas. As he plies doctrine on doctrine and conclusion on conclusion in the formation of some tremendous scheme of philosophy and religion, he is, in the only legitimate sense of which the expression is capable, becoming more and more human. When he drops one doctrine after another in a refined skepticism, when he declines to tie himself to a system, when he says that he has outgrown definitions, when he says that he disbelieves in finality, when, in his own imagination, he sits as God, holding no form of creed but contemplating all, then he is by that very process sinking slowly backwards into the vagueness of the vagrant animals and the unconsciousness of the grass. Trees have no dogmas. Turnips are singularly broad-minded. (CW 1:196-97)

Kent R. Hill

Defending Christianity from Its Critics

Besides pointing out fundamental flaws in modern thought, Chesterton turned his attention to attacks made on the church. His work here is essential for effective apologetics.

Christianity and the church are charged with being hostile to the natural world. We are told by some critics that the church was founded by ascetics who hated life. But this charge in Chesterton's view is far more true of the Gnostic heresies. Christian orthodoxy insisted that the world was created by God and was good. "It would be nearer the truth to call it [the church] the tamer of asceticism than the mere leader or loosener of it" (CW 2:357). Chesterton's biographies of St. Francis and St. Thomas reveal that both had a profound appreciation for nature.

It is often charged that Christianity and the church are at odds with reason and science. In fact, it is nearly always the reverse. "The truth is that the Church was actually the first thing that ever tried to combine reason and religion. There had never before been any such union of the priests and the philosophers" (CW 2:243). The church is blamed for the Dark Ages, when in fact it "was the one path across the Dark Ages that was not dark" (CW 1:352). And, of course, Chesterton's assertion is absolutely correct from a historical standpoint. Between the mid-sixth century, when Benedictine monasticism was established, and the mid-eleventh century, it is estimated that well over ninety percent of those who learned to read were taught by monks. The monasteries preserved many of the classics during those dark initial centuries following the fall of Rome in the fifth century. Yet, many critics continue to connect the medieval church with obscurantism.

There are few charges which have not been made against the church. Even when the charges contradict each other, they are advanced all the same. Chesterton recalls the rhetoric he listened to before he became a believer.

> One accusation against Christianity was that it prevented men, by morbid tears and terrors, from seeking joy and liberty in the bosom of Nature. But another accusation was that it comforted men with

a fictitious providence, and put them in a pink-and-white nursery. . . . Christianity could not at once be the black mask on a white world, and also the white mask on a black world. The state of the Christian could not be at once so comfortable that he was a coward to cling to it, and so uncomfortable that he was a fool to stand it. (CW 1:289-90)

Chesterton goes on to report that he was encouraged first to hate Christianity for being too passive and later to condemn it for being too violent. "It looked not so much as if Christianity was bad enough to include any vices, but rather as if any stick was good enough to beat Christianity with" (CW 1:293).

A typical "enlightened" secular thinker half a century after Chesterton still frequently parrots the view that religion, especially Christianity, spawns intolerance, fanaticism, and violence. If asked for proof, such a person will likely allude to the Crusades or the burning of heretics. Yet any coldly sober treatment of history will reveal a very different situation. It is all too true that the church has at times been a party to actions of which all Christians should be ashamed. But it is also true that the crimes committed in the name of Christianity in earlier centuries are but a mere shadow of the horrors to which humanity has been subjected in this century because of secular visions of paradise on earth. Victims of the latter run into the millions; victims of the former into the thousands. While it is of course terrible that there should be any victims, it is absurd not to ask why Christianity is able to check its abuses, while its secular replacements have so often slid hopelessly down a slippery slope into a hell on earth.

How do we account for this prejudice against Christianity and the resulting caricaturing of it which so often surrounds us? Chesterton is right that apparently any stick is good enough to beat it with. Part of the problem resides in misinformation and disinformation. But the malady goes beyond this. Chesterton comments:

Altruists, with thin, weak voices, denounce Christ as an egoist. Egoists (with even thinner and weaker voices) denounce Him as an altruist. . . . There is a huge and heroic sanity of which moderns can only collect the fragments. There is a giant of whom we see only the lopped arms and legs walking about. They have torn the soul of Christ into silly strips, labelled egoism and altruism, and they are equally puzzled by His insane magnificence and His insane meekness. They have parted His garments among them, and for His vesture they have cast lots; though the coat was without seam, woven from the top throughout. (CW 1:248)

The modern world, much like a madman, has a proclivity to ignore the complexity of reality in favor of the simplicity of singularity. Because the modern mind is unbalanced and insane, it has difficulty appreciating the crucial role that balance and sanity play in life. The modern tendency is to praise either St. Francis or St. Thomas, but not both; Chesterton loves them both dearly, and insists that the church's needs were such that it could not do without either one. Neither should be allowed to dominate the church. The modern tendency is to make the church pacifist or Crusader; Chesterton insisted the church has to include both elements, since they both have their roles to play. The modern mind wants to affirm either asceticism or family life; Chesterton contends that both have their place. Modern logic prefers to choose between Paul and James; the early church decided that the full truth was not present unless both were represented in the canon. Moderns would like God either to be almighty and transcendent or human and immanent; Christian orthodoxy insisted that God was both.

Orthodoxy as Truth

The third and final proposition which Chesterton wished to make for the honest nonbeliever was that there is a remarkable fit between the key of orthodoxy and the lock of the reality we experience.

According to Chesterton, "We are all agnostics until we discover that Agnosticism will not work" (CW 1:382). Given the weaknesses of modern thought and the emptiness of the strangely contradictory criticisms of the Christian faith, is there a better way to make sense of reality? Early in this century, in response to a question about the reasons he accepted orthodox doctrines,

Chesterton replied: "Because I perceive life to be logical and workable with these beliefs and illogical and unworkable without them" (Dale 87).

By orthodoxy Chesterton meant the historic truths of the Christian faith, including: God created the world; humanity fell away from God and became tainted by sin; God sent his Son who was fully human and fully divine to offer salvation to humankind; and Christ was crucified, died, and was raised from the dead, sent his Holy Spirit, and will come again one day. Though at first the definition of orthodoxy seems like abstract claims from a theological primer, so much here corresponds to what human beings experience—from the reality of sin to the deep hunger for a relationship with the Creator and Savior. For Chesterton, "theology is a product far more practical than chemistry" (CW 1:383). Chesterton comments on the creed as follows:

> In answer to the historical query of why it was accepted, and is accepted, I answer for millions of others in my reply; because it fits the lock; because it is like life. It is one among many stories; only it happens to be a true story. It is one among many philosophies; only it happens to be the truth. (CW 2:380-81)

Chesterton is convinced that there is a connection between the fact that Christianity has survived and its veracity:

> If it were an error, it seems as if the error could hardly have lasted a day. If it were a mere ecstasy, it would seem that such an ecstasy could not endure for an hour. It has endured for nearly two thousand years; and the world within it has been more lucid, more level-headed, more reasonable in its hopes, more healthy in its instincts, more humorous and cheerful in the face of fate and death, than all the world outside. For it was the soul of Christendom that came forth from the incredible Christ; and the soul of it was common sense. (CW 2:402)

Yes, there are many indications for the honest nonbeliever that Christianity at least needs to be considered seriously. To the extent Chesterton helps point the way, he deserves to be called an apologist.

Chesterton's wit and his insight, his keen mind and his penetrating analysis, his joy and his mirth have for decades endeared him to his readers. A "modern" pagan who has the audacity to criticize Chesterton might well be rebuffed and dismissed in the same way Hilaire Belloc once defended his long-time friend against an academic attacker:

> Remote and ineffectual Don
> That dared attack my Chesterton,
>
> . . . .
>
> Don dreadful, rasping Don and wearing,
> Repulsive Don—Don past all bearing,
> Don of the cold and doubtful breath,
> Don despicable, Don of death;
> Don nasty, skimpy, silent, level;
> Don evil; Don that serves the devil.
>
> . . . .
>
> My fires are banked, but still they burn
> To write some more about the Don
> That dared attack my Chesterton. (Belloc 182)

Needless to say, Chesterton would not have considered Belloc's outburst to have reflected sound apologetic methodology. But then Belloc was not trying to win any converts.

In contrast to Belloc's "remote and ineffectual Don," Chesterton is down-to-earth and highly effective. He begins where his readers are. He employs a concept of reason which recognizes both its strengths and its limitations. He demonstrates the shallowness of modern thought and the hollowness of its criticism of the Christian church. Moreover, he defends the beauty and the balance of orthodoxy—that priceless key which fits the lock of reality and opens up to us a proper relationship with the world and our Creator.

Works Cited

Belloc, Hilaire. "Lines to a Don." *Modern American and British Poetry.* Ed. Louis Untermeyer. n.p.: Harcourt, Brace, and Co., 1942.

Chesterton, G. K. *Collected Works of G. K. Chesterton.* Ed. George Marlin, et. al. San Francisco: Ignatius Press, 1986.

_____. *The Man Who Was Thursday*. New York: G. P. Putman's Sons, Wideview/Perigee Books, 1980.

_____. *Orthodoxy*. Garden City, NY: Doubleday, Image Books, 1959.

Dale, Alzina Stone. *The Outline of Sanity: A Life of G. K. Chesterton*. Grand Rapids: Eerdmans, 1982.

Dooley, David. "Introduction." *The Collected Works of G. K. Chesterton*. Ed. George Marlin, et al. San Francisco: Ignatius Press, 1986.

Lewis, C. S. *Surprised by Joy*. New York: Harcourt, Brace & World, Inc., 1955.

V. PURSUING THE RIDDLE OF JOY

C. S. Lewis's Argument from Desire

Peter J. Kreeft

This essay is about a single argument. Next to Anselm's famous "ontological argument," I think it is the single most intriguing argument in the history of human thought. When I teach it to my philosophy classes, I point out that, for one thing, it not only argues for the existence of God but at the same time it argues for the existence of Heaven, and for something of the essential nature of Heaven and of God—four conclusions, not just one. For another thing, it is far more moving, arresting, and apologetically effective than any other argument for God or for Heaven. (At least in my experience with students.) Finally, it is more than an argument. Like Anselm's argument, it is also a meditation, an illumination, an experience, an invitation to an experiment with yourself, a pilgrimage.

I shall first state the argument as succinctly as possible. Second, I shall show how C. S. Lewis, who more than anyone else is associated with it, uses it in three different contexts (autobiographical, practical-pastoral, and logical). Third, I shall trace historically four strands of influence (experiential, histori-

PETER J. KREEFT is professor of philosophy at Boston College and the author of numerous books, including *Heaven: The Heart's Deepest Longing, The Unaborted Socrates,* and *For Heaven's Sake.*

cal, epistemological, and practical) which feed into the modern form of the argument. Fourth, I shall try to answer the main objections against it.

I

The major premise of the argument is that *every natural or innate desire in us bespeaks a corresponding real object that can satisfy the desire.* The minor premise is that *there exists in us a desire which nothing in time, nothing on earth, no creature, can satisfy.* The conclusion is that *there exists something outside of time, earth, and creatures which can satisfy this desire.*

This something is what people call God, and Heaven. Thus the argument seeks to prove the existence of God and of Heaven via this one aspect of them, desirableness, just as Aquinas's five "ways" seek to prove the existence of God under five aspects, concluding with: "And this is what people call 'God.'"

A word about each premise.

The major premise — that all natural or innate desires have real objects — implicitly distinguishes desires into two kinds: innate and natural, or conditioned and artificial. We naturally desire things like food, drink, sex, knowledge, friendship, and beauty, and naturally turn away from things like starvation, ignorance, loneliness, and ugliness. But we also desire things like Rolls Royces, political offices, flying through the air like Superman, a Red Sox world championship, and lands like Oz. There are two differences between the two lists. First, we do not always recognize corresponding states of deprivation of the second, as we do with the first. And, most importantly, the first list of desires all come from within, from our nature; the second come from without, from society, or advertising, or fiction. The first desires come from spiritual heredity; the second come from the environment.

The minor premise of the argument—that we have an unsatisfiable innate desire — is an empirical observation, if "empirical" is extended to cover inner experience as well as outer, introspection as well as extrospection. The argument then depends on a personal appeal to introspective experience. Just as we cannot argue effectively about color with a blind man because he has no data, so we cannot argue about this desire with someone who cannot find the desire in question within, or who refuses to look for it, or who refuses to admit its presence once it is found. But, then, such a person cannot argue against us either. (In a sense the argument is an *ad hominem*, but a telling one, like Aristotle's argument against Protagoras's skeptical denial of the law of noncontradiction: if only the skeptic can be maneuvered into making some simple admission, he can be refuted, for he contradicts himself by claiming to know something when he says he cannot know anything. But he cannot be compelled to make that admission — in Aristotle's case, to utter a putatively meaningful sentence, in our case to admit the existence of a desire for a perfect object, or for perfect joy, that no earthly object and no earthly pleasure can fulfill. If someone blandly says, "I am perfectly happy playing with mud pies (or fast cars or money or political power)," we can query, "Are you, really?" but we can only try to inveigle him out of his childishness, we cannot compel him by logical force.

In a sense, the minor premise of the argument is more interesting than the argument itself. The phenomenon the Germans call *Sehnsucht* is psychologically fascinating, and when it occurs as subject rather than object, i.e., when we experience the desire rather than thinking about it, it is obsessive and imperious — in fact, even more imperious than erotic desire at its height. Faced with a choice between the perfect earthly beloved and the fulfillment of *Sehnsucht*, we choose *Sehnsucht*; for the object of *Sehnsucht* is the perfect heavenly beloved, whether we know it or not. As Lewis says, "Joy is not a substitute for sex; sex is often a substitute for Joy" (*Surprised by Joy* 170).

The conclusion of the argument, though, is *not* that everything which is meant by God or Heaven in the popular imagination or in the Bible must exist. What the argument proves to exist is unidentifiable with any image or representation. Lewis describes it thus in *Surprised by Joy*:

> . . . something which, by refusing to identify itself with any object of the senses or anything whereof we have biological or social need,

or anything imagined, or any state of our own minds, proclaims it-self sheerly objective. Far more objective than bodies, for it is not, like them, clothed in our senses: the naked Other, imageless (though our imagination salutes it with a hundred images), un-known, undefined, desired. (221)

The argument's conclusion is the concept of an unknown x, but an unknown whose *direction* is known, so to speak. God is *more* — more beauty, more desirability, more awesomeness. God is to great beauty what great beauty is to small beauty or to a mixture of beauty and ugliness. The same is true of God and other perfections. But the "more" is *infinitely* more; thus the anal-ogy is not proportionate. Twenty is to ten what ten is to five, but infinity is not to twenty what twenty is to ten, or five, or one. But it *is* "in that direction," so to speak. The argument is like a parable: it points down an infinite corridor in a finite direc-tion. Its object is not "God" as God has been conceived and defined for us already, but a movingly mysterious x which is al-ways more than any image, notion, or concept. This x, in other words, does not presuppose but supplies a definition of God, and one which reverses the normal positive notion of definition (*de-fino*) by asserting that God is the one *not* capturable in any finite terms. The "definition" of this "God" is "that which is more than any definition": the God whom "eye has not seen, ear has not heard, neither has it entered into the heart of man" (1 Cor. 2:9). In other words, this is the true God, the truly transcendent God.

II

There are three places in C. S. Lewis's work where the argument from desire is stated at length, though *Sehnsucht* itself seeps out from many a page of Lewis, most perfectly in "The Weight of Glory," the best sermon I have ever read. These three locations are in *Surprised by Joy*, *Mere Christianity*, and the introduction to *The Pilgrim's Regress*.

Surprised by Joy—which traces this desire, or "Joy" through Lewis's life — first defines the desire, in contradistinction to other desires, as follows: it is "an unsatisfied desire which is it-self more desirable than any other satisfaction" (17-18). Lewis then implicitly argues for the existence of the object of this desire when he discovers the fact that the desire is essentially "intentional," that is, reaching out and pointing beyond itself to its object. He confesses and turns from his earlier subjectivist error:

> I had smuggled in the assumption that what I wanted was a "thrill," a state of my own mind. And there lies the deadly error. Only when your whole attention and desire are fixed on something else . . . does the "thrill" arise. It is a byproduct. Its very existence presupposes that you desire not it but something other and outer. . . . (168)
>
> Images or sensations . . . were merely the mental track left by [its] passage . . . not the wave but the wave's imprint in the sand. The inherent dialectic of desire itself had in a way already shown me this, for all images and sensations, if idolatrously mistaken for Joy itself, soon confessed themselves inadequate. All said, in the last resort, "It is not I. I am only a reminder. Look! Look! What do I remind you of?"
>
> Inexorably Joy proclaimed, "You want—I myself am your want of—something other, outside, not you or any state of you." (219-21)

Like Augustine, ending Book X of his *Confessions*, so Lewis, on the last page of his autobiography, confesses his present state of soul with regard to *Sehnsucht*:

> I now know that the experience, considered as a state of my own mind, had never had the kind of importance I once gave it. It was valuable only as a pointer to something other and outer. While that other was in doubt, the pointer naturally loomed large in my thoughts. When we are lost in the woods the sight of a signpost is a great matter. . . . But when we have found the road . . . we shall not stop and stare, or not much; not on this road . . . "We would be at Jerusalem." (238)

These passages from *Surprised by Joy* describe the desire and head us off from the subjectivist error about it, but they do not so much argue from it to the existence of its object as look along the desire toward its mysterious object, or look at its intentionality and see at once that it must have an object, because it is thus essentially intentional. But Lewis does not distinguish natural or innate desires from other desires, nor yet argue, in this book, from the principle that all natural desires have objects.

Mere Christianity's use of the argument from desire is also essentially practical, meant to head the reader off from two popular mistakes. Lewis first calls our attention to the desire; then to two mistakes about it; then comes the argument itself:

> Most people, if they had really learned to look into their own hearts, would know that they do want, and want acutely, something that cannot be had in this world. There are all sorts of things in this world that offer to give it to you, but they never quite keep their promise. . . . Now there are two wrong ways of dealing with this fact, and one right way.
>
> (1) The Fool's Way. He puts the blame on the things themselves. He goes on all his life thinking that if only he tried another woman, or holiday, or whatever, then this time he would really catch the mysterious something. . . .
>
> (2) The Way of the Disillusioned "Sensible Man." He soon decides that the whole thing was moonshine. And so he represses the part of himself which used to cry for the moon. . . .
>
> (3) The Christian Way. The Christian says [and here is the argument]: Creatures are not born with desires unless satisfaction for these desires exists. A baby feels hunger; well, there is such a thing as food. A duckling wants to swim; well, there is such a thing as water. Men feel sexual desire; well, there is such a thing as sex. If I find in myself a desire which no experience in this world can satisfy, the most probable explanation is that I was made for another world. (104-5)

Note that Lewis does not claim certainty for the conclusion here, just probability. The conclusion is only a hypothesis that explains the data better than any other; he does not say it proves with certainty that this hypothesis is true.

Yet it does show the practical necessity of taking this desire seriously: "I must keep alive in myself the desire for my true country" (*Mere Christianity* 105). Like Pascal's "Wager," the argument here shows that you are a fool if you turn your back on this strong clue, this strong probability that infinite happiness exists and that you are designed to enjoy it.

In the introduction to *The Pilgrim's Regress*, Lewis does two things more clearly than he does anywhere else. First, he defines exactly how this one unquenchable desire differs from all others. Second, he argues from the principle that nature makes nothing in vain to the conclusion that the one who can satisfy this desire must exist.

> The experience is one of intense longing. It is distinguished from other longings by two things. In the first place, though the sense of want is acute and even painful, yet the mere wanting is felt to be somehow a delight. . . . This hunger is better than any other fullness; this poverty better than all other wealth. . . . In the second place, there is a peculiar mystery about the *object* of this desire. . . . Every one of these supposed objects for the desire is inadequate to it. It appears to me therefore that if a man diligently followed this desire, pursuing the false objects until their falsity appeared and then resolutely abandoning them, he must come out at last into the clear knowledge that the human soul was made to enjoy some object that is never fully given — nay, cannot even be imagined as given — in our present mode of subjective and spatio-temporal experience. This desire was, in the soul, as the Siege Perilous in Arthur's castle — the chair in which only one could sit. And if nature makes nothing in vain, the One who can sit in this chair must exist. (7-8, 10)

Here the conclusion is not called "the most probable explanation" but something which "must exist." *If* nature makes nothing in vain, if you admit that premise, then the conclusion necessarily follows. Of course, one who wants to refuse to admit the conclusion at all costs will deny the premise — at the cost of a meaningful universe, a universe in which desires and satisfactions match.

In other words, God can be avoided. All we need do is embrace "vanity of vanities" instead. It is a fool's bargain, of course: Everything is exchanged for Nothing—a trade even the Boston Red Sox are not fool enough to make.

III

Many virtues grace Lewis's work, but the one that lifts him above any other apologetical writer, I believe, is how powerfully he writes about Joy, or *Sehnsucht*, the desire we are speaking of here. Many other writers excel him in originality: he did not mean to be original. ("Our Lord never tried to be original," he noted.) Perhaps a few modern writers excel him in clarity (though offhand I cannot name one) or grace or beauty or accuracy or popular appeal. But no one has written better of Joy. Yet he never wrote a whole book examining this thing, though he admitted in his autobiography that it was the leitmotif of his whole life: "the central story of my life is about nothing else" (*Surprised by Joy* 17). He wrote, as he said, the kinds of books he wanted to read, the books he wished someone else would write (but they didn't, so he did). That is why I wrote *Heaven: The Heart's Deepest Longing*: because, incredibly, no one had ever written a whole book about the deepest longing in human life. This paper does not rehash my book, for this is, first of all, specifically about the argument, not the experience; second, it pretends to scholarliness; and third, it tries more precisely to relate this experience to the history of philosophy. We turn to that historical aspect now.

From a historical point of view I think one of Lewis's chief claims to fame is that he pulled together, coalesced, and sharpened to a fine point a number of important strands in the history of western religious and philosophical thought concerning this argument. The argument does not come to us floating on the surface of our past; it flowers from immense, deep tangles of growing things. Some of the most important names in our history are involved in this tangle: Moses, Solomon, Plato, Christ, Paul, Augustine, Bonaventure, Pascal, Jung. I discern four distinct aspects of the argument, four strands of influence contributing to its modern form: experiential, historical, epistemological, and practical. One name that crops up in all four strands is Pascal, whom Lewis evidently read and admired, though he quoted him only sparsely. (But such is the case with Kierkegaard, who fleshes out half the *Pensées* but never mentions Pascal's name.)

The first strand of influence is experiential, or psychological. It involves philosophical meditation upon a double experience, a negative and a positive. The negative experience is unhappiness, restlessness. The positive experience is longing, *Sehnsucht* itself. Let's look at the dark side first.

Solomon, or the author of Ecclesiastes, knew the emptiness, vanity, and wretchedness of human life, even at its best, as well as anyone ever did. Pascal says:

> Solomon and Job have known and spoken best about man's wretchedness, one the most fortunate, the other the most unfortunate of men; one knowing by experience the vanity of pleasure, the other the reality of afflictions. (403:146)

Herman Melville, in *Moby Dick*, and Thomas Wolfe, in *You Can't Go Home Again*, both called Ecclesiastes the greatest and truest book ever written about human life under the sun. Its conclusion is of course that life is "vanity of vanities." Why? I do not mean by that question: What evidence does Solomon use to prove his conclusion? That is painfully obvious: the oppression of the poor, the endlessly destructive cycles of time, the inevitability of death, the strength of evil over good, the indifference of nature to justice, the uncertainty of all our works, the impossibility of being at once wise and content, and above all the mystery, remoteness, and invisibility of a God whose ways are past finding out. No, I mean a more mysterious "Why?" Why do we rail against these things? Why do we not obey the reasonable advice of nine out of ten of our psychologists, who in book after book tell us to accept ourselves as we are, become well-adjusted citizens of the Kingdom of This World, and even accept death as a friend, not an enemy. Freud talked about making friends with the necessity of dying, but no one but a sheep or a scholar is fool enough to believe such inhuman nonsense. Instead, something in us thrills to the gloriously irrational passion of the poet Dylan Thomas when he says, "Do not go gentle into that good night/Rage, rage against the dying of the light" (lines 18-19).

What is that thing in us that passionately disobeys the rational advice of our comfort-mongering modern sages and rises to the dignity of despair? Death is the most natural thing in the world;

why do we find it unnatural? "Do fish complain of the sea for being wet?" asks Lewis, in a letter to Sheldon Vanauken. "Or if they did, would that not indicate that they had not always been, or were not destined always to be, sea creatures?" (Vanauken 90). But we complain about death—and about time. As Lewis says, "Time is just another word for death" (*A Grief Observed* 28). There is never enough time. Time makes being into nonbeing. Time is a river that takes away everything it brings: nations, civilization, art, science, culture, plants, animals, our own bodies, the very stars — nothing stands outside this cosmic stream rushing headlong into the sea of death. Or does it? Something in us seems to stand outside it, for something in us protests this "nature" and asks: Is that all there is? We find this natural situation "vanity": empty, frustrating, wretched, unhappy. Our nature contradicts nature.

Thus there is a double datum: the objective datum of all that is in nature, such as death and time (which makes us unhappy); and the subjective datum that these things *do* make us unhappy. The objective part of the datum can be described scientifically, but what of the subjective face of the datum? That needs to be explained, too.

There is a clue in Ecclesiastes 3:11, the one verse in the book that rings with hope, like a bell in a swamp. Solomon says to the Creator: "You have made everything fitting for its time, but you have also put eternity into man's heart." Time does not satisfy the restless heart: we cry out for eternity, because God has put such desire into our hearts. Our hearts are restless until they rest in God, because they were designed by God to rest in God alone. Resting in nature is unnatural for us. Our nature is to demand supernature.

This is the negative side of the coin: the wretchedness and dissatisfaction and restlessness of the heart, the spirit, the image of God, the God-child in us, alienated from Home and the Father. The positive side is the hopeful longing, the energy and homing pigeon's instinct that moves Augustine through the pages of the *Confessions*. It is the poignancy of E. T. looking for that magic place, "Home." Pascal writes that an infinite abyss can be filled only with an infinite object, i.e., God himself. We spend our lives trying to fill the Grand Canyon with marbles.

The pagans at their best knew this, knew this part of the argument from desire. Plato in the *Symposium* let the cat out of the bag. Eros, love, desire climbs the steps of a hierarchy and will not rest with lesser, lower, particular, limited, and material loves, beautiful as they are. Only Beauty Itself, absolute, pure, unmixed, perfect, and eternal, will satisfy the soul. Lewis thought that no one should be allowed to die without having read Plato's *Symposium*. And he surely speaks for himself when he has Professor Digory Kirke exclaim, "Why it's all in Plato! All in Plato! What *do* they teach them in the schools nowadays?" (*The Lion, the Witch, and the Wardrobe* 38, 40). Plato is eminently convertible, Christianizeable. Paganism at its best is a virgin, Christianity a wife, modernity a divorcée. I love Chesterton's three-sentence summary of the history of western thought in *The Everlasting Man*: Paganism was the biggest thing in the world, and Christianity was bigger, and everything since has been comparatively small.

A second ingredient in the background of our argument is the philosophical tradition of thought about a historical origin for our misery and displacement. If our present wretchedness and restless search is a historical fact, not "just" a myth, then the origin or cause of this fact cannot be a mere myth either; it must be a real event. The candidates for this Origin are Creation or Fall. Either God or Man created our wretchedness. The story of a Fall, a Paradise Lost, a Primordial Tragedy, is a nearly universal theme in the world's myths, for our myths are wiser than our science, which knows nothing of such archaic and spiritual events, or our psychology, which frequently knows little about our deepest longings and intuitions. Our science comes from our conscious mind, but our myths come from our unconsciousness, which remembers things the conscious mind has forgotten. The Priest of Glome is wiser than "the Fox" (the Greek philosopher) in Lewis's mythic novel *Till We Have Faces*, set in archaic history.

Much traditional thought has concluded that myths are even prophetic, pointing to the truth from afar, as Greek philosophy is prophetic. God has not left himself without witnesses even outside Israel, though none of these other witnesses is divinely

259

guaranteed and infallible. As the human soul has intellect, will, and emotions, and some knowledge of the true, the good, and the beautiful, so God has sent prophets to all three areas of the soul: philosophers to enlighten the intellect, prophets to exhort the will, and myth-makers to tease and touch the emotions with a desire for himself. The philosophers have an analogue in the soul: a philosopher within, our understanding. The prophets have an analogue in the soul, too: a divine mouthpiece called conscience. The myth-makers, too, have an analogue in the soul: a dreamer and a poet and myth-maker within. But the truths of the myths become distorted, like the message in the party game whispered around a large circle. That's why Lewis refers to myths as gleams of celestial strength and beauty—they are based on a far solider reality than we think.

The biblical account of the Fall in Genesis 3 explains our present experience as a scientific hypothesis explains observed data. The data here are very strange: that we alone do not fit the world of time and death, that we do not obey the advice of our own psychologists to accept ourselves as we are. The explanation must be equally strange. The human lock is weirdly shaped. The biblical key is also weirdly shaped: a story of a radical tragedy at our very roots. There are all sorts of difficulties with the story. But it fits — the key fits the lock. What happened in Eden may be hard to understand, but it makes everything else understandable.

Eden explains, for example, the strange complicity of our greatness and our wretchedness. As Pascal says, "All these examples of [man's] wretchedness prove his greatness. It is the wretchedness of a great lord, the wretchedness of a dispossessed king" (116:59). And: "Man's greatness can be deduced from his wretchedness, for what is nature in animals [e.g., pain and death] we call wretchedness in man, thus recognizing that he must have fallen from some better state which was once his own. Who indeed would think himself unhappy not to be the king except one who had been dispossessed? . . . Who would think himself unhappy if he had only one mouth and who would not if he had only one eye! It has probably never occurred to anyone to be distressed at not having three eyes, but those who have none are

inconsolable" (117:59). Our longing for a home and a happiness
that we do not experience in this world is a great mystery. The
story of the Fall is a great solution to it.

A third, epistemological strand in the history of our argument stems from Plato and his famous doctrine of Anamnesis,
or Recollection. In light of what we have just said about the historical events in Eden being an explanation of our present unhappy state — in light, that is, of the Christian doctrine of the
Fall — Plato's doctrine of Anamnesis also makes sense. For whenever we discover an eternal truth, we experience an "aha!" —a
moment of recognition (re-cognition, knowing-again). It is like
the aha! experience of remembering an empirical object like a
lost wallet when we meet it in a lost and found department. We
recognize it only because there is a memory image in us, which
came from our past experience of it. Similarly, when, like Meno's
slave boy, we discover an eternal truth of mathematics like the
Pythagorean Theorem, or an eternal truth of ethics such as the
fundamental conclusion of Plato's *Republic* (that justice is always
more profitable than injustice, for justice is health of soul) —
when we discover such eternal truths in the lost and found
department of ideas that is the history of western thought, we
experience a shock of recognition (re-cognition), a *deja vu*, an
aha! The innate truth-detector in us buzzes like a Geiger counter
— not infallibly, but nonetheless really. Knowledge need not be
infallible to be knowledge. Meno's slave boy's truth detector went
off too soon. He made a mistake before he found the truth. But
then, on the second attempt, he corrected his mistake. We also
often aha! too soon and seize on an error as a truth, or too late,
and miss a truth that is under our nose. But we do aha! We do
experience that sense of recognition.

From this aha! experience two lines of explanation are possible. Reductionism only explains it away, debunks it (or tries
to) as only empirical generalization, or projection of subjective
expectation, or habit, or even as a kind of *deja vu* resulting from
a new experience being misfiled into the brain's memory
category. But suppose we do not explain it away, but explain
it. Two dimensions of nonreductionistic explanation present
themselves: the ontological, as in Augustine's theory of Divine

Illumination, or the psychological, as in Jung's theory of the Collective Unconscious.

Augustine's idea of Divine Illumination as the source of *a priori* knowledge uses the image of *light* for truth and in so doing reveals something extremely important and usually forgotten in debates between Platonists like Augustine and Lewis and the empiricists or positivists or analytic philosophers who criticize them. As I shall try to show in the last section of this paper, a Platonist always puts *intellectus* above *ratio*, the fourth quarter of the Divided Line in the *Republic* over the third quarter, the First Act of the Mind, or Simple Apprehension of an essence, above or prior to the Second Act of the Mind, judgment of a proposition as true or false, and the Third Act of the Mind, reasoning or inference. Here is a more primordial notion of truth than the truth of a judgment. It is the truth of a concept, and this is something like light, something almost substantial. Thus Lewis speaks of edible and drinkable truth in *The Great Divorce* (chapter 5), just as Jesus did in John's Gospel.

An alternative nonreductionistic explanation of the aha! epistemological experience is Jung's theory of the Collective Unconscious. It may be used either as a substitute for or as a supplement to the ontological explanation of Augustine. It may also be used either as a substitute for or as a supplement to the historical explanation of Eden. It presupposes first that there *is* an Unconscious, as nearly every philosophical psychologist except Sartre and Behaviorists do, and second that Christopher Columbus Freud only landed on its beach. His mistake was not to overestimate its depth and complexity and innate power to inform and direct the conscious self, but to underestimate it, in identifying it with the sex drive (however broadly conceived). Scott Peck has shown in a practical, popular, and effective way in the first half of his bestseller *The Road Less Travelled*, how wise our unconscious is — so impressive is this wisdom to him, in fact, that in the second half of the book he voyages far beyond the shores of scientific psychology in the hypothesis, apparently shared by Jung, that the unconscious is God. For the Christian, this is heresy, of course, but every heresy is based on a truth that is bent. The heretic is mistaken, but some truth must be taken before it can

be mis-taken. The truth the Jungian takes is, I believe, precisely
the truth of the Augustinian Divine Illumination—which, by the
way, St. Thomas also teaches, though he clarifies it so that only
in God's light do we see light. Divine Illumination is not an object of consciousness; it is the sun shining behind us rather than
in front of us. As Chesterton says (in *Orthodoxy*), God is like the
sun: only in the light of the one who cannot be seen (because
he is too light, not too dark) can everything else be seen. Let
one thing be mystical and everything else becomes rational. Let
one thing be not a knowable object, and everything else becomes
a knowable object. Let one thing be an x and everything else becomes a why.

The Platonic epistemology of *a priori* knowledge is not as intellectually silly as its current reputation makes it. It is based on
data, evidence: the fact that we function like homing pigeons;
that we know what is *not* our home, like E.T.; and that we also
know what things are closer to Home, to Heaven, to God, than
other things, though we do not know this infallibly and we can
and do make many, many mistakes about it, even eternal mistakes. But we can and do judge that y is farther and z nearer to
x, to Home, even though we have never been Home, never experienced God or Heaven as we have experienced y and z. In
order to judge truly whether y is more or less perfect than z, we
must use a standard, x. Even if we do not know x as an explicit,
defined, experienced, or even experienceable object, we still *use*
x, and thus *implicitly* know x. "Better" implies "best." More or
less perfect implies perfectly perfect. Progress implies an unchang-
ing goal—how can you make progress toward a moving goal line?
How can a baserunner score a run if home plate keeps moving?

The program is in our computer because our Creator has
designed and programmed us. *Because* "Thou hast made us for
Thyself," therefore "our hearts are restless until they rest in Thee"
(Augustine 1:1). It is not a program that appears on our computer screen as data, as information to store and recall. Rather,
it is an operational program, a procedural rule, a practical command and direction we follow. It is program of the heart, not of
the head or conscious mind. But "heart" does not mean sentiment, emotion, or feeling in Scripture, as it does in modern par-

lance. It means our center, our I. Pascal is quite correct to say, "The heart has its reasons which the reason does not know" (423:154). The heart has *reasons*. The heart has eyes. Love is not blind. (How could love be blind? God is love. Is God blind? One of those three propositions must be false: that love is blind, that God is not blind, and that God is love.)

The "heart" that we have just spoken of is the central concept of the fourth strand of influence, the practical or pastoral. It is the heart that is the organ of the unconscious knowledge of the way home that we have just explored. The heart is our guide, our homing pigeon. Though it is fallen and desperately in need of correction by divine revelation, though it is "desperately wicked" (Jer. 17:9), yet its very wretchedness shows its greatness, as the height from which we have fallen measures the depths of our fall. We are not simply bad, not even just a good thing gone bad, but a sacred thing profaned.

Jesus appealed to the heart constantly, as when he said, "Seek and you shall find" (Matt. 7:7). It is the heart that seeks. Pascal comments, with this promise of Jesus in mind,

> There are three kinds of people: those who have sought God and found Him, and these are reasonable and happy; those who seek God and have not yet found Him, and these are reasonable and unhappy; and those who neither seek God nor find Him, and these are unreasonable and unhappy. (160:82)

There is no fourth class, those who find without seeking. Christ's promise that all who seek, find is simultaneously reassuring and threatening: reassuring in that everyone in Pascal's second class eventually graduates into his first class (all seekers find, all who are reasonable and honest and intend God, intend repentance and faith, will find him and become happy); but threatening in that no one who does not seek will find. It is the seeking heart that determines our eternal destiny. In the heart Heaven or Hell are decided.

Christ presupposed the primacy of the heart in John 7:17 when he answered his critics' hermeneutical question, "How can we know your teaching, whether it is from God?" with scandalous simplicity: "If you (or your heart) were to do the will of my

Father, you would know my teaching, that it is from him." When it comes to knowing persons rather than things or concepts, the heart rightly leads the head. Who understands you best, a brilliant psychologist who has spent 10,000 hours interviewing you as a case study for his doctoral dissertation but does not care about you personally, or your best friend, who is not terribly bright but loves you very much?

William Law, one of Lewis's favorite writers, is as embarrassingly simple as Jesus because he too sees that the heart decides all. He says, in A Serious Call to a Devout and Holy Life, that if you will honestly consult your own heart, you will see that there is one and only one reason why you are not even now a saint: because you do not wholly want to be. Augustine says the same thing in the Confessions: that it is the divided will, the divided heart, that accounts for sin in us, that accounts for the astonishing introspective discovery of Paul in Romans 7 that "I do not understand my own behavior. For the good that I would do, I do not, and the evil that I would not, that I do."

Heart, will, and desire are essentially one. The argument from desire is the argument from the heart. Even in the heart whose "fundamental option," as Rahner puts it, is to run from God, to reject God, there is still, until death, a spark of the fire of desire for God, thus hope for repentance, for turning. It is to such an unbeliever that Pascal addresses his argument from desire, the famous "wager."

The wager presupposes the same heart-desire for happiness that Lewis's argument presupposes but moves in a different direction: the practical calculation of winning or losing God rather than the theoretical insight that there must be a God. It is as if Lewis played with the blue chips of metaphysical argument while Pascal played with the red chips of the passion to possess God, to attain happiness. Lewis tries to prove God exists; Pascal, skeptical of all argument for God's existence, does instead what Scripture does: inveigles us to make a leap of faith, a wager. "It is a remarkable fact," Pascal writes, "that no canonical writer ever tries to prove the existence of God. Rather, they all strive to make us believe in Him" (160:82). The wager appeals to our desire for God, our love of God though on a very low and selfish level. Lewis begins with the desire, at least implicit, to leap into God's arms and concludes that therefore God must exist. Pascal begins with, "You can't be certain God exists, but you can't be certain He doesn't, either" (189:85) and concludes that we *should* leap into his arms.

The wager works like Martin Buber's nonargument to an atheist who came to him demanding that Buber prove to him God's existence or else he would never believe. When Buber refused, the friend rose to leave angrily. Buber's parting words were: "But can you be *sure* God does not exist?" Forty years later, that atheist told that story and added that he was still an atheist, but that Buber's words continue to haunt him every day. If that man is honest and continues to seek and to let himself be haunted, he will one day leap and find.

Augustine uses a little thought-experiment to the same effect in his sermon "On the Pure Love of God." He says: Imagine God appeared to you and said he would make a deal with you, that he would give you everything you wished, everything your heart desired, except one thing. You could have anything you imagine, nothing would be impossible for you, and nothing would be sinful or forbidden. But, God concluded, "you shall never see my face." Why, Augustine asks, did a terrible chill creep over your heart at those last words unless there is in your heart a love of God, the desire for God? In fact, if you wouldn't accept that deal, you really love God above all things, for look what you just did: you gave up the whole world, and more, for God.

Augustine's experiment can help you prove to yourself that the minor premise of Lewis's argument is true, that the strange desire exists, and that it is a desire for nothing less than God. Once again, the heart has led the head. Love has instructed understanding. The fear of the Lord has proved to be the beginning of wisdom.

IV

Finally, I want to defend this argument against five objections that have been made (or could be made) against it.

First, one might simply deny the minor premise, saying, "I do not observe any such desire for God, or Heaven, or infinite joy, or some mysterious x which is more than any earthly happiness." This denial can take two forms. First, one may say, "I am not perfectly content now, but I can imagine myself to be perfectly content if only I had a million dollars, a Lear jet, an immortality pill, and a new mistress every week." The reply to this, of course, is: "Try it. You won't like it."

The second form of the denial of the minor premise is not "I would be perfectly content if only," but rather, "I am perfectly content right now." This, I suggest, verges on culpable dishonesty, the sin against the Holy Spirit, and requires something more like exorcism than refutation. This is Merseult in Camus's *The Stranger*; it is subhuman, vegetative, pop psychology. Even the hedonist utilitarian John Stuart Mill, one of the shallowest minds in the history of human thought, said that it was better to be Socrates dissatisfied than a pig satisfied.

A second objection concerns the major premise. John Beversluis offers this objection in his book *C. S. Lewis and the Search for Rational Religion*, one of those rare books that is even worse than its title. Beversluis seems to believe that every argument Lewis ever concocted is not only fallacious but downright foolish. In other words, we have in Lewis something like a negative pope speaking ex cathedra: infallibly wrong rather than infallibly right. Beversluis formulates this particular objection as follows:

> How could Lewis have known that every natural desire has a real object *before* knowing that Joy [*Sensucht*] has one? I can legitimately claim that every student in the class has failed the test *only* if I first know that each of them has individually failed it. The same is true of natural desires. (19)

This argument amounts to saying that only through sense experience and induction is any knowledge possible, that there is only *a posteriori* knowledge, not *a priori* knowledge. This is positivism, or at least empiricism. The classical empiricists and the logical positivists objected to all deductive reasoning as never really proving what the reasoning appeared to prove and claimed to prove, because there is no way, they contended, to know the

truth of the major premise, the general principle, except by
enumerative induction, i.e., by first knowing every example of it,
including the conclusion. Thus knowledge really always works,
according to them, in the opposite order from the way a syllogism
claims to work: never from the universal to the particular but always from the particular to the universal.

But surely this is simply not so. We can and do come to a
knowledge of universals through abstraction, not only by induction. We know that all people must be mortal, or capable of
speech or laughter or prayer, not in the same way that we know
that no one has green skin, by mere sense observation, but by
understanding something of human nature, which we meet in,
and abstract, from the individuals we experience. The objector
denies the fourth quarter of Plato's Divided Line, Wisdom or
Reason, as distinct from reasoning or hypothetical deduction, "if
. . . then" calculation, inference. He denies *epistēmē* as distinct
from *dianoia*, or, as the medieval scholastics put it, *intellectus* as
distinct from *ratio*. Descartes, for example, denies *intellectus* at
the beginning of the *Discourse on Method*, in order to insure agreement among all people, for all have the same "reason" in the
sense of logic — there is, for example, no Protestant or Catholic
logic, no French or English logic. But, we must answer, there *are*
differences in wisdom. All people are *not* equal here, and Descartes simply denies or ignores this.

The issue between ancients like Plato, Aristotle, Aquinas,
and Lewis, and moderns like Descartes, Hume, the logical
positivists, and Beversluis can be put this way: Is there a third
way of knowing in addition to sense perception and logical calculation? Is there a third kind of meaningful proposition in addition to empirically verifiable propositions and logical tautologies, Hume's "matters of fact" and "relations of idea," Kant's
synthetic *a posteriori* judgments and analytic *a priori* judgments?
Are synthetic *a priori* judgments possible?

My answer is, Of course they are. In empirical propositions
the predicate is accidental to the subject. In tautologies, the predicate is essential to the subject. But in metaphysical propositions,
in synthetic *a priori* propositions, in propositions which express
acts of understanding, the predicate is a *property* of the subject

in Aristotle's technical sense: not the explicitly defined essence of the subject, as in "all effects need causes" or "red things are red," nor accidental to the subject, as in "some effects are red," but understood as contained in and "flowing from" the essence of the subject, formally caused by the essence of the subject. (Formal causality is the one of Aristotle's four causes which drops out of the vocabulary and the sights of the empiricist.) *Because* man is a rational animal, he must be mortal (caused by his animality), loquacious (caused by his rationality), humorous (caused by the combination), and prayerful (caused by his rationality's awareness of God).

Thus the proposition "every natural, innate desire has a real object" is understood to be true because nature does nothing in vain, and this in turn is seen to be true by understanding the concept expressed in the use of the word "nature." Nature is meaningful, teleological, full of design and purpose. It is ecological, arranging a fit between organism and environment, between desire and satisfaction, between appetite and food.

All reasoning begins with some understanding of this type, some seeing. Seeing is not just sensory, but also intellectual. Some people just don't see things as well as others. All important disagreements in the history of philosophy come from this fact. That's why they are practically irresolvable, and why the history of philosophy does not lead to eventual general worldwide agreement as the history of science does.

A third objection against Lewis's argument from desire, also from Beversluis, is that its major premise, like all metaphysical propositions, confuses grammar with reality and reads grammar into reality. This is a typical logical positivist objection. "Lewis was correct, of course, in claiming that every desire is a desire *for* something. But this is nothing more than an observation about the nature of desire. From this purely conceptual observation nothing follows about what really exists. All desires must have *grammatical* objects, but they need not have *real* ones. People desire all sorts of imaginary things" (16).

This is simply a misunderstanding and quite inexcusable. Lewis's argument does not begin with a purely grammatical observation but with a metaphysical observation: that real desires really do have real objects. But he does not say that *all* desires do, only that all natural, innate, instinctive desires do. Desires for imaginary things, like Oz, are not innate. Desire for God is.

A fourth objection is that the major premise that an innate hunger proves a real food is simply untrue. Beversluis says, "The phenomenon of hunger simply does not prove that man inhabits a world in which food exists. . . . What proves that we inhabit a world in which food exists is the discovery that certain things are in fact 'eatable' . . . " (18).

This is simply to presuppose empiricism and to blind oneself to the sign-nature, the significance, of desire, as empiricists tend to do to everything. Thus Beversluis says, "The desire in and of itself proves nothing, points to nothing" (19). But surely it does. My finger points to my dog's food. My dog, a true empiricist, comes and sniffs my finger. Dr. Beversluis is a dogged empiricist. To this mentality nothing has a built-in, real, metaphysical significance. Only words are signs, things are not, to the empiricist. In other words, the world is not full of the grandeur of God, and Paul must have been philosophically wrong (perhaps *mythically* right?) in saying, in effect, that the world is a sign and that we should be able to read it, that "the invisible things of God are known through the things that are made" (Rom. 1:20).

A fifth objection from Beversluis: "If Joy's object really is God, and if all desire is really desire for him, why when he was brought face to face with him did Lewis *cease* to desire him and search for a way of escape?" (20). Lewis himself admits he did this. He was brought in "kicking and struggling, the most reluctant convert in all England." For God was "a transcendental Interferer," and "no word was more distasteful to me than the word *Interference*" (*Surprised by Joy* 172, 228-29). Beversluis says, "Either God is the ultimate object of desire or he is not. If he is, then it makes no sense to talk about shrinking from him the moment he is found" (21).

I think this is the silliest and shallowest objection of all. It shows an outstandingly immature understanding of human nature, fit perhaps for a merely logical mind but not for a human mind that exercises even a little of that nonempirical and nontautological kind of knowing called understanding or insight or wisdom or mental seeing. By this way of knowing, everyone knows that we often love and hate, desire and fear, the same object at different times or even at the same time, especially if that object is a person. How did a virgin feel about her wedding night in the days before the sexual revolution? Was there not often a fear of the great, the mysterious, the unknown, the "bigger than both of us," as well as a desire for it? Did Beversluis never have a hero, even a sports hero, when he was a child, whom he both desired and feared to approach? Did he never have a *parent*? Has he never met God in prayer?

Lewis has. The deep self-knowledge that lies behind his argument from desire comes from that experience, an experience no mere positivist or empiricist can understand. The argument from desire cuts to our hearts. Its critics try to head Lewis off at the pass between the empirical and the logical walls of the canyon. But not only do they fail to head him off, they head themselves off, for their positivistic assumption is self-contradictory, being itself neither empirical nor tautological. Lewis's head feeds off his heart. Therefore his thought pulsates with real blood. Their bloodless formal critiques proceed from the ghostlike head already cut off from the heart. But any organ cut off from the heart atrophies and dies. Thus the critiques perish, but the argument from desire goes on beating, like Augustine's restless heart, until it rests in God.

I began by referring to Anselm's "ontological argument." Let me end there too, by asking whether the argument from desire is similar to Anselm's argument, as its objectors usually maintain.

It seems so, for (1) it is a privileged, unusual desire, as the idea of God is a privileged idea; (2) it is the most moving desire, as the idea of God is the most moving idea; (3) and it seems that the very fact of the psychological occurrence of this desire in consciousness is claimed to prove the real, objective existence of its object, just as the idea of God is claimed to prove the real God.

But there are significant differences, so that objections to Anselm's argument are not valid against Lewis's. For one thing, unlike the ontological argument, the argument from desire begins with data, facts, rather than simply the meaning of a word or concept. For another thing, Lewis does not begin with God, or a definition of God, as Anselm does, but ends with God, as Aquinas does ("and this [this thing we have proved] is what people call 'God.'"). For a third thing, there is a major premise in the argument from desire, a general principle about all natural desires. Thus desires follow a general rule, while the idea of God in the ontological argument is an exception to the rule, the rule that no idea includes or proves existence.

Most importantly, the argument does not derive existence from the desire alone as the ontological argument derives existence from the idea alone. Rather, the argument from desire first derives a major premise from the world (that nature makes no desire in vain) and then applies that principle about the nature of the world to this desire. Thus the argument is based on observed facts, both outer (about the world) and inner (about desires).

Works Cited

Augustine. *Confessions.*

Beversluis, John. *C. S. Lewis and the Search for Rational Religion.* Grand Rapids: Eerdmans, 1985.

Chesterton, G. K. *The Everlasting Man.*

———. *Orthodoxy.*

Kreeft, Peter. *Heaven: The Heart's Deepest Longing.*

Lewis, C. S. *The Great Divorce.*

———. *A Grief Observed.*

———. *The Lion, the Witch, and the Wardrobe.*

———. *Mere Christianity.* New York: Macmillan, 1952.

———. *Perelandra.*

———. *The Pilgrim's Regress.* 3rd ed. Eerdmans, 1943.

———. *Surprised by Joy.* New York: Harcourt, Brace paperback, 1955.

Pascal. *Pensées.* Trans. Krailsheimer. Penguin Books, 1966.

Thomas, Dylan. "Do Not Go Gentle Into That Good Night." *The Collected Poems of Dylan Thomas.* New York: New Directions, 1957. 128.

Vanauken, Sheldon. *A Severe Mercy.* New York: Bantam paperback, 1978.

Williams, Charles. *The Place of the Lion.*

Derrida Meets Father Brown: Chestertonian "Deconstruction" and that Harlequin "Joy"

Janet Blumberg Knedlik

This chapter is for three kinds of people: first, for devotees of G. K. Chesterton's Father Brown; second, for devotees of detective fiction in general; and third, for people who have an interest in the French literary critic Jacques Derrida (however hostile that interest might be). But far and away the best audience for me would be composed of people who, like myself, contrive to be in all three of these groups at once.

(Jacques Derrida is the leading literary theorist in the interdisciplinary movement called "deconstruction," based in part on the linguistics of Ferdinand de Saussure's *Course in General Linguistics*, 1915. For Saussure, words became "signs," composed of "signifieds" and "signifiers," all fluid perceptual categories — created and sustained by cultural codes — rather than fixed entities referring to a stable reality outside language. Derrida "deconstructs" Saussure's sign and identifies its implied hierarchy of SIGNIFIED/signifier as the same false "move" that enables all the traditional hierarchies in western thought [GOD/man, SPIRIT/matter, INTELLIGIBLE/sensible, KING/commoner, MASCULINE/feminine]. Derrida's sweeping critique of western

JANET BLUMBERG KNEDLIK is professor of English at Seattle Pacific University and a contributing editor to the *John Donne Varionum*.

metaphysics condemns its "logocentric" assigning of "presence" to the "unembodied," and implicates all transcendence (the SIG-NIFIED) in "the play of signs". . . . Edgar Allan Poe's "The Purloined Letter" has been invoked as a sort of deconstructive parable: a compromising letter is "hidden" in plain view, never literally "delivered," while its surmised significance is constituted differently by each interpreter.)

In any case, whether you are a Derridean adept, a novice, or a foe, it will surely help you, just now, if you should ever have followed the adventures of a certain somewhat shabby little priest, who is sitting at this moment on a bench in Hampstead Heath, sometimes gazing up at the sky with a vacant, moonfaced stare, sometimes poking absently about in the dirt at his feet with the tip of an old black umbrella. He is (of course) the guardian of a valuable cross studded with sapphires, which he is carrying up from Essex to the International Eucharistic Congress in London. But now he listens quietly to a much taller priest who sits beside him. The tall priest gestures animatedly toward the starry sky as he talks, exuding something of the air of a magician, or perhaps an actor, although certainly both figures, clad in black, are only somber clerics on their way to attend an ecclesiastical gathering, precisely what they appear to be . . . are they not?

Let *us* assume a third persona and play ourselves the role of Aristide Valentin, head of the Paris police and the greatest detective in the world. We will hover near the two priests in the figure of Valentin, accompanied by a pair of London policemen, carrying on surveillance from behind the cover of a big branching tree. With them, we will eavesdrop upon the "metaphysical gossip" of "two mild old parsons":

> The taller priest nodded his bowed head and said:
> "Ah, yes, these modern infidels appeal to their reason; but who can look at those millions of worlds and not feel that there may well be wonderful universes above us where reason is utterly un-reasonable?"
> "No," said the other priest; "reason is always reasonable, even in the last limbo, in the lost borderland of things. . . ."
> The other priest raised his austere face to the spangled sky and said:

"Yet who knows if in that infinite universe —?"

"Only infinite physically," said the little priest, turning sharply in his seat, "not infinite in the sense of escaping from the laws of truth."

Valentin behind his tree was tearing his fingernails with silent fury. [It seemed he had not tracked down the greatest and cleverest of all the great French criminals after all.] He seemed almost to hear the sniggers of the English detectives. . . . In his impatience he lost the equally elaborate answer of the tall cleric, and when he listened again it was again Father Brown who was speaking:

"Reason and justice grip the remotest and the loneliest star. Look at those stars. Don't they look as if they were single diamonds and sapphires? Well, you can imagine any mad botany or geology you please. Think of forests of adamant with leaves of brilliants. Think the moon is a blue moon, a single elephantine sapphire. But don't fancy that all that frantic astronomy would make the smallest difference to the reason and justice of conduct. On plains of opal, under cliffs cut out of pearl, you would still find a noticeboard, 'Thou shalt not steal.'"

. . . The tall priest [sat very still]. . . . When at last he did speak, he said simply, his head bowed and his hands on his knees:

"Well, I still think that other worlds may perhaps rise higher than our reason. The mystery of heaven is unfathomable, and I for one can only bow my head."

Then, with brow yet bent and without changing by the faintest shade his attitude or voice, he added:

"Just hand over that sapphire cross of yours, will you? We're all alone here, and I could pull you to pieces like a straw doll."

The utterly unaltered voice and attitude added a strange violence to that shocking change of speech . . .

"Yes," said the tall priest, in the same low voice and in the same still posture, "yes, I am Flambeau." (*The Innocence of Father Brown* 24-25)

Such is the first encounter of Father Brown with the extraordinary French criminal, Flambeau. But perhaps it may have occurred to you, as it has to me, that "Flambeau" is only a pseudonym. It is one of the countless proper names invented by this most clever of artists and tricksters, who is so fleet of foot and such a master of disguise. If we were to make the correct moves in an elaborate etymological game, the meaning of the name would unveil itself, disclosing the palimpsest of another name that lies behind it, at once the origin and cancellation of the first. The primary name — the name under the sign of erasure — is "Derrida." And if Father Brown's adversary, that "tall figure" with its "titanic energy," is in fact "Flambeau-Derrida," then we perceive afresh the exchange — or the failure of exchange — which now passes between them. It is a text waiting to be opened:

> ". . . yes, I am Flambeau."
> Then, after a pause, he said:
> "Come, will you give me that cross?"
> "No," said the other, and the monosyllable had an odd sound.
> Flambeau suddenly flung off all his pontifical pretensions. The great robber leaned back in his seat and laughed low but long.
> "No," he cried; "you won't give it me, you proud prelate. You won't give it me, you little celibate simpleton. Shall I tell you why you won't give it me? Because I've got it already in my own breast-pocket. . . . I had the sense to make a duplicate of the right parcel, and now, my friend, you've got the duplicate, and I've got the jewels. An old dodge, Father Brown — a very old dodge."
> "Yes," said Father Brown, and passed his hand through his hair with the same strange vagueness of manner. "Yes, I've heard of it before."
> The colossus of crime leaned over to the little rustic priest with a sort of sudden interest.
> "*You* have heard of it?" he asked. "Where have *you* heard of it?"
> "Well, I mustn't tell you his name, of course," said the little man simply. "He was a penitent, you know. He had lived prosperously for about twenty years entirely on duplicate brown-paper parcels. And so, you see, when I began to suspect you, I thought of this poor chap's way of doing it at once."
> "Began to suspect me," repeated the outlaw with increased intensity. "Did you really have the gumption to suspect me just because I brought you up to this bare part of the heath?"
> "No, no," said Brown with an air of apology. "You see, I suspected you when we first met. It's that little bulge up the sleeve where you people have the spiked bracelet."
> "How in Tartarus," cried Flambeau, "did you ever hear of the spike bracelet?"

"Oh, one's little flock, you know!" said Father Brown, arching his eyebrows rather blankly. "When I was a curate in Hartlepool, there were three of them with spike bracelets. So, as I suspected you from the first, don't you see, I made sure that the cross should go safe, anyhow. I'm afraid I watched you, you know. So at last I saw you change the parcels. . . . Then, don't you see, I changed them back again. . . . I went back to that sweet-shop and asked if I'd left a parcel, and gave them a particular address if it turned up. Well, I knew I hadn't; but when I went away again I did. So, instead of running after me with that valuable parcel, they have sent it flying to a friend of mine in Westminster. . . ."

Flambeau tore a brown-paper parcel out of his inner pocket and rent it in pieces. There was nothing but paper and sticks of lead inside it. He sprang to his feet with a gigantic gesture, and cried:

"I don't believe you. I don't believe a bumpkin like you could manage all that. I believe you've still got the stuff on you, and if you don't give it up—why, we're all alone, and I'll take it by force!"

"No," said Father Brown simply, and stood up also; "you won't take it by force. First, because I really haven't still got it. And, second, because we are not alone."

Flambeau stopped in his stride forward.

"Behind that tree," said Father Brown, pointing, "are two strong policemen and the greatest detective alive. How did they come here, do you ask? Why, I brought them, of course! How did I do it? Why, I'll tell you if you like! Lord bless you, we have to know twenty such things when we work among the criminal classes! Well, I wasn't sure you were a thief, and it would never do to make a scandal against one of our own clergy. So I just tested you to see if anything would make you show yourself. A man generally makes a small scene if he finds salt in his coffee; if he doesn't, he has some reason for keeping quiet. I changed the salt and sugar, and you kept quiet. A man generally objects if his bill is three times too big. If he pays it, he has some motive for passing unnoticed. I altered your bill, and you paid it."

The world seem waiting for Flambeau to leap like a tiger. But he was held back as by a spell; he was stunned with the utmost curiosity.

"Well," went on Father Brown, with lumbering lucidity, "as you wouldn't leave any tracks for the police, of course somebody had to. At every place we went to, I took care to do something that would get us talked about for the rest of the day. I didn't do much harm—a splashed wall, spilt apples, a broken window; but I save the cross, as the cross will always be saved. It is at Westminster by now. I rather wonder you didn't stop it with the Donkey's Whistle."

"With the what?" asked Flambeau.

"I'm glad you've never heard of it," said the priest, making a face. "It's a foul thing. I'm sure you're too good a man for a Whistler. I couldn't have countered it even with the Spots myself; I'm not strong enough in the legs."

"What on earth are you talking about?" asked the other.

"Well, I did think you'd know the Spots," said Father Brown, agreeably surprised. "Oh, you can't have gone so very wrong yet!"

"How in blazes do you know all these horrors?" cried Flambeau.

The shadow of a smile crossed the round, simple face of his clerical opponent.

"Oh, by being a celibate simpleton, I suppose," he said. "Has it never struck you that a man who does next to nothing but hear men's real sins is not likely to be wholly unaware of human evil? But, as a matter of fact, another part of my trade, too, made me sure you weren't a priest."

"What?" asked the thief, almost gaping.

"You attacked reason," said Father Brown. "It's bad theology."

And even as he turned away to collect his property, the three policemen came out from under the twilight trees. Flambeau was an artist and a sportsman. He stepped back and swept Valentin a great bow.

"Do not bow to me, *mon ami*," said Valentin, with silver clearness. "Let us both bow to our master."

And they both stood an instant uncovered, while the little Essex priest blinked about for his umbrella. (25-29)

A most satisfying first encounter between our rustic priest and the dazzling criminal who will eventually become his convert, follower, and friend. But if the great robber should not be merely Flambeau, but "Flambeau-Derrida," then certain questions present themselves. In what sense is the sapphire cross, we must ask, the object of Flambeau-Derrida's desire? Does not the importunate asker slyly know that what he demands is merely the substitute, the supplement, of that which is always already deferred, even in its constitutive nature of being *wanted*? No one, we may be sure of it, knows better than our magnificent thief, our Flambeau-Derrida, that the sapphire cross *is in the mail*— that it must always, everywhere, already *be* in the mail, a parcel that even in the act of delivery can never be delivered (except by an invisible postman?). No, the sapphire cross must be, for Flambeau-Derrida, a purloined letter, a dead letter, always, everywhere *absent*. He, the great French criminal, is beyond the reach of the deceptions of the sapphire cross. He is a high and distant and lonely star, living at the margins of the universe, where reason itself must be utterly unreasonable.

Faithfully, then, he will pursue the only path of disclosure available to a man at the margin, in the "lost borderland of things" (24). He recites the totality of the faith at the center, asking, as so many have asked before him, that the priest *give it to him*— give him the cross and all that it promises, give him the Logos in its full presence. This is his characteristic move, faithfully to repeat the faith in its totality while making it insecure in its most assured evidences (*Of Grammatology*), knowing that the cross cannot be given to him because it is in the post — always everywhere promised and yet deferred. Thus he, the high and lonely star, the Star of the Morning, uses the fabric of the poor deluded little priest's own onto-theology, and uses it against it-self, to deconstruct it and to think absence where presence has been thought before. Thus, by the scattering of a light which must in its nature be a kind of darkness, he, Flambeau-Derrida, might save the dusty little cleric from the colossal blindness of metaphysics.

Let us not suppose — as is thought too often — that Flam-beau-Derrida entertains a mere garden-variety crime, the old crime of moral relativism, the "death of God," an end of values. This would be a gesture fully thinkable within the concepts of traditional metaphysics, as Nietzsche perhaps and others have thought and inscribed it already. No, it is the deadlock of the grid of assumptions enabling metaphysics which must be negated —negated, therefore, only by *something which cannot be thought* by any concept in metaphysics, because it is the absence glimpsed in the subtle derangement of the system.

279

Flambeau-Derrida knows that moral relativism, the death of God, unlimited limitation, belong to the onto-theology they fight against, even as all semiotic polarities, in the very gesture of excluding one another, constitute one another. What Flambeau-Derrida is after — the trace, the play of difference — is not only unthinkable in terms of pure transcendence, but it is "also something other than finitude" (68). (Infinity and finitude, absolute and contingent, divine and human, spirit and matter, all can be read merely as one another's obverses, and it is their dualistic "embrace" which must be rejected, because of the falsity of that false union, its absence of presence. Flambeau-Derrida is after something else, something much *more* than that, something signified by that absence. . . .)

Hence Flambeau's speeches against reason, his recitals of possible impossible worlds, his acts of thievery and tricksterism borrow their resources from the language of metaphysical faith and from the logic he seeks to deconstruct. He risks being engulfed by what he must turn against itself, and each time he escapes, he escapes only by a hairsbreadth. When he argues rationalistically against reason, he is within the system of reason. When, without change of tone or posture, he writes himself in the proper name of betrayal and deceit — "Yes, I am Flambeau" — he puts both that system and that self which deranges the system under erasure, in the act of unveiling them.

But the little priest, we recall, is not surprised. He plays the role assigned to him. He withholds the cross, "keeping it safe," he says, but at the expense of its purpose and significance. For does not the cross, like the kingdom to which it promises access, claim to be takable by force? Yes, even to surrender itself into the hands of all who seek it? No wonder Father Brown's monosyllabic negation, his "no," has "an odd tone." Is it not a deception greater than any perpetrated by Flambeau, this gainsaying which cancels out his priesthood and his faith, by refusing to give *It* to him, the object of Flambeau's restless desire? Father Brown's no (I will not give it to you) appears now to be an extorted moment of honesty, an honesty that makes his claim to priesthood a lie. Or, if he be a true priest with salvific intentionality, then his no is a sly and dishonest word that equally proves him false.

But wait. Flambeau himself reads yet another meaning in the priest's refusal.

"No," he cried; "you won't give it me, you proud prelate. You won't give it me, you little celibate simpleton. Shall I tell you why you won't give it me? Because I've got it already in my own breast-pocket." (26)

But of course! If Flambeau thinks he has it, then it cannot be given to him, not in any way that is thinkable by him. Father Brown's no is thence allowable as concession to Flambeau's certitude, a no conditional upon duration of certitude. As that certitude crumbles, the no dissolves as well. Father Brown begins to give Flambeau the moon, that great blue sapphire, that fairy tale of a Real Presence for which he listens with such intense curiosity, briefly acknowledging a master.

But we are getting ahead of Chesterton's story. Flambeau has many lessons in humility to learn. It will not be Flambeau, after all, but the obscure little priest who will demystify the mystery of "The Invisible Man." Father Brown will find the trace of footprints in the snow, the arche-writing of absence articulating a mentally invisible presence. Or we may think back in *The Innocence of Father Brown*, from the snowy footprints to the earlier episode of "The Queer Feet," audible footprints this time, but again the flickering track of invisible absent presence, a presence manifesting among the gentlemen that negation of presence called a waiter, and among the waiters that negation of presence called a gentleman. The tricky moment for the superb Flambeau is to manage to be manifest — or not manifest — in both companies simultaneously, seen and not seen under the signs of gentleman and waiter at once. But so powerful are the preconditioning systems of reference that the single figure leaning against the wall presents itself to each group under the sign of its constitutive polarity. Yet it is Father Brown who understands the delusive presence-in-absence and finds the "facts" constituting it.

What Flambeau-Derrida learns, most of all, is that Father Brown is always already there before him. Flambeau is the novice and Father Brown the adept in the diabolism of *l'ecriture*. What Derridean depths, after all, has not Father Brown plumbed?

In a story whose title speaks the language of dissemination
—"The Sign of the Broken Sword"—Father Brown tells Flambeau: "I am only looking for [a] word. A word that isn't there"
(214). Or consider "The Honour of Israel Gow," an "honor"
constituted surprisingly out of all the features of dishonor. In this
tale of marginality, Father Brown singlehandedly explodes the
myth of the center with a dazzling rhetorical *tour de force*. You
recall the challenge offered in the story by Inspector Craven of
Scotland Yard: "For the central riddle we are prepared," says
Craven (116). "The core of the tale we could imagine; it is the
fringes that are mysterious. By no stretch of fancy can the human
mind connect together snuff and diamonds and wax and loose
clockwork" (117). Father Brown at once produces three succes-
sive exegeses of the snuff, the candles, the diamonds, and the
small wheels, declaring each time, just as he has captured the
belief of his audience: No, that is not the truth. "I only suggested
that because you said one could not plausibly connect snuff with
clockwork or candles with bright stones" (119).

Appropriately, it is in this same tale of marginality that Father
Brown states the deconstructive technique in its essence. "We
have found the truth," he announces, "and the truth makes no
sense" (124). Is this Father Brown really the "guardian of the
relic," after all, or is he, even more than Flambeau-Derrida, the
exposer of the fraudulence of the reasonable explanation?

No wonder Flambeau repents—repents first of tearing Father
Brown apart "like a straw doll" when that opportunity ad-
vantageously presents itself in a cloakroom ("The Queer Feet").
He cannot destroy Father Brown without destroying too much
that is his own. Nor is it surprising that both Father Brown and
his creator, Chesterton, are so fond of Flambeau—so much more
fond of the trickster and con artist than of that paradigm of logic
and truism, Aristide Valentin, Chief of the Paris Police, whom
Chesterton kills off in the second Father Brown story ("The
Secret Garden"). Chesterton is no believer in pure ratiocination
and the fanaticisms it breeds. His Father Brown reasons, like Derrida, because that is the only available way to journey beyond
reason to that "voice from nowhere" (229)—the "voice," I suggest, not of the logos but of the trace—that tells us the peculiar

"facts" of the matter. The reasoning fanatic Valentin dies a suicidal death of stoic pride; Flambeau, who entices real people into the fairie land of a wild harlequin comedy, finds life, and finds it more and more abundantly.

In the beginning, Father Brown spoke to Flambeau of reason and justice, reaching the loneliest and most distant star. He spoke of the tenacity of moral law, of the superiority of generosity to meanness, in all universes. In the story called "The Flying Stars," Father Brown finally brings reason and justice home to Flambeau, rescuing the Flying Star before he has become the Falling Star. But it is *moral* reason, we notice, not ratiocination *per se* that transcends boundaries. Flambeau's dilemma, as Father Brown knows, is not finally philosophical or speculative, but ethical. What makes Flambeau's conversion is the discovery that the universe is even more flabbergasting than he is, signing a character more Flambeau-esque than his own, a character so brilliant *and* good as to be unutterably paradoxical and wild and surprising. Flambeau finds that he must rejoice to bespeak and be spoken to by such a mind, just as he has found that he must always evade the heartless reductive logic of the pseudo-policeman Valentin.

Flambeau, Father Brown perceives, is still an innocent child in crime, delighting in the artistic deception and making Father Brown laugh with his daring and whimsy. He is not so very far gone yet in badness—not so far as to have become truly mean or petty. He is a joyous criminal, and a criminal with a conscience. Valentin is a man of logic and order, but a man without a conscience, without any notion of a thing so devilishly constraining and liberating—so inexplicable and quixotic and noble—as conscience is.

Just as for Flambeau, so for Derrida, let us suppose that the problem is finally not philosophical or speculative, but ethical. Why does Derrida deconstruct the universe? Not "because it is there"—the motive of some of his followers. Not because deconstructing confers power, money, prestige, and full professorships—the motive of others of his followers. Not because it works—the motive of some doctrinaire Marxists or feminists who borrow his techniques and toss them aside when they have ceased to be useful. Not even because deconstructing is right—

Janet Blumberg Knedlik

in the sense of having a new truth to establish as dogma in place of the old truth. No, Derrida deconstructs for a better reason, a higher reason, than these — a reason which constitutes one of those "gleams" which it is Father Brown's profession to discern, even "in assassins" ("The Hammer of God"). Just as Flambeau is driven to steal by a wild impulse of delight, so Derrida deconstructs *because deconstructing is good.*

I mean that deconstructing seems to Derrida good (however he puts the term under erasure) because it is an activity, a choice, that carries in it the wild elfin qualities that Chesterton and some of the rest of us know belong, inexplicably, disquietingly, to the Beautiful and the True.

The act of Derrida's writing abounds with Sherlockian phrases, phrases of sheer pleasure, of knowing the game is afoot and the world's Watsons await. Derrida's favorite connective is "in fact." "If it is true, as I believe. . . ," the grammatologist hypothesizes (127). Later, he gleefully explodes "a consequence that cannot be rigorously deduced from these premises" (132). Elsewhere, he shouts with triumph: "that restores the true meaning of the remarks . . ." (122). Should we then be at all surprised that this is a thinker to labor Holmeslike at "a science of writing" (4), and to inveigh about the ever present necessity of "patient meditation and painstaking investigation" (4)? Everywhere, we hear "in fact . . . in fact." In fact, he would use "in truth," were it not necessary "to be wary of that phrase" (111), for it "privilege[s] the instance of a vision filled and satisfied with presence" (337).

Reading Derrida is like reading a detective novel, breathlessly in pursuit of the facts of the matter—and always finding the facts of the matter, even though here "truth" is deferred. Some of the post-moderns have made their own what the mythopoeic writers of the Oxford circle exploited back in the hostile days of modernism (or what Chesterton and MacDonald pioneered earlier): the power of popular and "escapist" genres to capture an audience. What was vilified then as puerility, demagoguery, or sensationalism is elevated today—at its best —into a sophisticated and zestful play of critical intellect that seeks to sabotage old-fashioned "serious" discourse altogether, turning exposition and argument into witty poetic play. Post-modern critics, (un)like

Chesterton, Lewis, Tolkien, Williams, or Sayers, persuade best by being (diabolically) *fun*.

Derrida's detective-like-ness is *on the one hand* a rhetorical strategy, a deliberate playing to the logocentric hungers of the western mind—our need for the illusion of presence—engaging us in the thrill of the chase in order to unveil the emptiness at the end of each tunnel. To deconstructive critics, after all, the detective story is the privileged mode of the western Cartesian mind, with its logocentric hope that the care and compassion of the intellect can find out truth. Faithful sons and daughters of western onto-theology, we read mysteries to get our "logos fix," to be reassured that we can know the truth, and the truth will make us free. As William Spanos applies this line of thought in "The Detective and the Boundary: Some Notes on the Postmodern Literary Imagination," the detective novel is part and parcel of that meretricious ordering of the world insisted upon by the bourgeois mind, a *Bovarisme*, we might say, of the Romantic intellect. All this we may grant, *on the one hand*. *On the other hand*, Derrida invests in *play of mind*. So much so, as to suggest a sincerity so sincere as to be ethical. I make this astounding claim on one basis only: the sheer intellectual artistry which makes Derrida one of history's major creative individuals, a poet whose medium is theory: or better, is the ceaseless play of difference constituting human awareness itself.

Derrida, like Flambeau, is too rich and innocent a jester not to be enjoyed. I use the term "innocent" advisedly, for great crimes against humanity are laid at his feet. But there is joy in his work; his play is not mean. His critiques are works of understanding, understanding that teases itself and us with its own enabling deceptions. Who has read others so minutely and with such ironic compassion? (The illusion of) Lucidity of mind is everywhere; his deceptions are self-disclosed and self-disclosing. He has focused on the metaphysical gesture in every recent figure whose claim to meaning is great—he has problematized, hence privileged (cathected) the relations of metaphysics and meaning. He has helped to send western scholarship back to the medieval world, to its meditations upon God, the Sign, Necessity, and Freedom, back to Aquinas and Augustine, with the respect implicit in scrutiny. He has opened and reclaimed the language of theology as the operative system of metaphors across disciplinary boundaries. If he had set out, as did Chesterton, Lewis, Tolkien, Williams, and Sayers, to reinvigorate the past, I do not see how he could have done a better job.

His gestures, like Flambeau's, must deconstruct themselves. For as Flambeau is caught by an invisible hook, and a line long enough so that if he should run to the ends of the earth, he could still be brought back with a single twitch upon the thread ("The Queer Feet"), so Derrida is (who knows better than he?) the servant of that which he must outwit. The hook set in his jaw is baited, of course, with the logos. The slightest odor of its sanctity and Derrida is there to do battle. Thus, I think, no recent thinker has done more to draw attention to the logos, or to disclose the powers of presence. No recent thinker can so purify and reinvigorate truly metaphysical thought—that metaphorical and mythic way of knowing that articulates itself in archetype and pattern, cutting across every boundary and reuniting every field of discourse, every arena of life. Who else has, since the great Christian metaphysical John Donne, so indefatigably and wittily made the human body a map of intellectual discovery, or teased out of the physiology of erotic love the subtlest dynamics of epistemological doubt?

We are accustomed to Derrida as the destroyer and demystifier of the logos, because he is the champion of everything that the logos is said to efface in order to exist (the trace, the play of difference, *differance*). But the logos Derrida explodes as a pretense and a slavery is not the Logos guarded by Father Brown —nor is it the logos elucidated in its natural sacramental analogue, the linguistic sign, by Ferdinand de Saussure. Derrida misreads both Words — the Words of Father Brown and of Saussure — because if he did not, either might incarnate for him the paradox upon which all his paradoxes feed. Our lostness and marginality is what God IS (not), to the Christian as well as to Derrida. The trace he seeks so assiduously as the exploder of the false logos is indeed the death and resource out of which is constituted our desire/Desire, that which cannot be thought by any concept of metaphysics and hence validates and engenders metaphysics every bit as much as it deconstructs metaphysics: the true Logos, the unthinkable fact, the paradox which metaphysics cannot think, but which cannot be thought without metaphysics. Christians call this living nest of contradictions savior, and worship therein the most baffling of persons — a God "stripped" of transcendence and so good that he must everywhere be convicted of criminality by fair-minded persons, a God whose mind is yet more elfin, even, than the mind of Father Brown.

I have said that Derrida deconstructs because it is good. I partly mean that it is good to use the powers and resources of the mind to deny that heartless immaterial "logos" which claims to be a transcendental signified, not implicated in the play of signifiers. Such a logos could not die to itself. It is also good to deny that same heartless immaterial "logos" which must suffer a fall into sin if it is to become true language and true sign. That logos never created the glories of the flesh. That logos is only, as Father Brown would tell us, the god of Gnosticism, and he is a demon. Derrida deconstructs, in part, because the false logos he reads in western metaphysics *is* a devil, and deconstructing that devil is good. Let us examine carefully to be sure what side we are on. As Chesterton wrote of an early experience which shaped his mind: "I rushed out without daring to pause; and as I passed the fire I did not know whether it was hell or the furious love of God" (Ward 45). They can be very much alike.

The story that is Derrida is based upon peculiar facts, upon, among others, the peculiar facts found by Saussure early in this century in the constitution of the earthly logos: that is, in the signs and sign-systems that originate meaning. *Meaning*—not *thought* or *memory*, for although both thought and memory rely so heavily upon language, they can exist vestigially without it. But *meaning*, which is just so much of things, including ourselves, as can be socially negotiated, translated, and communicated, and by being so negotiated, translated, and communicated, come to exist for us as the things they are taken to be. Derrida skews and reduces Saussure's profoundly metaphysical findings, not because they are too "logocentric" and "metaphysical," but because by associating Saussure's sign with a straw figure of the western logos he can carry on his explication of marginality without facing the most peculiar fact of all. Not only has Father Brown been there before him . . . but God—if God is indeed Word and not Idea—has been there before him.

Derrida's mode of thought and discourse is profoundly liberating and profoundly vulnerable to Christian analysis, especially insofar as he is Saussure's most brilliant reader. We celebrate the Oxford Christians for their mythopoeic imaginations and their sacramental understanding of the universe. If we claim a sacramental universe, ought we not to expect that radically new linguistic insights into the peculiar facts of words should enable a powerful restatement of the Word Who is God?

Deconstruction, at least in the form practiced by Derrida, constitutes an exhilaratingly fresh critique of traditional western thought—and critiques are always constitutively good. It is also a magnificent opportunity for the Christian mind, if we are willing to absorb the language theory of Saussure. For one example, by deconstructing Saussure, among others, Derrida can demonstrate that the liberal arts, and indeed the enterprises of humanistic liberalism in general, are founded upon the metaphysics of the God-talk they frequently and superficially deny. Can we be entirely unhappy if this kind of "crooked honesty" is brought to bear upon the contemporary intellectual scene?

Meanwhile, Derrida remains intoxicated with the pursuit of his beloved enemy, the logos he must unmask. He is living out the great detective odyssey; he is the Holmes who has found Moriarty, masquerading as God. If he persists in playing his own Holmesian god to Moriarty's cosmic devil, he will end in the cold-blooded anarchistic self-murder of Aristide Valentin. But if the gleams are indicative, the "anarchist" Derrida may yet prove to carry in his breast pocket a small blue card. He may turn out to be one more member of that strange Chestertonian band of philosopher-detectives, always true to a quirky honor of their own (*The Man Who Was Thursday*). If so, he will come to acknowledge that the incomprehensible state-of-affairs which he seeks to elucidate through play, that of the elfin trace, imprints and is imprinted with the one(?) who is(?) God . . . and Man (is God? is Man?) . . . the one who bears about in his (elusive) body the marks of his own marginality and harlequin joy, even while his voice keeps right on writing a universe with voices like Chesterton's and Derrida's in it.

In which case, after Derrida has drawn even nearer the uncanny (non)presence that speaks in the flickering traces of a burning bush (*burning bush?*), he will no doubt say something akin to what one of Chesterton's converts said in *The Man Who Was Thursday*:

> "Why do I like [Him]? . . . how can I tell you? . . . [I like Him] because he's such a Bounder." (171)

WORKS CITED

Chesterton, G. K. *The Autobiography of G. K. Chesterton.* 1936; rpr. 1939. New York: Sheed & Ward.

_____. *The Innocence of Father Brown.* 1910; rpr. 1980. New York: Penguin Books.

_____. *The Man Who Was Thursday.* 1908; rpr. 1979. New York: Paragon Books.

Derrida, Jacques. *Of Grammatology.* Trans. Gayatri Chakravorty Spivak. Originally published in France as *De la Grammatologie*, 1967; rpr. 1976, Baltimore, MD: Johns Hopkins Paperbacks.

Saussure, Ferdinand de. *Course in General Linguistics.* Trans. Wade Baskin. Ed. Charles Bally and Albert Sechehaye. New York: Philosophical Library, 1959.

Spanos, William V. "The Detective and the Boundary: Some Notes on the Postmodern Literary Imagination." *Existentialism 2, A Casebook.* Ed. William V. Spanos. New York: Harper & Row, 1976. 163-89.

Ward, Maisie. *Gilbert Keith Chesterton.* 1944; rpr. London: Sheed & Ward, 1945.

The Psychology of Conversion in Chesterton's and Lewis's Autobiographies

David Leigh, S.J.

"A young man who wishes to remain a sound atheist cannot be too careful of his reading." C. S. Lewis makes this remark in *Surprised by Joy* (191), just at the point where he describes his first reading of Chesterton. At the time, Lewis was a nineteen-year-old second lieutenant in the British infantry recovering in 1917 from trench fever in a hospital at Le Trepart. Although Lewis disagreed with Chesterton's essays at the time, he admits that the humor, paradox, and goodness of the author made "an immediate conquest." In fact, the book led him to regard Chesterton as "the most sensible man alive 'apart from his Christianity'" (223). Nine years later, while teaching philosophy and English back at Oxford, Lewis read Chesterton's *Everlasting Man*. This second book led him to affirm "that Christianity itself was very sensible 'apart from its Christianity'" (223). Thus, at two crucial periods in his life—the first during a moral conversion in World War I, the second during his final conversion to belief in God—Lewis read G. K. Chesterton. Any study of the psychology of conversion in their religious autobiographies might well search out the similarities and dif-

DAVID LEIGH, S.J., is director of the Honors Program at Seattle University and the author of numerous articles in literature and theology.

ferences in their respective stories of the journey from unbelief to Christian faith.

By "psychology of conversion," of course, I do not mean to reduce the authentic religious transformations of Lewis or Chesterton to mere psychic or emotional phenomena. Lewis himself was the first to recognize and discard any merely Freudian interpretation of his experiences. As he puts it, "If [Freud] can say that It [Joy] is sublimated sex, why is it not open to me to say that sex is sublimated It?" (Griffin 64-65). Likewise, he was aware of Jungian and archetypal interpretations but did not see these as incompatible with historical and realistic interpretations of Christian experiences. Just as Christianity is a myth but a true myth, so his own experiences were perhaps archetypal but nonetheless valid. What remains for me is to use some of the broader and friendlier categories of developmental psychology to explore the stages of the faith journeys of our two autobiographers. In either case, the use of psychological categories does not necessarily preclude a theological interpretation; in fact, as Emilie Griffith has shown in her excellent study of conversion experiences, *Turning*, any theology in which grace builds on and transforms nature calls for a natural psychological pattern to be present in the development of the religious self.

Here is the burden of the present essay. I will begin by discussing the similar routes (through other genres) taken by Lewis and Chesterton to the writing of their autobiographies. Next, I will examine three common literary elements within their autobiographies proper, namely (a) the circular journey form of their narratives; (b) the intentional images and emotions of each author; (c) the mediation of friends and books. In the final section, I will provide a preliminary examination of Lewis's autobiography as a movement through the five levels of conversion which Bernard Lonergan and Walter Conn have identified in religious development: the levels of imaginative, affective, moral, intellectual, and religious conversion.

Chesterton once said: "If [autobiography] is really to tell the truth, it must . . . at all costs profess not to. . . . [A] touch of fiction is almost always essential to the real conveying of fact. . ." (*Dickens* 139-40). The similarity in the use of "a touch of fiction" in various genres for autobiographical purposes by Chesterton and Lewis deserves a separate study, for the similarity is too remarkable to be merely coincidental. Both Lewis and Chesterton first wrote the story of their intellectual and religious conversions around age thirty-three in allegorical form — *The Man Who Was Thursday* (1908) and *Pilgrim's Regress* (1935). The use of such a form suggests, perhaps, similar psychological insecurity about revealing their deepest personal transformations in direct first-person autobiography, but it also reveals the intensity of their convictions about their conversions. Their next attempts were through a second literary form, the argumentative essay; for Chesterton in *Orthodoxy* (1908), for Lewis in a series of short books beginning with *The Problem of Pain* (1940). Both came to the use of formal autobiography only at a later age, Chesterton in his early sixties, Lewis in his mid-fifties. Even in these later books, however, both shied away from the revelation of personal details not directly relevant to their religious conversions. Chesterton, in fact, relegated his religious conversion to relatively few pages of *Autobiography* (1936), a book which is primarily a series of memoirs on the influence of others. Lewis concentrated, as we shall see, on events and persons directly relevant to his movement away from and back to Christian faith. But the general movement from allegory to apologetical essay to conversion autobiography reflects the relatively private character of these very public Christian converts.

Other studies of Lewis have shown in detail how *Pilgrim's Regress* embodies in its allegory what Lewis summed up in his 1943 preface: "On the intellectual side my own progress had been from 'popular realism' to Philosophical Idealism; from Idealism to Pantheism; from Pantheism to Theism; and from Theism to Christianity" (5). What is significant for our present study is that Lewis highlights the allegorical journey as primarily intellectual. Chesterton also uses the allegorical form of *The Man Who Was Thursday* and the essays of *Orthodoxy* (both published in 1908) to express his intellectual conversion to Christian faith. In the former, Chesterton describes in a detective story the search for ultimate meaning and reality by a poet who is much like the young Chesterton. The autobiographical impulse is so strong in

both *Orthodoxy* and *The Man Who Was Thursday*, however, that
they provide a much clearer picture of the stages of Chesterton's
conversion than does his later *Autobiography*. Thus, in an allegory
and in a book of essays which Chesterton describes as "unavoidably affirmative and unavoidably autobiographical,"
Chesterton heralded the way for Lewis to follow thirty years later.
But enough of genre; let us examine the common elements of
their autobiographical works: *Surprised by Joy* for Lewis, *Orthodoxy*
and part of *Autobiography* for Chesterton.

Orthodoxy (1908) and *Surprised by Joy* (1955) exhibit notable
common patterns, in spite of the fact that no two books of
Chesterton and Lewis may seem less alike than the books which
they each claimed and disclaimed to be an autobiography. The
former is a series of essays written when Chesterton was thirty-
two and not yet a Christian, the latter a conversion story written when Lewis was fifty-eight and a long-time convert to
Anglicanism. Yet both books take the reader on a circular
romance narrative in which the author arrives where he started,
only to recognize the place for the first time. This form, familiar
to students of autobiography from the time of Augustine's *Confessions*, lent itself to these two authors who had common
childhood experiences of a quasireligious nature, who then spent
many years of wandering in search of an adequate version or fulfillment of their first experience, and who finally arrived at a faith
which did fulfill their earlier longings in a surprising but familiar
manner. Chesterton describes the circular journey image as the
motif of his story in his introduction to *Orthodoxy*:

> I have often had a fancy of writing a romance about an English
> yachtsman who slightly miscalculated his course and discovered En-
> gland under the impression that it was a new island in the South
> Seas. . . . But I have a peculiar reason for mentioning the man in
> the yacht, who discovered England. For I am that man in a
> yacht. . . . The man from the yacht thought he was the first to find
> England; I thought I was the first to find Europe. I did try to found
> a heresy of my own; and when I had put the last touches to it, I
> discovered that it was orthodoxy. (14, 16, 19)

Chesterton discovers, as he tells it through the subsequent eight

essays, a series of truths about his experience, only later to realize that these truths had previously been available under the title
"Christianity."

Lewis's circular journey, as we shall see, was much less an
intellectual homecoming than an imaginative rediscovery of the
ultimate meaning of his early emotional experiences. He begins
his story with a central childhood experience of what he calls
"Joy," then loses the experience for many years, only to rediscover it in a way that leads him to the surprising joy of Christianity. Like Augustine with his repeated experiences of a "restless heart," both Lewis and Chesterton move through an odyssey
of islands on their journey to discovery of their true and first
home.

Green and Hooper have shown that Lewis first tried the circular sea voyage form of Chesterton in an unsuccessful attempt
in 1932 to write a long narrative poem on his own conversion.
The only remaining thirty-four lines of the aborted autobiographical epic contain the verses: ". . . to follow the retreating shore /
Of this land which I call at last my home, where most / I feared
to come" (Green and Hooper 127). Lewis picks up the sea voyage
imagery only occasionally in *Surprised by Joy*, for example at his
mother's death near the end of "The First Years": "It was the sea
and islands now; the great continent had sunk like Atlantis" (21).

At the start of their circular journeys, Chesterton and Lewis
each describes a basic "mental picture" (as Chesterton calls it)
from his childhood, what psychologists might call a directional or
"intentional" image, a sort of archetype which leads one on one's
lifelong search for ultimate meaning. For Chesterton, it was a "toy
theater" built by his father; for Lewis it was a "toy garden" made
by his brother. Chesterton describes the toy theater in chapter
two of his 1936 memoirs (misleadingly entitled *Autobiography*):

> The very first thing I can ever remember seeing with my own eyes
> was a young man walking across a bridge. . . . I saw it through a
> window more wonderful than the window in the tower: through
> the proscenium of a toy theater constructed by my father. . . . And
> the scene has to me a sort of aboriginal authenticity impossible to
> describe; something at the back of all my thoughts; like the very
> back-scene of the theatre of things. (24-25)

For Chesterton, this theater provided an heuristic picture, as Chesterton explains, of several qualities he searched for all his life and eventually found in Christianity: a sense of limits and connections amid the mysteries of human life; a sense of romance, creativity, and imagination; and a sense of personal meaning symbolized by the man with the golden key in the theater's story. Chesterton not only used childhood images to open and close his *Autobiography* (24, 355), but he even transformed them into philosophical qualities which he discovered on his journey through the intellectual and religious landscape of *Orthodoxy*.

Lewis tells us of the similar archetypal importance of the "toy garden" in the first chapter of his autobiography:

> Once in those very early days my brother brought into the nursery the lid of a biscuit tin which he had covered with moss and garnished with twigs and flowers so as to make a toy garden or a toy forest. That was the first beauty I ever knew. What the real garden had failed to do, the toy garden did. It made me aware of nature. . . . As long as I live my imagination of Paradise will retain something of my brother's toy garden. (7)

At the time, Lewis recalls, this was an aesthetic experience, but throughout his journey such aesthetic moments gradually merge with and then become distinguished from religious moments. The "toy garden" sums up for him both his love of romance and his love of nature. In both he found a combination of satisfaction and dissatisfied desire which was the central *emotional* experience of his childhood. From this experience, all the energy for his life journey flowed; the experience provided the name and center of his autobiography, simply called "Joy":

> . . . an unsatisfied desire which is itself more desirable than any other satisfaction. I call it Joy. . . . I doubt whether anyone who has tasted it would ever . . . exchange it for all the pleasures in the world. (18)

Lewis had already described this experience, which he then entitled "Romanticism," in the 1943 preface to his quasi-autobiographical allegory, *Pilgrim's Regress*: "The experience is one of intense longing . . . yet the mere wanting is felt to be

David Leigh, S.J.

somehow a delight. This hunger is better than any other fullness;
this poverty than all other wealth" (7). He goes on to describe
the importance of this "joy" in human experience, as well as in
his own allegory: "It appeared to me therefore that if a man
diligently followed this desire, pursuing the false objects until
their falsity appeared and then resolutely abandoning them, he
must come out at last into the clear knowledge that the human
soul was made to enjoy some object that is never fully given—
nay, cannot even be imagined as given—in our present mode of
subjective and spatio-temporal experience" (10). This primal experience, as we shall see, will serve Lewis as the recurring motif
during the turning points of his autobiography, driving him beyond satisfaction with any partial good, inadequate meaning, or
"false object."

The equivalent of Joy in Chesterton seems to be his notion
of romance. Joy is also a driving emotion for Chesterton, but in
a slightly different sense, one which he describes most fully not
at the beginning but at the conclusion of *Orthodoxy*:

> It is said that Paganism is a religion of joy and Christianity of sor-
> row; it would be just as easy to prove that Paganism is pure sor-
> row and Christianity pure joy. . . . Christianity satisfies suddenly
> and perfectly man's ancestral instinct for being the right way up;
> satisfies it supremely in this: that by its creed joy becomes some-
> thing gigantic and sadness something special and small. (294, 297)

In this focus on early childhood images and experiences as
crucial to their later conversions, both Chesterton and Lewis make
similar statements about the *role of memory*. Chesterton speaks of
his memory of the toy theater as "more our own memory of the
thing rather than the thing remembered" (*Autobiography* 29). He
gives several other examples of these lifetime remembered images
—one the picture of his sister falling, the other of a white horse.
Lewis makes such "memory of a memory" the core of his autobiography, beginning with the toy garden and repeated in experiences
of the currant bush on a summer day, of reading *Squirrel Nutkin*,
and so on (*Surprised by Joy* 16).

This combination of satisfaction and dissatisfaction in the
remembered experiences of both Lewis and Chesterton (not un-

296

related to the *cor inquietum* of Augustine) drives both the narratives and each man's movements through the levels of conversion in his autobiography. Both begin with "joy" in a "toy" romance; both end with "joy" in a real romance, Christianity.

What helps them along the way? Both Chesterton and Lewis received little formal help on their religious quests from either parents or parsons. Psychologically and culturally, both were men born into the modern age, an age which, as John S. Dunne describes it, suffers from a loss of spiritual and temporal mediation. As searchers without mediators from church or culture, Chesterton and Lewis were driven into their own inner experience to find their authentic selves and a sense of the transcendent. But on their journeys through the islands of dissatisfactions, both Chesterton and Lewis found quasimediators in friendships and in books.

Because he writes a more traditional religious autobiography, Lewis provides for us a sketch of these mediators at each stage. The first and most important single mediator in his youth was Arthur Greeves, a classmate at Campbell's school near Belfast, who shared Lewis's love of *Myths of the Norsemen*. In Lewis's words, "both knew the stab of Joy and . . . for both, the arrow was shot from the North" (*Surprised by Joy* 130). After the war Lewis found a "second friend" at Oxford in Owen Barfield. The difference between the two friends reveals the two sides of Lewis:

> There is a sense in which Arthur and Barfield are the types of every man's First Friend and Second Friend. The First is the *alter ego*, the man who first reveals to you that you are not alone in the world by turning out (beyond hope) to share all your most secret delights. There is nothing to be overcome in making him your friend; he and you join like raindrops on a window. But the Second Friend is a man who disagrees with you about everything. He is not so much the *alter ego* as the antiself. (*Surprised by Joy* 199)

As we shall see later, Arthur helped Lewis in the imaginative level of conversion, Barfield in the intellectual. A third friend, Nevill Coghill, whom Lewis met in 1922 while studying English in his fourth year at Oxford, mediated his religious conversion. For Coghill was both "the most intelligent and best informed man in that class" but also "a Christian and a thoroughgoing supernaturalist" (212). Outside of his father and brother, who had strong but ambiguous influences on Lewis, these three friends —Arthur Greeves, Owen Barfield, and Nevill Coghill—embody the three types of friendships which Lewis tells us drew him from childhood imaginative Joy to the adult Joy of Christian faith.

Equal if not more powerful influences came to Lewis (as to Chesterton) from his reading. As Lewis confesses near the time of his final conversion:

> George MacDonald had done more to me than any other writer . . . Chesterton had more sense than all the other moderns put together . . . Johnson was one of the few authors whom I felt I could trust utterly . . . Spenser and Milton by a strange coincidence had Christianity too. Even among ancient authors the same paradox was to be found. The most religious (Plato, Aeschylus, Virgil) were clearly those on whom I could really feed. (213)

From the time of his first experience of childhood Joy, Lewis, as he tells us, was "the product . . . of endless books" (10). In fact, one of the three childhood examples he gives of his experience of Joy occurred while reading "Balder the beautiful / Is dead, is dead" in Longfellow's *Saga of King Olaf* (17). Later, at Campbell's school, Lewis says that the most important event was reading Arnold's *Sohrab and Rustum*, perhaps the truest beginning of his imaginative conversion through literature. But Lewis explicitly denies this was an experience of Joy (72), for the title that called him back to "the memory of Joy itself" was *Siegfried and the Twilight of the Gods.* As he describes this turning point of his life: "at once I knew (with fatal knowledge) that 'to have it again' was the supreme and only important object of desire" (73). Lewis subsequently read all of Norse mythology and became a devotee of Wagner.

Although Lewis read the Greek, Roman, and English classics in his school years and developed intellectually under the tutelage of his two great mentors, Smewgy and Kirkpatrick, he tells us that the most important literary mediator in his spiritual journey was George MacDonald, the Victorian fantasy writer. Lewis describes the October train trip when he first read *Phantastes:*

It was as if I were carried sleeping across the frontier, or as if I had died in the old country and could never remember how I came alive in the new. For in one sense the new country was exactly like the old. I met there all that had already charmed me in Malory, Spenser, Morris, and Yeats. But in another sense all was changed. I did not yet know (and I was long in learning) the name of the new quality, the bright shadow, that rested on the travels of Anodos. It was Holiness. (*Surprised by Joy* 179)

He goes on to describe this experience in language which echoes that of Chesterton on the discovery of the familiar: "It seems to have been always with me . . . never had the winds of Joy blowing through any story been less separable from the story itself." (180). Finally, as we have seen, Chesterton himself was an important literary mediator for Lewis during the latter's respite from the war. Lewis sums up the cumulative effect of all his reading in a famous passage: "All the books were beginning to turn against me" (213).

Once all of these writers had helped Lewis to an act of faith in God, Chesterton appeared again, this time to "make sense" of history in Christian terms in his *The Everlasting Man*. Lewis pulls together in one sentence all the mediators on his journey —experience, friends, and books—as he draws near the end of his autobiography: "And nearly everyone was now (one way or another) in the pack: Plato, Dante, MacDonald, Herbert, Barfield, Tolkien, Dysen, Joy itself. Everyone and everything had joined the other side" (225).

In contrast to Lewis, Chesterton followed literary mediators who were not at all Christian. As Chesterton tells it: "I never read a line of Christian apologetics. I read as little as I can of them now. It was Huxley and Herbert and Spencer and Bradlaugh who brought me back to orthodox theology. They sewed in my mind my first wild doubts of doubt" (*Orthodoxy* 154). Because his conversion story focuses most fully on his intellectual "argument" for Christianity, Chesterton finds his enemies to be his mediators. As he describes his thoughts after reading a series of lectures on atheism, "almost thou persuadest me to be a Christian" (154). Throughout his earlier books, he had debated against the giant freethinkers of his generation—from Kipling to

David Leigh, S.J.

Shaw to H. G. Wells—and in *Orthodoxy* he showed how these
debates led to his personal philosophy, which turned out, to his
surprise, to be the same as Christianity.

In fact, Chesterton gives almost no clues to any positive
mediators among his readings before his conversion. With regard
to the mediation of friends, however, Chesterton is slightly more
helpful. Even in his late *Autobiography* he credits four persons
with mediating his conversion—his wife, his brother Cecil, his
friend Hilaire Belloc, and his confessor, Fr. John O'Connor (the
latter was also the model for Fr. Brown). His wife mediated his
early conversion to Christianity and his affective conversion;
Cecil and Belloc mediated his intellectual growth and social conscience; Fr. O'Connor mediated the final steps of his religious
conversion to Catholicism.

We have noted in passing that Chesterton gives us glimpses
of three aspects or levels of conversion in his autobiographies.
Recent theories of conversion have distinguished four stages in
the process of transformation from childhood to adult Christian
faith. For Walter Conn, building on the work of Bernard Lonergan, there are four major conversions: moral, affective, intellectual, and religious. In each stage, the person breaks through to a
new horizon and restructures old and new contents of belief
(Conn 27). The movement of one's life is, then, one of "self-
realization" as "self-transcendence" through the distinctive conversions to goodness (moral), to love (affective), to objectivity
(intellectual), and to faith (religious). The lives of Chesterton
and Lewis suggest a fifth and perhaps even more fundamental
type of conversion, *imaginative conversion*. By this is meant the
discovery and transformation of one's innermost intentional symbols so as to be led beyond oneself and driven to search for ultimate meaning throughout a lifetime. (As we have seen, for
Chesterton this symbol was the toy theater, for Lewis the toy garden. Each of these symbols appears early in their respective lives
and serves as an image which both drives them back from false
paths and on to further search for God.)

Lewis's autobiography embodies the power of this fundamental symbol in the conversion process. As we have seen,
his early experience of Joy at seeing the toy garden becomes a

300

lifelong image of Paradise. It repeatedly emerges in his memory "as if from a depth not of years but of centuries" (*Surprised by Joy* 16) and is associated with experiences of nature, books, friends. Even in the years of wandering which make up most of the central chapters of his autobiography, Lewis finds that he tries in various aberrant ways to rediscover and control Joy, only to be disappointed and led, like Augustine, to further searchings. As he describes these middle years, "I was sent back to the false gods there to acquire some capacity for worship against the day when the true God should recall me to Himself" (77). As we have seen in our study of the mediation of books in Lewis's life, he considered several of his childhood readings to be preludes to his imaginative conversion. Only later did he come to learn how to discern merely imaginative from religious symbols. As he says of his readings of the Norse sagas, "Only very gradually did I realize that all this was something quite different from the original Joy. . . . Finally I woke from building the temple to find that God had flown" (165). Like Wordsworth whose "glory" had passed away, Lewis had to learn the levels of conscience and faith:

> I do not think the resemblance between the Christian and the merely imaginative experience is accidental. I think that all things, in their way, reflect heavenly truth, the imagination not least. (167)

From this distinction, Lewis learns two lessons — first, that he could not achieve Joy directly, and second, could not produce or control it at all. Only later, when he read George MacDonald's religious fantasies, did he undergo a full-fledged conversion of the imagination. In Lewis's words, "That night my imagination was, in a certain sense, baptized; the rest of me, not unnaturally, took longer" (181). "The rest of me" included his moral, intellectual, and religious conversions. Like Chesterton, he gives very little clue in this book to any affective conversion, except for a listing of his best friends. But he gives a fairly detailed account of some of the circumstances of his moral conversion during World War I. This transformation was mediated by a man named Johnson, with whom he used to argue and who proved to be "a man of conscience." The result of these conversations for Lewis was a conversion to "strict veracity, chastity, or devotion to duty. . . . I accepted his principles at once" (192-93).

Lewis's intellectual conversion covered many years and many doctrines. Like Chesterton, he debated with and tried out a variety of theories—necessitarianism, absolute idealism, romanticism, etc.—but never found true and complete Joy in any of them. What was lacking, he later tells us, was any full notion of transcendence. In reading Samuel Alexander's *Space, Time and Deity*, Lewis came to see the crucial difference between direct experiential awareness (which Lewis called "Enjoyment") and reflective consciousness (which he called "Contemplation"). He found this distinction "an indispensable tool of thought," especially for understanding why and how he had lost his original Joy:

> I saw that all my waitings and watchings for Joy, all my vain hopes to find some mental content on which I could, so to speak, lay my finger and say, "This is it," had been a futile attempt to contemplate the enjoyed. . . . I knew now that the images and sensations were merely the mental track left by the passage of Joy—not the wave but the wave's imprint on the sand. (*Surprised by Joy* 219)

From this insight into the distinction between objectivity and subjectivity, Lewis came to appreciate the presence of God, not as merely subjective human experience itself or as scientific object of consciousness "out there," but as the implicit, unknown, undefined source and goal of human desire. Joy, then, proved not to be a delusion, but, as he says, "its visitations were rather the moments of clearest consciousness we had, when we became aware of our fragmentary and phantasmal nature and ached for that impossible reunion which would annihilate us or that self-contradictory waking which would reveal, not that we had had, but that we *were*, a dream" (222). But he did not remain in this state of merely intellectual conversion.

Lewis's final and specifically religious conversion followed soon upon reading another book, Chesterton's *Everlasting Man*. This final move was not merely an intellectual insight or judgment. Rather, faith came as a choice.

> The odd thing was that before God closed in on me, I was in fact offered what now appears a moment of wholly free choice. I was

going up Headington Hill on the top of a bus. . . . I felt myself being, there and then, given a free choice. I could open the door or keep it shut; I could unbuckle the armor or keep it on. (*Surprised by Joy* 224)

Like Augustine in the garden or Chesterton at his desk, Lewis was left to choose whether to believe in God. His religious conversion was not merely a final step in an imaginative or intellectual process; rather, it was a choice of belief in a personal God, a choice that felt like a letting go — "I chose to open, to unbuckle, to loosen the rein." The result of this choice, of course, had its emotional and imaginative aspects, neither of which was pleasant, as Lewis recalls: "Then came the repercussion on the imaginative level. I felt as if I were a man of snow at last beginning to melt. . . . I rather disliked the feeling" (225).

Let us conclude with two reflections on Lewis's final stage of religious conversion. First, in the final stage of Lewis's conversion—as of Chesterton's—the more difficult step was to "admit that God was God"; the second step from Theism to Christianity (although two years long in his life) takes up no more than a few pages of *Surprised by Joy* and ends with that delightful description of the drive to Whipsnade one sunny morning:

When we set out I did not believe that Jesus Christ is the Son of God, and when we reached the zoo I did. Yet I had not exactly spent the journey in thought. Nor in great emotion. "Emotional" is perhaps the last word we can apply to some of the most important events. (237)

Second, the lack of ecstatic or even pleasant emotions in the final movement to faith suggests what Emilie Griffith has noted in her study of Lewis and other converts — "the conversion does not automatically convert the emotions as well" (140). Unlike what is suggested by some contemporary psychologists of religion, holiness is not necessarily wholeness. This was especially true of both Lewis and Chesterton, who continued to struggle, as most humans do, with disagreeable and even bizarre emotional patterns. This lifelong struggle for emotional integration, however, did not prevent either of these men from showing in their autobiographies the truth of Chesterton's words at the conclusion

David Leigh, S.J.

of *Orthodoxy*: "Man is more himself . . . when joy is the fundamental thing in him" (296).

Works Cited

Chesterton, G. K. *The Autobiography of G. K. Chesterton*. New York: Sheed and Ward, 1936.
———. *Charles Dickens*. London: Methuen, 1906.
———. *Orthodoxy*. New York: Dodd, Mead, 1908.
———. *Sidelights*. New York: Dodd, 1932.
Conn, Walter. *Christian Conversion*. New York: Paulist, 1986.
Dunne, John S. *The Search for God in Time and Memory*. New York: Macmillan, 1969.
Green, Roger, and Walter Hooper. *C. S. Lewis: A Biography*. New York: Harcourt, 1974.
Griffin, William. *Clive Staples Lewis: A Dramatic Life*. New York: Harper, 1986.
Griffith, Emilie. *Turning: Reflections on the Experience of Conversion*. New York: Doubleday, 1980.
Lewis, Clive Staples. *Pilgrim's Regress*. Grand Rapids: Eerdmans, 1943.
———. *Surprised by Joy*. New York: Harcourt, 1955.